S 7.50
7

MAGDALEN SCHOOL

THE SCHOOL HOUSE OF 1894

MAGDALEN SCHOOL

A History of
Magdalen College School
Oxford

By R. S. STANIER
MASTER OF THE SCHOOL

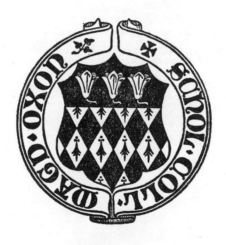

OXFORD
BASIL BLACKWELL
MCMLVIII

B581911600

L18241

37342

Printed by The Ditchling Press, Ltd, Ditchling, Sussex
and bound by the Kemp Hall Bindery, Oxford

THOMAE S. R. BOASE
COLLEGII BEATAE MARIAE MAGDALENAE
PRAESIDI QUI SCHOLAM HANC NOSTRAM
CONSILIO INDUSTRIA BENEVOLENTIA
EGREGIE ADIUVAT

PREFACE
TO THE FIRST EDITION

O N Commemoration Day, 1937, the Warden of
All Souls, giving away the prizes, wondered
that a School with so much about it that was
unique should have no published History. Much of the
material upon which such a History must be based is
to be found in the Register of Magdalen College by
Bloxam and Macray; but in their sixteen volumes the
relevant facts are inevitably, for the general reader,
obscured rather than illuminated. These facts I have
taken upon myself to exhume, interpret, and amplify
with such other material as I could gather, in an effort
to present a consistent and accurate picture of
Magdalen School in all its peculiar variety of constitution and fortune from the first beginnings to the present
day. My debts to other printed works are acknowledged in the notes, but there are many, Old Boys and
others, who have answered questions, supplied information and encouragement, and helped me in other
ways; it is my pleasant duty to thank for such help Dr
W. E. Audland, Mr A. R. Bayley, Sir Basil Blackwell,
Mr J. P. T. Bury, Mr G. H. Charsley, Professor G. R.
Driver, Canon W. H. Ferguson, Mrs Gamlen, Mr
Strickland Gibson, Rev. P. B. Halewood, Mr C. J.
Highton, Dr Claude Jenkins, Dr J. Johnson, Mr G. P.
Jones, Mr A. Keen, Mrs Lobel, Mr Cecil Page, Mr
L. S. Powell, Rev. E. C. Sherwood, Mr R. G. W.
Smeaton, Mrs Stanier, Mrs Terry, Mr T. D. Tremlett,
Mr W. S. Unwin, Rev. E. M. Walker.

A word as to the School's name. I suspect that to
the City, if not to the University, of Oxford it has
always been 'Magdalen School', and that even among
purists there can be few who have not at times found
'Magdalen College School, Oxford' something long.
If so, they are in good company. Anthony Wood,
indeed, in recognition of the fact that the School was
not an independent foundation, generally uses some
such designation as 'the Free School adjoining Magdalen College', but Hearne seems to say 'Magdalen
School' or 'Magdalen College School' indifferently,
and Bloxam invariably, I think, says 'Magdalen
School'. That must be my apology for putting the
shorter title on the cover.

PREFACE
TO THE SECOND EDITION

SINCE the first edition of this school history was produced several new chapters have been written in bricks and mortar; and I hope that the time may now be thought ripe for them to be recorded on paper as well. I have tried to describe these changes and other developments in an additional chapter (Recent Times) and I have also re-arranged and amplified the last three chapters of the old edition. In the earlier part of the book the only alterations are those due to new discoveries, the attendance at the school of Thomas More (chapter III), the biography of Thomas Whythorne (chapters II and III), and the Fifteenth Century Schoolbook (chapter II), which combine to throw a good deal of fresh light on the school's first seventy years.

New illustrations are a portrait of Sir Thomas More and a view of the school taken from a helicopter by Captain S. M. W. Hickey, R.A.S.C., *O.W.*, whose kindness I take this opportunity of acknowledging.

R.S.S.

CONTENTS

LIST OF ILLUSTRATIONS

LIST OF ILLUSTRATIONS.

LIST OF BOOKS
REFERRED TO BY ABBREVIATED TITLES, GIVING THE FULL TITLE OF EACH

Annals=Anthony Wood's *Annals* included in *The History and Antiquities of the University of Oxford*, ed. Gutch. (The reference is usually given by years, but occasionally by volume and page.)

Athenae=Anthony Wood's *Athenae Oxonienses*, ed. Bliss.

Bloxam=J. R. Bloxam's *Register of the Presidents, &c. of Magdalen College.*

Buckler=J. C. Buckler's *Observations on the Original Architecture of St Mary Magdalen's College, Oxford.*

Chandler=Richard Chandler's *Life of William Waynflete.*

D.N.B.=*The Dictionary of National Biography.*

E.S.R.=A. F. Leach's *English Schools at the Reformation.*

Foster Watson=Foster Watson's *English Grammar Schools down to 1660.*

Gibson=Strickland Gibson's *Statuta Antiqua Universitatis Oxoniensis.*

Macray=W. D. Macray's *Register of the Members of St Mary Magdalen's College, Oxford.* New Series.

Mallett=C. E. Mallet's *History of the University of Oxford.*

O.H.S.=Publications of the Oxford Historical Society: Volumes lxvii-lxix comprise the *Cartulary of the Hospital of St John the Baptist.*

Rashdall=Hastings Rashdall's *The Universities of Europe in the Middle Ages.*

S.M.E.=A. F. Leach's *Schools of Medieval England.*

Statutes=*Statutes of the Colleges*, published 1853.

Vulgaria=Beatrice White's *The Vulgaria of St John Stanbridge and the Vulgaria of Robert Whittinton.*

Wilson=H. A. Wilson's *Magdalen College* (in the Series of College Histories).

Worthies=Fuller's *Worthies.* The edition of 1840.

CHAPTER I
WILLIAM WAYNFLETE & HIS TIMES

The Bishop's Career—The Founding of Magdalen College—The Educational System in England before the Renaissance—Waynflete's Educational Scheme

THE BISHOP'S CAREER

THE founder of Magdalen College, and therewith of Magdalen College School, was born, probably shortly before 1400,[1] at Wainfleet in Lincolnshire, son to Richard Patten or Barbour of that town. When he changed his double surname to the better known Waynflete is not certain, but it is a probable conjecture of Chandler[2] that it was on his ordination as sub-deacon in 1420.

He was educated as a boy at Wykeham's College at Winchester, if Leach[3] is right in identifying him with the William Pattney who appears on the Roll in 1403. The identification is uncertain; but that Waynflete was at Winchester is suggested by a statement of one Chaundler, who was there in 1430. He speaks as if Waynflete had had his origin at Winchester and mentions the debt he owed to Thomas Beckington, Bishop of Bath and Wells, who was himself a contemporary of William Pattney at Winchester.[4]

Waynflete proceeded to Oxford and obtained the degree of B.D., but what college, if any, he was a member of is not known. He was ordained priest in 1426 (if he is the William Waynflete of Spalding mentioned in the register of the see of Lincoln). We are

[1] Wilson, p. 3. [2] p. 10, corrected by Wilson, p. 3.
[3] *History of Winchester*, p. 204.
[4] 'ex tantae fundationis pullulans radice, florescens quasi virgula, ope et adjutorio Thomae Beckingtonii . . . ferme in cedrum crevit magnam, quasique lignum plantatum secus decursus aquarum, uberrimos fructus protulit' (quoted by Chandler, p. 21).

on more certain ground in his appointment as Master of Winchester in 1429. It is from this time that we see him started on his double career as statesman and promoter of learning. It was no doubt his work as a teacher that recommended him to Cardinal Beaufort, then Bishop of Winchester, and the Cardinal who recommended him to Henry VI, when that enthusiastic but unbalanced devotee of education visited Winchester in 1440 to learn how to set about founding Eton. At any rate Henry, in 1441, named Waynflete as one of the first Fellows of Eton, and Waynflete became Master there in 1442, Provost in 1443. He rose rapidly in the King's favour, became a member of the Council before 1447, and in that year, when Beaufort died, was immediately, at Henry's request, elected Bishop of Winchester.

William of Wykeham (1367–1404) and Cardinal Beaufort (1404–47) had ruled the see of Winchester for eighty years, and Waynflete rivalled his two great predecessors in political and educational activity no less than in length of tenure. He was active among the chief ministers during Cade's rebellion and that of the Duke of York and during the madness of King Henry; and in 1456 he became Lord Chancellor. Waynflete resigned office just before Henry VI was defeated by Edward IV at the battle of Northampton in 1460; and therewith his political career ended, though, no doubt owing to his piety, submission, and readiness to contribute to the royal chest, the rapid changes on the throne which followed left Waynflete unharmed, if endangered, in his bishopric till his death in 1486. The overthrow of Edward IV in 1470, his restoration in the following year, the accession and murder of his son in 1483, the accession of Richard III and his death on Bosworth Field, the accession of Henry VII in 1485

—all these changes with their alarming accompaniments did not prevent Waynflete from pursuing the works of piety and learning for which not only his previous eminence as a schoolmaster but also his talents peculiarly fitted him.

THE FOUNDING OF MAGDALEN COLLEGE

Before Magdalen School can be discussed some account must be given of the founding of the College of which it is a part, and of the educational system with which Waynflete had to work.

In 1448, the year after his appointment as Bishop, Waynflete founded a college by the name of Magdalen Hall, between Merton Street and High Street, west of the present Examination Schools. In 1456, immediately after becoming Lord Chancellor, he began the operations which led to Magdalen Hall's supersession by Magdalen College as it now is, the licence to found the College being granted on July 18th, 1457.[1] Waynflete designed to abolish the ancient but decayed Hospital of St John the Baptist, and establish instead a new college on the same site by the Cherwell, thus 'changing earthly things to heavenly and things temporal to things eternal';[2] and his position as Chancellor and the admitted decadence of the Hospital enabled him to win the papal blessing on this anticipation of the Reformation. By June 1458 the Master and brethren of the Hospital were pensioned off, the new Magdalen College was founded and in possession of the Hospital's buildings, and Magdalen Hall had disappeared. Its members, no doubt, were largely absorbed in Magdalen College, but continued to live in their old quarters

[1] For a full account of these proceedings see Wilson, pp. 9 ff.
[2] Pope Calixtus III's authorization of the conversion of the Hospital (O.H.S. lxviii. 414).

till the Hospital buildings had been sufficiently supplemented to receive them. Building started in 1467, and
the College was occupied in or shortly before 1480, the
year in which the first statutes were delivered to it.

THE EDUCATIONAL SYSTEM IN ENGLAND BEFORE THE RENAISSANCE

To trace the rise of the medieval university, its em-
broilment in a somewhat arid scholasticism, and its
emergence into the humane light of the Renaissance,
volumes would be needed; but enough must be said
here of the subject as a whole, and of Oxford in particular, to indicate the importance of Waynflete's
reforms.

Universities arose from the schools of the Dark Ages.
As a need came to be felt for a higher education than
the schoolmaster could provide, teachers and students
congregated for mutual benefit, and associations of
teachers analogous to the mercantile guilds developed
into universities. The studies consisted of the higher
faculties of Theology, Law (both Canon, or Church,
and Civil Law), Medicine, and the primary faculty of
Arts. The conception of the seven liberal arts was a
part of Western Europe's debt to the ancient world.
The trivium (grammar, rhetoric, dialectic or logic) and
the quadrivium (arithmetic, geometry, music, astro-
nomy) were regarded as a preliminary training to
enable the student to proceed to higher studies; but
many years were needed to obtain degrees in Theology,
Law, or Medicine (fourteen to sixteen years for Theology at Oxford),[1] and few students aspired to such
heights; so that the Arts faculty's vastly greater
numbers gave it a practical importance which theoretically it did not deserve. However, the rediscovery

[1] Rashdall, ii. 452-3.

of Aristotle's works led to the inclusion of Philosophy in the Arts course, and helped to make it a more complete education.

In Oxford's development an important factor was the rise of the College system. Two colleges (Balliol and Exeter) had no aim, originally, beyond the sustenance of poor Arts students who would otherwise have lived at their own expense in halls, but most of the early colleges had a more definite purpose, to encourage graduates in Arts to proceed to higher faculties, especially Theology, and thus both to further higher education and also to counteract the monopoly in Theology which the Friars seemed likely to establish. For the Friars were not hampered like the secular clerks by the long and expensive course for the theological degree, as they had no economic worries; and moreover they claimed, and were often allowed, to proceed to Theology without an Arts degree. Most founders designed to pick out a number of the best men and foster them during the long struggle for one of the higher degrees; and all colleges were meant for students rather than teachers. The University in early days supplied the teachers by the rule that every Master, on graduating, should lecture for one or two years; and the pupils paid the lecturer. But the pay was insufficient to attract the best men when their compulsory years of teaching were over, and, as Rashdall says, 'Want of adequate support for University teaching, and the youth and inexperience of the "necessary regents", led eventually to the breakdown of University teaching, at least in the Faculty of Arts.'[1]

There were further weaknesses in the system as Waynflete found it. In the thirteenth and fourteenth

[1] Rashdall, ii. 460.

centuries students had grappled boldly with the
deepest problems of theology and philosophy; and,
even when the despotic claims of the Church in the
one field and of Aristotle in the other had begun to
stifle research, the ticklish task of reconciling the two
authorities had given a field for exercise to the keenest
wits. By the beginning of the fifteenth century, however, not only had the possibilities of this rather
limited subject been exhausted, but freedom of thought
in Oxford had been suppressed owing to the University's support of the doctrines of Wycliffe.

Accompanying, and, to a great extent, causing this
dehumanisation of education was a decay in the study
of Grammar, that is to say, of the Latin language and
literature, the only connotation of the word in medieval
times. No doubt in some country grammar schools,
especially in such magnificent foundations as Winchester and Eton, the teaching and the range of studies
was as good as could be expected,[1] but in Oxford,
Grammar was in a sorry state. From early days
Grammar had been a distinct faculty under the control
of the University, with Masters (often M.A.s themselves) who paid a poll tax to the regent Masters of
Arts who supervised them;[2] and salutary statutes pre-
scribed the nature of the studies and ordered regular
conferences of Grammar Masters.[3] In 1442, however,
the Grammar Masters attempted to cut the payments
to their supervisors, 'the said collections, it seems,
being not so fully paid as formerly, occasioned by the
decrease of scholars';[4] and in 1466 the University
appealed to the Bishop of Lincoln to do something to
help.[5] The decay was partly due to the general feeble-
ness of the University at this time, but mainly to the

---

[1] *S.M.E.*, p. 235.   [2] Gibson, p. lxxxvi.
[3] Ibid., p. lxxxv.   [4] *Annals*, an. 1442.   [5] Ibid., an. 1466.

excessive claims of Logic. Erasmus, criticizing the neglect of Grammar in monastery schools, says, 'Youths, after a bare term's study of Grammar, are whirled forthwith to sophistry, dialectic, suppositions, ampliations, restrictions, expositions, resolutions, and the questionistic labyrinths, hence straight to the shrines of theology'; and, no doubt, his words were true of Oxford.[1] The Arts course allowed one term for Grammar, the presumption being that students were not enrolled till they 'knew' Latin; but the only test was a prepared speech, which could be learned parrot-fashion;[2] and the wiser heads were well aware that the decay of Grammar was a great, if not the main, cause of the decadence of Oxford.[3] Patrons of learning, such as the Good Duke Humphrey,[4] had brought to Britain a whiff of the literary Renaissance of fourteenth-century Italy; and Oxford, whether she knew it nor not, was hungry for more.

WAYNFLETE'S EDUCATIONAL SCHEME

Waynflete's originality and vision can best be judged by the way in which his foundation met and remedied

[1] Erasmus, *Dial. de Pronuntiatione:* 'adolescentes, vix trimestri studio grammaticae data protinus rapiuntur ad sophisticen, dialecticen, suppositiones, ampliationes, restrictiones, expositiones, resolutiones ad gryphos, et quaestionum labyrinthos, hinc recta in adyta theologiae'.

[2] Wood, in the *Annals* for 1456, tells of an Archdeacon of Oxford who was 'not only a Natural, but also a Sot. He would be also drunk every day. He could understand little or no Latin, no more than a parrot that is taught.'

[3] In the appeal to the Bishop of Lincoln mentioned above, the University speak of Grammar as *reliquarum scientiarum radicem*. In 1444 (Wood's *Annals*), 'the King took order that the Latin sermons should be duly observed as before, to the end that the Latin tongue which was now decaying should be revived'.

[4] For his study of Latin literature and his encouragement of Italy's Renaissance scholars, see Sandys, *History of Classical Scholarship*, ii. 220f. 221.

these evils. His Magdalen Hall of 1448 was just such another college as Oriel, All Souls, or New College, but his retirement from politics in 1460 and his constant interest in the University[1] enabled him to think out numerous improvements. Desultory remedies had been applied by earlier founders. At Merton and Queen's a Grammar Master existed; but, though the Merton seniors were urged to have recourse to the Grammarian without a blush (*absque rubore*) if in difficulties, it is to be feared that the poor boys or *parvuli* attached to the two foundations were in fact the only people to profit. Wykeham at New College ordained that the older Fellows should give instruction to the younger, so that he is rightly regarded as the originator of the college tutorial system; but his measure may have produced as much harm as good: for the College, perhaps, suffered from the torpor of isolation, and the University certainly got no better teaching.

Waynflete's reform was sweeping. He divided his College between forty graduates (Fellows) and thirty undergraduates (Demies), and he also allowed the admission of twenty *commensales* (Commoners), the sons of noble and powerful friends of the College. Through this undergraduate element he was able to make the College education a rational whole from the earliest stages. At the same time he attached to the College a Reader in Theology, another in Natural Philosophy, a third in Moral Philosophy or Metaphysics, and a School with Master and Usher. The services of these officers were thrown open to all who cared to make use

[1] *Annals*, an. 1459, quotes part of several complaints by the University to Waynflete against the Friars; and Chandler (Appendixes 8, 20, 21) cites letters by the University to Waynflete in 1447, 1479, 1477 appealing to him on various matters.

of them; and the handsome salaries[1] allowed them ensured that the teaching should be the best possible.
The result was that the members of Magdalen College
were certain of a good education from the first stages
to the last; and everything was done that the benefits
might spread throughout the University.

More important even than this provision of teachers
was the nature of the teaching. Waynflete did not
favour letters at the expense of religion—his endowment of a chapel with four chaplains, eight clerks, and
sixteen choristers shows that—but it was the humanistic
teaching at Magdalen that distinguished it in its early
days. The School, as will be seen below, was meant to
ensure that no member of the College should proceed
to higher studies unlearned in the humanities; and it is
because of this emphasis and because of the excellence
and fame of the early Grammar Masters that Rashdall[2]
can say, 'Magdalen—the College of Grocyn (who
received his earliest education at New College) and of
Colet, the temporary abode of Erasmus—was essen-
tially the home of the Classical Renaissance in Oxford.'
The College was so far aware where its peculiar eminence lay that when the School was in danger of
suppression in 1550, the Fellows, in their protest,
spoke of it as 'the most principal treasure they or the
University have'.[3]

---

[1] The Master received £10 per annum, Usher £5, Reader in Theology
£10, Readers in Philosophy £6. 13s. 4d. At first sight these salaries do
not seem lavish; but the best way of assessing them in modern figures
is to compare them with the wages of the skilled workman of the day.
Those who built Magdalen College received from 3½d. to 6d. a day;
if they worked six days a week all the year round, which is not likely,
they would thus earn from £4. 11s. to £7. 16s. per annum. Thus it
can be seen that the salaried officers of the College were, on the average,
receiving, in addition to their board, lodging, and clothes, rather more
than the full pay of the skilled workman.

[2] Vol. ii. 515.   [3] See below, p. 88.

CHAPTER II

THE EARLY SCHOOL

*Date of Origin—The Early Buildings—The Grammar Hall—The Members
of the School—Commoners and Demies of the College—Magdalen Hall—
Choristers and Song School: Thomas Whythorne—The Magdalen School
Grammarians—Curriculum and Manner of Life*

DATE OF ORIGIN

ABOUT the exact date when Magdalen School
started to exist there is some doubt. In the lawsuit of 1847[1] 'The defendants [i.e. Magdalen
College]', said Lord Langdale, giving judgment, 'seem
doubtful whether they ought to admit that the school
was ever founded in the proper acceptance of the
term.' The College were attempting to draw a distinction between their School and the usual type of Free
Grammar School, whose governors are responsible
to the public for seeing that endowments left for the
specific purpose of providing free grammar education
are used for that purpose. In this the College were
quite correct. Magdalen School was a department of
the College with no separate legal existence or endowment. Waynflete's statutes provided for the perpetual
maintenance of a School just like any other element in
his College, and the only authority to see that the
statutes were carried out was the Visitor, the Bishop
of Winchester.

This constitutional peculiarity, however, did not in-
volve any practical difference between Magdalen
School and other Free Grammar Schools; whether it
can rightly be said to have been founded or not,
Magdalen School certainly came into existence, in
popular estimation, when the College first provided a

[1] See below, pp. 149-53.

Grammar Master. Unfortunately, to quote Lord Langdale again, 'It does not, I think, certainly appear when
the establishment of a school, as connected with or in
the College, was first thought of'.

The earliest direct evidence is to be found in the
College Register, and is quoted by Bloxam:[1]

'Eodem anno et mense incepit extra portas Collegii
edificium pro schola grammaticali cum cameris superioribus,
et cum coquina dictae Scholae necessaria: et Magister
Ricardus Bernys ibidem praefuit, ut magister et praepositus
operis. Prius tamen grammatici omnes et singuli gratis erant
instructi expensis Dni Fundatoris per unum Informatorem
et unum Hostiarium, et hoc per medium annum ante, vide-
licet, a Festo Paschuae ultimo praeterito, in quadam aula
bassa intra Collegium ex parte australi Capellae in antiquo
edificio.'

This may be translated:

'In the same year and month [August 1480] he began
outside the College gates the building of a grammar school
with upper rooms and the necessary kitchen for the said
school: and Master Richard Bernys was in charge of the
same, as master in charge of the works.[2] Previously, however,
the grammar students ,one and all, had been freely instructed
at the expense of the Founder by a Master and an Usher, and
that through the middle of the past year (i.e. from the Easter
immediately preceding) in a certain low hall within the
College to the south of the Chapel in the old building.'

From this it would, I suppose, be possible to deduce,
as Wilson[3] apparently does, that the grammar teaching
referred to as starting in the low hall in 1480 was the
first given. But surely the *et hoc*, 'and this', implies
that the teaching in the low hall is only part of the

---

[1] Bloxam, iii. 3.
[2] Richard Bernys, or Berne, was Vice-President from 1469 to 1499
and superintended all the Founder's building operations (Wilson, p. 21).
[3] Id. p. 28.

previous free teaching at the Founder's expense; that is to say that Easter 1480 is the date when teaching began in the low hall, and not the date when teaching began. When, then, did the grammar teaching first start? Leach[1] couples it with the original foundation of the first Magdalen Hall in 1448. I can find no direct evidence for this, and the series in which Leach was writing excluded reference to authorities.[2] No doubt he was arguing that, as practically all colleges had schools founded in connexion with them,[3] it was unlikely that Waynflete, 'the greatest schoolmaster of the era', should allow thirty years to elapse between the foundation of his college and the start of its school. If true it is certainly surprising, but if he did start a school in 1448 it is surprising that the complaints about inadequate grammar teaching in Oxford continued;[4] and that Wood, who mentions a good many grammar schools as existing in Oxford in the reigns of Henry V, Henry VI, and Edward IV, says nothing to suggest that Magdalen School existed so early.[5]

[1] *S.M.E.*, p. 270.   [2] Ibid., p. vi.

[3] Of the colleges founded before Magdalen, Balliol and University were founded before the linking of schools and colleges became customary, and, in any case, were of an unorthodox type; Merton and Queen's had small groups of boys attached to the College and educated by a Grammar Master; New College was closely linked to Winchester; the founders of Exeter and All Souls founded schools in their native counties; and the Burghersh charity founded a Grammar School at about the same time as Bishop Burghersh was giving Oriel its statutes (1326). Lincoln alone of the fourteenth and fifteenth-century colleges had no school, owing to its inadequate endowment and its special theological purpose—to defend orthodoxy against 'the swinish snouts who presumed to root among the pearls'.

[4] See above, pp. 6, 7.

[5] His words are, 'Another at Magdalen College, instituted by the Founder, which being free, not only the Choristers of that College are taught there, but also the sons of Oppidans and strangers, &c.' Wood's account of the Oxford grammar schools is to be found in the *History and Antiquities of the University of Oxford*, ii. 712 ff.

If these arguments, from analogy and silence, cancel one another out, further evidence supports the later date. It will be remembered that Grammar Masters in Oxford from early days paid a poll tax to the University. On April 10th, 1478, the University passed a statute exempting from this tax any free school that should be founded.[1] Waynflete, as we have seen, kept in close touch with the University; and it is surely probable that this statute was passed at his request when he was about to start a free school. The beginnings of Magdalen College School may therefore be placed with probability in 1478, though one cannot be absolutely certain of the School's existence before 1480. We do not know where the instruction was given before its transference to the 'low hall to the south of the chapel'.

THE EARLY BUILDINGS

The first known Schoolroom was the low hall south

The front of Magdalen College showing the old Chapel of the Hospital of St. John the Baptist.

of the Chapel, referred to in the document quoted on page 11. It was a vaulted chamber below the Chapel

[1] Gibson, p. 291.

of St John's Hospital, which stood between the present porter's lodge and Great Tower. Some of the stone-work of this old building still exists, though the whole building was adapted towards the end of the seven-teenth century and made uniform in appearance with the row of chambers that had been built between it and the Great Tower; these are the chambers that now form the College's front facing High Street. A picture of date about 1660 reproduced above shows the Chapel and Tower and intervening buildings before the adaptation.[1]

After the completion of the present College Chapel the old one was used as a lecture-room and the chamber beneath it, after its temporary service as a schoolroom, was equipped by President Claymond (1507–16) with four beds, in order that the old alms-giving tradition of the Hospital which Waynflete had suppressed might not entirely die out. The room measured about fifty feet by fifteen, its floor was about two feet below the level of the street, and its fitness, whether as bedroom or classroom, may be gauged from the report which the College drew up of its alms-giving in 1596.

'In sommer the resort (i.e. of poor folk to the free beds) is greater, in winter verye smale, bycause of the coldnes and unwholesomeness of the vault, which is in verie deed so moyst and dampish that we have the last yeare removed the beddes into another house not far off: for that everie winter they are subject to rottennes; and have provided some tymber, and meane God willinge this springe to provide more, for the bordinge of the floure of the said allmeshouse, as well for the safetie of our beddes as the health and ease of the poore.'

[1] The picture is in the possession of the College, and is reproduced in O.H.S. lxix; a full account of the old Chapel is there given, and the account given here is based on it.

MAGDALEN COLLEGE—ST. JOHN'S QUADRANGLE

In the centre is the former President's Lodging. On the left is the eastern side of Waynflete's Schoolroom

From a water-colour by Buckler in Magdalen College

If anything more is needed to show the pleasure the *grammatici* must have felt at moving from this temporary schoolroom to Waynflete's new building, it may be mentioned that, when the 'allmeshouse' was being renovated in the nineteenth century, a large quantity of human bones were found 'sorted and closely packed', as Buckler, the architect, records, against its eastern wall.

THE GRAMMAR HALL

The building of the first Schoolroom proper was begun, as has been seen, in August 1480. The so-called Grammar Hall now standing consists of the bell-turret and northern end of the Schoolroom and some additions built in 1614. The original Schoolroom stretched from this bell-turret to about where the present St Swithun's Buildings have their south-east corner. Between its eastern side and St John's Quadrangle ran a road and a wall, in which was the Great Gate of the College; and the School is frequently described as the school outside Magdalen College great gate. This gate looked up the Gravel Walk, which until recent years separated High Street from those buildings of the College and of Magdalen Hall that lie between St John's Quadrangle and Longwall.

Something of the Schoolroom's appearance when complete can be seen in many old prints of Magdalen Hall;[1] but all existing pictures show it after alterations had been made to it in the seventeenth century, the most important being the addition of a third floor. Originally the building rose to the height of the battlements seen in the illustrations, the roof, no doubt, being nearly flat. It consisted of two stories, the lower one being the Schoolroom, 72 feet long and 24 feet 9 inches[2]

[1] See the illustrations facing pp. 15, 21, 134.   [2] Bloxam, iii. 6.

wide,[2] and the upper containing the rooms for Master and Usher. When Magdalen Hall grew up around and above the School in the manner described below various alterations were made. As early as 1518 there was built on at the south-west end of the Schoolroom a wing which was later the main front on High Street of Magdalen Hall. In 1614 the buildings forming most of the present Grammar Hall were added, and in 1632 the Schoolroom was completely remodelled, and 'nothing of Waynflete's work remained excepting the walls, even the windows being destroyed and three stories placed where only two were formerly seen'. The Schoolroom thereafter was a low room with a roof supported by beams and twelve wooden pillars in two rows.[1]

THE MEMBERS OF THE SCHOOL

From its earliest days Magdalen School was recruited from a wide diversity of types. Demies and Commoners of the College, the more advanced Choristers, sons of noblemen, sons of townsmen, Choristers of other colleges, and those undergraduates who were soon to form Magdalen Hall, all attended the new School, which may be said to have had one foot in the University and one in the City. Bloxam, indeed,[2] with his memory still full of the recent attempt by the citizens of Oxford in 1845 to secure free education for their sons at the School,[3] is emphatic that when the Founder laid down in his statutes that the Master and Usher should teach all comers gratis and for nothing[4] he 'did not and could not contemplate that any would resort to the grammar school . . . except Academical persons belonging to the recognized

---

[1] For the whole story of the buildings see Buckler, pp. 18 ff.
[2] iii. 3 ff.   [3] See p. 150f.
[4] 'quoscunque ad Scholam Grammaticalem . . . accedentes, libere et gratis sine cuiusque rei exactione.'

class of Academical Grammar Scholars'. Arguing apparently from the statement of Wood[1] that Matriculation rolls were made as early as the time of Henry III, and that Grammar Masters were subject to the statutes of the University, he deduces that 'no Scholars were permitted to reside within the precincts of the University, much less to resort to any school there, unless they were matriculated and subject to a Tutor according to the rules of the place'. His facts and his deductions are doubtful,[2] and even if the deduction is correct it is certain that any Grammar Master could accept any pupil he chose: so that we may say— either the Grammar pupils needed not to be matriculated members of the University (which is most likely), or else they became matriculated members of the University on becoming Grammar pupils. In either case no restriction was placed by the Founder on attendance at his school. He used the same form of words about his school at Wainfleet as about that in Oxford, and there is no doubt that he meant both to give education to any one who wished for it.

COMMONERS AND DEMIES OF THE COLLEGE

The commoners or *filii nobilium et valentium personarum*, whom Waynflete allowed to frequent the College, wrote their names in water; for, not being strictly members of the College, they do not appear on official lists. Nevertheless, the fact that chance has preserved the information that the sons of the Marquess of Dorset were at school under Wolsey (p. 63) and those of the Earl of Bedford under Cooper (p. 84) suggests that if full lists were available, it would appear that many

---

[1] *Annals*, i. 372.
[2] Cf. Rashdall, ii. 581, 582. It is unlikely that there was any Matriculation Book before the reign of Queen Elizabeth.

C

nobles interested in educating their children sent them to Magdalen School.

But with the Demies clearer information appears. We have seen that Waynflete made the Demies an essential part of his educational scheme, and from the statutes it is possible to gain a very fair notion of what that scheme was. He saw the danger of approaching philosophy before mastering literature, and laid it down that 'because a weak foundation, as experience shows, ruins the work', none of the Demies were to proceed to sophistry and logic until the President, Master, and one of the Deans had passed them as sufficiently instructed in Grammar,[1] 'the mother and foundation of all sciences'. The Demies were to be of good character and promise, 'competently instructed in reading and plain song, and to have attained their twelfth year';[2] and, provided that they did not acquire an income greater than five marks (£3. 6s. 8d.) they could stay until their twenty-fifth year. The age and qualifications, which are those of boys who have passed through the Song School (the medieval elementary school), indicate that Waynflete expected, though he did not ordain, that the Demies should come to his College for their grammar learning, and so have all their education from the College.

The average age of appointment in the earliest days was apparently not so low as Waynflete expected,[3]

[1] 'Grammar', of course, means, as always, Latin literature and language.

[2] 'in lectura et plano cantu competenter instructi, qui annum attigerunt duodecimum.' The statutes about Demies are to be found on pp. 15, 16 of the printed version of 1853.

[3] The ages of appointment are not known till 1534, except for the period 1485-95, when Bloxam gives the following records: one aged 13, four 15, twelve 16, seven 17, six 18, one 19, four 20 (four of the 16's, one 17, one 15, had been choristers and therefore caught young). From 1534 to 1563 the average age of appointment is 15.3.

probably because his scheme needed time to take root and become known, but there can be no doubt that nearly all the Demies attended the School. Even those who came at a more advanced stage than ordinary probably found that the high literary standards at Magdalen necessitated some work at the School before they could proceed to philosophy. A striking instance is that of Lawrence Humfrey, the celebrated Puritan scholar, and later President of the College. Coming as Demy in 1547, after being, as Wood[1] says, 'educated in Latin and Greek learning at Cambridge' he, if any one, might have been expected to have no need to study at the School; yet we have his own authority that he did so.[2] In 1550, when the unsuccessful attempt, described below, was made to suppress the School, the College still looked on the School as instituted to train up Demies for the College, being a 'Norisshe' (whether that means 'nurse' or, source of nourishment') for it as Eton School is to King's College in Cambridge, and the School at Winchester to the New College in Oxford'. (See pp. 86–9 for the whole story and the appeal of the College.)

Waynflete, moreover, designed to train teachers as well as students. At least two or three of the thirty Demies were to apply themselves 'so long to grammatical and poetical and other humane arts that they could not only profit themselves but be able also to instruct and educate others'. It is this statute, I suppose, more than anything else that gave Magdalen its pre-eminent educational position as the mother and origin of almost all the innovations and institutions that enthusiasm for the New Learning begot in the

[1] *Athenae*, i. 557.
[2] *Vita Juelli*, p. 36: 'Joannem Harlaeum (Master 1542–8), praeceptorem olim meum observantissimum.'

years about 1500. Grocyn became the first teacher of
Greek in Oxford when he returned from the East to
Magdalen in 1491; Richard Croke, first Public
Orator and Reader in Greek at Cambridge, was
Grocyn's pupil; Cardinal Wolsey, founder of Christ
Church and of a school at Ipswich, got his start in life
as Master of Magdalen School and was probably a
pupil in it as well; Fox, who, founding Corpus
Christi College in 1516, established the first public
Greek Lecture in England, was probably a Magdalen
man; and so was Colet, the re-founder of St Paul's;
and Fox, Wolsey, and Colet got from Magdalen the
Heads of their foundations, Corpus Christi, Christ
Church, and St Paul's. Magdalen School both
acquired and seemed likely to produce the best
Grammar Masters, and it was Grammar—in the fullest
and best sense of the word—that engrossed the keenest
minds of the period.

MAGDALEN HALL

What is both free and good is always popular, and
it is not surprising to find the School attracting numbers of pupils who were not members of the College.
Colleges, though their number had grown, were still
mainly for graduates, and the mass of what we should
now call undergraduates had to find accommodation
for themselves in halls or elsewhere. Waynflete's
schoolroom had above it rooms for the Master and
Usher, and as John Anwykyll, who was probably
Master when the new school was first ready for occupa-
tion, had a wife and family, it came about that he was
given a house elsewhere by the College, and the
students flocking to the School were allowed to camp
in the rooms meant for the Master and Usher.[1]

[1] Bloxam, iii. 7–9, quotes the agreement made between Anwykyll
and the College.

MAGDALEN HALL AND WAYNFLETE'S SCHOOLROOM FROM THE GRAVEL WALK

The Greyhound Inn can be seen on the extreme left

From a print in the School Dining Hall

These rooms were known at first as Grammar Hall and soon as Magdalen Hall; and the numbers of students may be judged from the fact that further accommodation had to be provided in 1518. The relation of this community to the College is peculiar.

The Schoolroom and the land as far as Longwall belonged to the College; and the first students paid, through their Principal, a rent of forty shillings to the College; there is not much doubt, on *a priori* grounds, that the College paid for the extensions of 1518; and the early Principals seem to have been Fellows of the College, appointed by it to supervise what might be called the boarders of the College School. Magdalen Hall was, in fact, a charitable institution, a corollary of Waynflete's provision of free grammar teaching; the College received nothing but a rent for their buildings.

The rent remained for many years at the original figure in spite of the fall in the value of money, and, as the Grammar School came to be separated as in modern times from the University, old custom gradually gave the Hall an independent standing as a community of undergraduates and a Principal. In 1694 Magdalen College claimed the right to appoint the Principal, arguing that it was merely exercising the normal right of a landlord to select its own tenant for its own property. So far from winning the case was the College that it was decided not only that the right of appointment lay with the Chancellor of the University, but also that as the College could not absolutely prove that it had appointed the early Principals, and as it had not increased the rent of the Hall, those original forty shillings must be regarded as a quit-rent and Magdalen Hall was irremovable. As the historian of Magdalen Hall (later Hertford College) says that this verdict was 'what might be expected', and the

historian of Magdalen College calls it 'hardly surprising', the layman must contain his astonishment
and close the story by relating that in 1816 the College
was glad to recover the use of its own ground by paying
for new buildings for Magdalen Hall on the site of the
then defunct Hertford College.[1]

THE CHORISTERS AND THE SONG SCHOOL:
THOMAS WHYTHORNE

On the foundation of Magdalen College Waynflete
placed sixteen choristers. These nowadays receive their
education at the College School, but in early times they
did not all do so. The boy in medieval England obtained his elementary education in what was called
sometimes a Song School, sometimes an absey (from
ABC), and most choristers were appointed at an age
more suited to the Song School than the Grammar
School. Accordingly the founder laid it down that the
choristers should be taught singing by one of the
Chaplains or Clerks or some other well-qualified
person, who should also give them their elementary
education: this office soon became equivalent to that
of Organist.

A recent discovery makes it clear that the Song
School was not confined to choristers. This is the
autobiography of Thomas Whythorne,[2] perhaps the
first autobiography ever written in English. He was
appointed Demy of Magdalen in 1544. His actual
words give a vivid picture of how at any rate one
sixteenth-century boy came to attend Magdalen

[1] For a full account of the proceedings see S. G. Hamilton's *History
of Hertford College*, pp. 100–3, 119–22, 129–30, and Wilson, pp. 29, 32,
214, 215.
[2] Discovered by Professor James Osborn of Yale, and presented by
him to the Bodleian Library.

School. After telling how he was virtually adopted at an early age by an uncle, who was a priest with a benefice 'within fyve myles of the University of Oxenfoord',[1] he goes on to explain how this uncle

'would sometime demand of me whether I would be a priest or no, or whether I would be a physician or a lawyer; to the which professions (because I had then no taste or savour in learning) I had no devotion or liking. At another time he said unto me, "Be not afraid to tell me your mind plainly, in that which I will demand of you . . . how incline you then to Grammar with the knowledge in the Latin tongue? or else to music, as to learn to sing, and to play on the organs, the which be good qualities and much esteemed in these days, and by them many men do live very well, and do come to preferment thereby. To this said question I answered . . . that I liked very well of them both, but yet of both I liked music best. Then quoth my uncle you shall learn them both, and because that you do like Music best of both, you shall learn somewhat of that first, and afterward you shall learn the other also. . . . He shortly after brought me to Oxford aforesaid, and . . . set me to school in Mawdelyn (*sic*) college. . . . When I had remained in the college aforesaid nigh about seven years (of the which I spent nigh about six years at the music school, and one at the grammar school) nigh about the end of the same, my said uncle deceased, after whose death I was desirous to see the world abroad, and so I left and forsook Oxford and went . . . to London, where by the mean of a friend of mine I was placed with Mr John Haywood, to be both his servant and scholar; for he was not only well skilled in music and playing on virginals, but also such an English poet, as the like, for his

---

[1] Whythorne was an early spelling reformer. His principles as explained by himself can be read in my article about him in the *Lily* of April, 1957. His main variations from the normal are (i) to put a dot under a vowel to lengthen it instead of putting an 'e' at the end of the word (e.g. 'sam' instead of 'same') and (ii) to spell phonetically words of the types 'Jezus' (for 'Jesus') and 'abull' (for 'able'). In the passage quoted here I have modernised the spelling.

wit and invention, with the quantity that he wrote, was not as then in England nor before his time since Chaucer's time.'

It can be seen from this passage that the Song School or Music School must have been a highly organized affair if Whythorne, who was not a Chorister, spent six years there. It seems that at some point before 1538, probably by a gradual process, the Organist or Chaplain or Clerk who undertook the elementary and musical education of the choristers had developed his charge into a regular music and elementary school, open, like the Grammar School, to all (though perhaps non-foundationers such as Whythorne was until 1544 had to pay a fee). This conclusion is reinforced by a passage in the *vulgaria* or phrase book used in the Grammar School in the fifteenth century, which is discussed below (p. 35). It refers to a boy 'that was sent to his absey (=primary school, from ABC) hereby at the next door'. One may legitimately deduce that the Grammar School and this junior institution, whether we call it Music School, Song School or absey, had the same close relationship as the Senior and Junior departments of many a school today.

From very early days certain buildings were allotted to the Choristers and other members of the Song School. A tower called the Vyse, from the vyse or spiral staircase it contained, was erected in 1472–3, and a school was built near it in 1487. This is undoubtedly the building called, a few lines back, 'hereby at the next door'. The Vyse is called in Aggas's map (1578) the Song-School, and by Hearne in 1733 the Organist's House. It stood where the eastern end of the present New Buildings is, and was demolished to make room for them in 1734. The whole block was evidently the music section of the College, placed at such a distance from the rest of it as not to distract study with song.[1]

Obviously, however, though these arrangements may have suited most of the choristers, many of them, before their voices broke, must have reached a stage where they could profit by attending the Grammar School. Bloxam, indeed, because of his theory about Matriculation discussed above,[2] thinks it probable that 'originally they did not pass the limits of the song-school, unless they became Clerks or Demies or at least matriculated members of the University'. But the theory, as we have seen, is untenable; and not only does common sense suggest that the College must from the earliest times have sent those of their choristers who could profit by it to school, but we are told by Wood[3] that Edward Wootton, later Greek Reader at Corpus Christi College, and a famous physician, who became Chorister in 1503, was made Demy 'after he had been educated in the Grammar School joining to Magdalen College'; and the same is true of others later.

THE MAGDALEN SCHOOL GRAMMARIANS

Before we proceed to discuss the curriculum of Magdalen School some account must be given of the Magdalen School grammarians. Their work not only forms the greatest glory of the School, but also throws much incidental light on the way the boys must have worked and lived.

The advance in the study of Latin in England that was made in the half century following 1480 was due to three causes: the invention of printing; the revived

[1] See Wilson, pp. 24, 48; Bloxam, i, p. iii.   [2] p. 17.
[3] *Athenae*, i. 94.

interest in the classical authors that spread from Italy to England; and the scientific study of the art of teaching, in particular of teaching Latin to English boys.

The teaching that prevailed before the invention of printing must have been extremely dreary, aiming only at giving pupils such a knowledge of Latin as would enable them to talk, understand, and write it as their business or professional studies might demand. Oxford University enforced a due attention to parsing and prose and verse composition, and, far from encouraging the study of literature, forbade 'cursory lectures' (i.e. lectures consisting of a running commentary on a text), and laid down, not what authors should be read, but which, like Ovid and Pamphilus' *De Amore*, should be avoided lest they 'should provoke or allure the reader to things unlawful'.[1] As Foster Watson says:[2]

'The main resource of the teacher was his memory of such texts as he had heard lectured on. Knowledge, therefore, of texts must have been very fragmentary, and, the method being traditional, pupils at a grammar school were dependent largely upon the place of training of their teacher. . . . Before the invention of printing, as, in the office of the Church, the use of Sarum, York, Hereford, &c., pointed to variety of traditions which became unified in a Book of Common Prayer, so local usages, books and traditions probably obtained in a school's work in a way we are apt to overlook.'

Even without the increased literary interest of the Renaissance, printing would have brought a pooling of skill and brains, and a consequent improvement in teaching.

But, apart from printing, Latin in England at the end of the fifteenth century was undergoing a revo-

[1] Gibson, p. lxxxv.   [2] Foster Watson, p. 230.

lution. On the one hand men were ceasing to think of it as the normal language of the educated; on the other they were realizing again that it was the language of Cicero. There was loss as well as gain: it was the end of Latin's development as a living tongue; but the stimulus to the study of language was enormous. Imagine English taught in schools today entirely as a vehicle for self-expression, with no writers studied except Paley's *Evidences for Christianity*, a book of parsing, and some selections from Pope; then picture the sudden entrance to the curriculum of Shakespeare, Milton, Sheridan, Dickens, and all the glories of English literature. The reinvigoration and reorientation of language studies would hardly be greater than that which actually occurred in the reigns of Henry VII and Henry VIII.

To speak as if the change were merely from non-Ciceronian to Ciceronian Latin is beside the mark. The Renaissance was the beginning of a new stage in the life-cycle of Language as a whole. Latin as a cosmopolitan language was dead; but its children, the national tongues of modern Europe, were alive, ready to shoot up like seedlings, no longer overshadowed and stunted by the parent tree, but still drawing nourishment from its dead mould. For the Renaissance study of Latin was not mere pedantry; it was language and not merely Latin (or, later, Latin and Greek) that was being studied; new ideals were being put before the student, and generations would soon arise that would not rest content until they could rival in their mother tongue the beauty, the wisdom, and the clarity of Sophocles and Cicero.

It is in the reflected brightness of this prophetic vision of Shakespeare, Spenser, and Milton that one must view the humble grammarians who laid the foundations of the humane education, under whose stimulating yet chastening influence all English literature was produced from their time almost to our own. As these grammarians were nearly all masters or pupils of Magdalen School we must not shrink from the somewhat arid task of examining their work in detail. Their concern was the exposition of Latin Grammar, rather than original research into it. Discoveries were made and knowledge grew, but even today we do not know very much more about Latin than Priscian and Donatus did. It was in the art of teaching that real progress took place.

The foundation on which it was necessary to build was extremely inadequate. Priscian and Donatus were all very well for grown-up philologists, but what they wrote to explain Latin to the Romans was not very helpful to English schoolboys; nor were the simplified grammars that boys used much better. The so-called *Donatus Minor* was the regular handbook of the medieval beginner; it contained in Latin a list of the parts of speech with the regular declensions and conjugations, but no more. For syntax and irregular verbs and nouns the boy turned to the *Doctrinale* of Alexander de Villa Dei, a depressing work in unmetrical Latin hexameters. Verse has its uses in assisting the memory and Alexander's successors made much, perhaps too much, use of it; but the *Doctrinale*, besides being inaccurate, was so obscure that it was usually published with enough interlinear or marginal explanation to make a fresh grammar, so unmetrical that much of it must have been no easier to memorize than prose, and so verbose that even when it ran trippingly the schoolboy would probably have preferred to have the matter put compendiously in prose. Hear Alexander explaining preterites and supines!

TITLE-PAGE OF ANWYKYLL'S (?) PARVULA

The woodcut is not a portrait, being a stock frontispiece used by Wynkyn de Worde for books by various authors, but gives a good idea of what Anwykyll's and Stanbridge's classes must have looked like

DE PRETERITIS ET SUPINIS

Ut tibi per metrum formatio preteritorum
Atque supinorum pateat, presens lege scriptum
Et primo disce quae sit formatio primae.
Vi vel ui vel di vel ti formatio primae
As in preterito vi suscipit s removendo
Non sic formantur ter quinque sed excipiantur
Cre, do, do, mi, iu, sto, pli, co, fri, so, ne, ue, la, se, cu, to
Nam cubo sive crepo domo deinde micoque fricoque . . .

and so on.

The first demand of the new age was for greater accuracy. John Anwykyll, the first known Master of Magdalen School, attempted to meet the demand with his *Compendium totius Grammatice ex Laurentio Valla Servio et Perotto*, published about 1483 by Roode and Hunte at Oxford.[1] The book is written in Latin prose, each section being paraphrased in Latin hexameters for ease of memorization, and is an attempt to present to English boys the recent improvements in grammatical knowledge due to the grammarians mentioned in the title; the excellent selections from classical authors contained in the text are a sign of the times.

More interesting, however, is the *Vulgaria quedam abs Terentio in Anglicam linguam traducta*, published in the same volume as the *Compendium*, and therefore generally accepted as the work of Anwykyll. It consists of phrases from Terence translated into English. Most of these are clearly designed to help the boy in the Latin conversation to which he was limited:

---

[1] In the Bodleian copy there is a modern note saying that the grammar was composed at the request of Archbishop Warham, but as Warham was only a Fellow of New College till 1488 this does not seem likely.

'Odd spede you, save you or rest mery.'[1]

'Gramercy or i thanke you or thee.'

'iii or iiij days yitt i was evyll att ese in my hede/. Be of goode chere thow shalt amende and faare right wele.'

'All odyr thyngys left or sett asyde i muste giff me to my book.'

'I shall ley my or this fyste on thy cheke anon. I wolde thou durste assaye.'

Many are moral precepts:

'Me semys thoos chylder lose evyl ther tyme which are goven so muche to play and sportyng that thei sett nought by their scole and lernynge.'

'Scolers shuld love togyder lyke as thei were bredys.'

'It is better to holde chylder undir with shame & gentillnes sofnes or esyness than be fere or drede.'

There are also pithy comments on matters not usually covered by a school curriculum.[2]

'The condicyon or disposicyon of wymen is whan a man will thei will not and whan a man will not than thei desyre moste.'

'Knowist thou nott the gyses of women. It is a yere while they kembe them tyre them or aray them.'

'There is allwey mich troble amonge shrewys.'

And for the melting mood,

'Women luff or desyre to be mich made off.'

'Com hydere that i may strooke thyn hede.'

In the word of Beatrice White,[3] 'The palm for endeavouring to adapt classical Latin to the exigencies of contemporary English should, then, go to Anwykyll.'

Anwykyll is sometimes credited also with the authorship of *Parvula*, the first Latin grammar in the

---

[1] The corresponding Latin is here and in the following extracts omitted.

[2] It will be remembered that Anwykyll was a married man.

[3] *Vulgaria*, p. xvii.

English language; the first known edition of this book was printed at Oxford by Rood and Hunte in about 1481, and A. E. Shaw[1] thinks that Stanbridge, to whom the book used to be attributed when only later editions were known, was too young to have written it in 1481. Stanbridge was born in 1463, became Fellow of New College in 1481, and succeeded Anwykyll as Master of Magdalen School in 1488, having been his Usher for an unknown time before that. A worked-up version of *Parvula* is included in the *Parvulorum Institutio ex Stanbrigiana Collectione* of which editions in *c.* 1513, 1520 and after are known; but, so far as I know, no edition of *Parvula* itself bears the name of Stanbridge. It is, therefore, possible that Anwykyll wrote *Parvula* and Stanbridge improved it and included it in his *Collectio* of grammatical writings. But 1513 is three years after Stanbridge's death, and it may therefore have been the printer, Wynkyn de Worde, who had the book brought up to date and included in the *Collectio Stanbrigiana*, hoping that it would sell better under the aegis of the famous protagonist of 'Stanbridge Grammar'. Stanbridge's name was certainly a draw; his pupil Whittinton thought it worth while to print a long letter to Stanbridge and verses from him in grammatical works printed long after Stanbridge's death, presumably by way of enlisting the eminent shade as an ally in his battle with Lily and Horman (see below, p. 38).

Whoever the author, *Parvula* was certainly a revolutionary book, because it was in English. Contrast its opening lines, for example, with the hexameters of Alexander de Villa Dei.

'What shalt thou do whan thou hast an englysshe to make

---

[1] In *Transactions of the Bibliographical Society*, 1899. F. Madan (*Oxford Press*, ii. 4), however, attributes *Parvula* to Stanbridge.

in Latyn? I shal reherse myne englysshe ones or twyes /
or thryes / & loke out my pryncypal (sc. verb) & aske the
questyon / who or what. And the worde that answereth
the questyon shall be the nominatyf case to the verbe /
excepte it be a verbe impersonall / as in this example. The
mayster techeth scolers / techeth is the verbe / Who techeth /
the mayster techeth. This worde mayster answereth to the
questyon here & therefore it shall be the nominatyf case
& the worde that cometh after the verbe shall be the accusatyf
case comynly / as Magister docet me.'

Modernize the spelling and punctuation of this, and
you have a simpler and more straightforward introduction to Latin, probably, than any other that was used
in English schools until modern times.

Other books, more certainly by Stanbridge, continue
the work of making Latin easier for the young. *Accedence* is an English substitute for the *Donatus Minor*;
Comparatio Nominum (Comparison of Adjectives), and
Sum, es, fui, a handy summary of the main irregular
verbs, supplemented the *Accedence*; *Vocabula*, a classified
array of Latin words and their English equivalents,
was, to judge by the number of editions known,[1] the
most popular of his books; nor is this surprising when
one remembers that there were no English-Latin
dictionaries then.

To *Vocabula* was added in later years a *Vulgaria*. I
know of no dated edition of this before 1519, nine
years after Stanbridge's death; it may be that earlier
editions were made but have perished; but I cannot
help suspecting that the great name of Stanbridge has
again attracted to itself a book by some other author,

---

[1] The Short-title Catalogue lists editions by Wynkyn de Worde
and Pynson in 1510, 1513, 1516, 1519, 1525, 1531, as well as others
undated or later; and Magdalen College School possesses an edition by
Wynkyn de Worde dated 1523 (with Pynson's heading, *primum iam
edita sua saltem editione* garbled into *sui saltem editione edita*).

more especially as the title bears the addition 'As used at St Paul's' (*iuxta consuetudinem ludi litterarii divi pauli*). These compilations were becoming popular, and this one, like Horman's *Vulgaria*, the most famous of them, consists, not of classical Latin phrases put into English, but of English phrases put into Latin. Most of them are clearly for the use of schoolboys and help to give us a picture of the school life of the day.

'I shall begyn my grammer on mundaye.'
'wolde god we might go to playe.'
'I have no leaser to conne my Latyn.'
'I have blotted my boke.'
'the chyldren be sterynge about in the maistre's absence.'
'lende me the copy of thy latyn and I shall gyve it the agayne by and by.'

Magdalen School and St Paul's may dispute for whose use were added the phrases 'thou stynkest', 'wype thy nose', 'my heed is full of lyce'.

John Holt, who became Usher at Magdalen School in about 1494, tried to combine the merits of Anwykyll's and Stanbridge's various books in one elementary volume, *Lac Puerorum or Mylke for Children*. This was notable for its attempt to present the elementary accidence in picture form; an outstretched hand has a case of the second declension written on each finger, and the ablative on the ball of the thumb; and a bunch of six candles shows all the declensions in a similar way. The book also tried to avoid technical terms by calling the indicative the 'shewynge' mood, the imperative the 'biddynge' mood, and so on. Characteristic of the practical usefulness of this excellent primer is the suggestion that verbs taking the dative should be 'englysshed' in a way that should force the beginner to put the correct case after them. 'Wherefore these verbes Noceo and placeo and suche other

D

the whiche have after theim a datyf case must have these englysshes, I do greve (grief) I do pleasure etc.'

It may well be that Holt should also be credited with the authorship of another *Vulgaria*. This is the one recently discovered in the British Museum[1] by Professor W. Nelson and published by the Oxford University Press as *A Fifteenth Century School Book*. The whole book is of extraordinary charm, and it conveys —quite unselfconsciously—a most sympathetic picture of the writer, who was obviously a schoolmaster of the best sort: an enthusiast for his subject, something of a humorist, wise, kindly and capable of entering into the boy's mind and interests.

Numerous passages that concern the boy's relationship with his master range from the hortatory to the humorous and ironical.

The rules that I must say to my master are scantly half written, wherefore I am worthy to be beat.[2]

Though I should be beat now, and not without a cause, for I was so lewd and so negligent to lose my books, yet I am glad that at the last I have found them again.

Fellows, what is your mind? Are ye glad that the master is recovered of toothache? Whatsoever ye think in your mind, I know my mind. Without doubt, and I were a rich man I would spend a noble worth of ale among good gossips so that he had been vexed a fortnight longer.

There is much serious and sound advice, examples for letter-writing and for conversation. The following extract reveals a typical schoolmaster's philosophy, though not expressed without moderation.

—All the richest men's children everywhere be lost

[1] Arundel ms. 249, fols. 9r–61r.

[2] The spelling has been modernized. The original spelling can of course be found in *A Fifteenth Century School Book*, as published by the Oxford University Press.

Ĥat ſhalt thou do ŵhan thou haſt an englyſſhe to make in latyn? J ſhal reherſe myn englyſſhe ones tŵyes/oʒ thʒyes/ɫ loke out my pʒyncypal ɫ aſke ÿ queſtyon/ŵho/oʒ ŵhat. And the ŵoʒde that an= ſŵereth the queſtyon ſhall be the noiatyf caſe to ÿ verbe/excepte it be a verbe imperſonall/as in this example. ¶The mayſter techeth ſcolers/techeth is ÿ verbe. ŵho techeth/ the mayſter techeth. ¶This ŵoʒde mayſter anſwereth to the queſtyon here/ɫ therfoʒe it ſhall be the noiatyf caſe/ɫ the ŵoʒ de that cometh after ÿ verbe ſhall be the accuſatyf caſe compʒi ly/as Magiſter docet me/ɫ ŵhan J haue ad adiectyf no ŵne pʒono ŵne oʒ partyepple/adiectyf oʒ relatyf J ſhall aſke this queſtyon ŵho oʒ ŵhat. And ÿ ŵoʒde that anſwereth to the queſtyon ſhall be the ſubſtantyf to ÿ adiectyf/ɫ the antecedent to the relatyf. ¶Ŵhan tŵo ſubſtantyues come togyder lon= gynge bothe to one thynge/they ſhall be put bothe in one caſe. As my fader a man loueth me a chylde. Pater me⁹ vir diligit me puerū. ¶Hoŵ ſhalte ÿ knoŵe the pʒyncypall verbe in a reaſon yf thou haue in it moo verbes than one. Euermoʒe my fyrſt verbe ſhall be my pʒyncypal verbe/excepte he come nygh a relatyf oʒ a coniunccyon/oʒ be lyke ÿ infinityf mode. Ŵherby knoŵeſt ÿ ŵhan he cometh nygh a relatyf/ euermoʒe ŵhan he cometh nygh ony of theſe englyſſhe ŵoʒdes/that/ŵhome oʒ the ŵhiche. Ŵherby knoŵeſt ÿ ŵhan he is lyke an infini tyf mode. Euermoʒe ŵhan there cometh this englyſſhe ſygne to oʒ to be befoʒe a ÿbe as to loue oʒ to be byloued/to be taught ¶Ŵhat hath a relatyf/an antecedent. Ŵherby knoŵeſt ÿ an antecedent. Foʒ he cometh befoʒe the relatyf ɫ is reherſed of ÿ relatyf. Ŵherby knoŵeſt ÿ a relatyf. Foʒ he maketh the reher ſynge of a thynge that is ſpoken of befoʒe/ŵhan there cometh a noiatyf caſe bytŵene the relatyf ɫ the verbe perſonall/than the relatyf ſhall be ſuche caſe as the perſonall ŵyll haue after hym. As ego quē pʒeceptoʒ docet aduerto. And there cometh no nominatyf caſe bytŵene the relatyf ɫ the verbe perſonall

THE FIRST PAGE OF PARVULA

From the edition of 1526 in the Bodleian Library

A transcript is given on pages 31–32

(corrupted) nowadays in their youth at home, and that with their fathers and mothers, and that is great pity, plain. But to tell you how, trust me and ye will, it will make me weep.

—Nay, there you pass your bounds. 'But for all the most part', ye should have said. I know many one myself that be sped right well, both in nurture and in cunning. And if I set them among the best, I trow I did no man wrong. But what the devil aileth me to let you of your tale? Ye may say I lack courtesy, and better fed than taught. Say forth, I pray you. Your words may hap to turn some man to good.

—The mothers must have them to play withal stead of puppets (dolls), as children were born to japes and trifles. They bold them both in word and deed to do what they list, and with wantonness and sufferance shamefully they run on the head (headlong). Furthermore, if they hap to call the dame 'whore' or the father 'cuckold' (as it lucketh sometime), they laugh thereat and take it for a sport, saying it is kind (natural) for children to be wanton in their youth. They hold it but folly to put them to school, trowing it good enough whatsoever they have learned at home. They may not forth them beat (manage to beat them) all the world to win, for and they should see them weep, they were then utterly lost. I will make you an example by a cousin of mine that was sent to his absey (ABC) hereby at the next door. And if he come weeping after his master hath chared (driven) away the fleas from his skin, anon his mother looketh on his buttocks if the stripes be a-seen. And the stripes appear, she weepeth and waileth and fareth as she were mad.

Further quotation will be necessary when we come to consider the schoolboy's life in these early days.

For some thirty years after the foundation of Magdalen School the monopoly of Anwykyll, Stanbridge, and Holt in the production of Latin grammars in England appears not to have been challenged; but in 1515 a rival appeared. William Lily, one of those Magdalen Demies trained in the School as Grammar

Masters, was selected by Colet as first Master of his re-founded St Paul's School; and Lily, Colet, and Erasmus between them produced a Latin Grammar which differed from the earlier Magdalen schoolbooks in several respects. The attempt to address the boy in language he could understand was given up; the book was in Latin, and even when an English version was added it was in formal language not unlike that of the modern 'Kennedy'. Much use was made of Latin hexameters for mnemonic purposes, and Robertson, Master of Magdalen School from 1526 to 1534, added many such verses. All of them are clearer, more accurate, and briefer than the verses of Alexander; compare Lily's rules for the formation of tenses in the first conjugation with those of Alexander, quoted above.

As in praesenti perfectum format in avi:
Ut, no nas navi, vocito vocitas vocitavi.
Deme lavo lavi, juvo juvi, nexoque nexui,
Et seco quod secui, neco quod necui, mico verbum
Quod micui, plico quod plicui, frico quod fricui dat, etc.

Lily's methods are certainly less attractive than those of his forerunners and in some ways inferior; but his grammar was meant to be used as a reference book, the main study of Latin being done by the reading of texts; his copious examples taken actually from Latin writers (again like those of Kennedy) point in the same direction. Nevertheless, it soon became customary to learn masses of the grammar by heart, in a way that Wolsey at any rate deplored (see below, page 45), and Lily cannot be acquitted of having pointed the way by his hexameters to a technique of Latin study that turned the subject for many boys into sheer plod for some three hundred years.

Lily's great contemporary rival was Robert Whittinton, a pupil of John Stanbridge at Magdalen School, and a great admirer of his old master. Whittinton is often spoken of as the improver of Stanbridge's grammatical works; but to modern eyes his grammars seem rather to resemble those of his foe, Lily, in that they are both more advanced than Stanbridge's and in Latin. In method, indeed, he goes back to Anwykyll's system of hexameters with prose commentary. More interesting, however, is his *Vulgaria*, a collection of English phrases with their Latin equivalent, framed with the greatest ingenuity so as to perform a double function; they not only illustrate his own grammatical rules but also fit together in groups so as to amount almost to little essays or dialogues, which throw much light not only on contemporary conditions at schools and elsewhere but also on the character of their author. This is the more useful as Whittinton was a stormy petrel, and amid the lightnings loosened around his able but provocative head it is difficult to discern his real nature. Fuller[1] admits he was 'no mean grammarian', but adds, 'Indeed he might have been greater, if he would have been less; pride prompting him to cope with his conquerors, whom he mistook for his match. The first of these was W. Lillie, though there was as great difference betwixt these two grammarians as betwixt a verb defective and one perfect in all the requisites thereof.' Wood[2] is kinder: 'his delight being much in the teaching of youth, he became so excellent in that way, that it was thought, especially by those that favoured him, that he surpassed W. Lilye'. He adds, 'He was . . . esteemed by many for his great skill he had in the Greek and Latin tongues, for his lepid and jocular discourse also, but much blamed by scholars for the biting and sharp reflections used in it,

[1] *Worthies*, ii 335 (1840 edn.).   [2] *Athenae*, i. 55.

and in his books against several noted persons of his age'.

Whittinton was certainly vain; his naïve pride in the degree in grammar which Oxford granted him in 1513 induced him to head all his books with the words, 'Grammatices magistri et prothovatis Anglie in florentissima Oxoniensi achademia laureati',[1] which, to quote Wood again, 'was much stomached by William Horman and William Lilye, and scorned by others of his profession, who knew him to be conceited, and to set an high value on himself, more than he should have done'.

Whittinton appears to have started the grammatical war by fastening some verses against Lily to the door of St Paul's, but Lily and his ally Horman, Head-master of Eton, retorted vigorously, and thereafter none of Whittinton's numerous grammatical works appear without piteous complaints against his enemies and detractors. The main question at issue seems to have been whether authors should be imitated in composition before the relevant grammatical rules are known. Whittinton airs his views pointedly in the *Vulgaria*, illustrating such apparently non-controversial subjects as the agreement of nouns with adjectives by a crushing series of maxims.

'Imitacyon of autours without preceptes & rules is but a longe betynge about the busshe & losse of tyme to a yonge begynner.'

'That teycher setteth the cart before the horse that prefer-reth imitacyon before preceptes.'

'Chyldre brought up only by imitacyon wandre bloun-drynge as a blynde man without his staffe or guyde.'

---

[1] 'Of the Grammar Master and Prime-seer of England crowned with laurel in the most flourishing University of Oxford.'

'Tendre wyttes with suche derke ambage be made as dull as a betle.'

'A scholer by suche tryfullynge hath as moche losse in one daye as he getteth profet in iiij dayes.'

But, though hard on Lily, Whittinton could appreciate merit when he believed in it, as he shows by his references to his contemporaries, Linacre, Erasmus, and Sir Thomas More.

'Lynacre hath translated Galyen out of greeke tongue into latyn. and that in a clene style lately.'

'He is depely experte in greke tongue soo that dyuerse men judge that ther is smal difference bytwene Erasmus and hym.'

'Moore is a man of an aungel's wyt and syngler lernyng.'

'He is a man of many excellent vertues (yf I shold say as it is) I knowe not his felowe.'

'For where is the man (in whome is so many goodly vertues) of that gentylnes, lowlynes and affabylyte.'

'And as tyme requyreth a man of meruelous myrth and pastymes & sometyme of as sad grauyte as who say. a man for all seasons.'

Further quotations from the *Vulgaria* will show that Whittinton was not without insight into the minds he taught. Here follow several passages of consecutive sentences.

'Peace, the mayster is comen into the school. He is as welcome to many of us as water into the shyppe. I shall playe hym a cast of leger demayn & yet he shall not espye it, as quykke eyed as he is. Whyles he declareth the lecture of tully I wyll convey myselfe out of the doores by sleyght. . . . I played my mayster a mery pranke or playe yesterdaye and therfore he hathe thaught me to synge a newe songe to daye. He hath made me to renne a rase (or a course) that my buttokkes doeth swette a blody sweat.'

'I wote not who myght worse saye it than thou. For thou shalte as soone robbe Tully of all his eloquence as prove a latynyste or latyn man. It cometh to the by nature to be a dullarde, therfore it were pyte to put the fro thy enheritaunce. It is clerkly spoken of you [i.e. about you], a man myght as soone pyke mary [marrow] out of a mattok as dryve iij good latyn wordes out of your fortop.' [Is not this the language of Falstaff and Sir Toby Belch?]

' "What maketh the loke so sad?"
' "I am thus sadde for fere of the rodde and the brekefaste that my mayster promest me."
' "Be of good chere man. I sawe ryght now a rodde made of wythye for the, garnysshed with knottes, it wolde do a boy good to loke upon it. Take thy medicyne (though it be somwhat bytter) with a good wyll it wyll worke to thy ease at length."
' "Leve of thy mokkes & japes. Yf thou were in my coote thou woldes have lytle luste to scoffe."

' "I warne the fro hensforth medle not with me bookes. Thou blurrest and blottes them as thou were a bletchy sowter [greasy cobbler]."
' "It is not so but thou hast envye that I shold have profet by them. by cryste I shall quyte [requite it]." '

' "One hath pyked out al the pennes of my pennarde. I pray you lende me a pen."
' "I am in worse case, for one hath plucked fro my gyrdle both pennarde and ynkhorne." '

The frequent references to beatings are sometimes used to give an alarming picture of the brutality of the schools of the day: the reader may judge whether they are not rather examples of the somewhat crude humour that still has an appeal for the average boy. Whittinton himself was certainly an enlightened teacher as the dialogue between Praeceptor and Discipulus shows:

'The gentell exhortacyons of my mayster allured my

mynde merveylously & made me more diligent than all his austeritye coude do.'

'It belongeth to a mayster prudently to consydre the qualyte of his scholers after theyr capacyte & tyme: so to nourysshe them in lernynge as yonge begynners at the fyrst entryng, to use them with easy lessons & playn, also fayre wordes to corage them.'

There is much more sound advice, too long to quote here. Further details of Whittinton's life, his translations from Latin, his connexion with Henry VIII's court, and his appointment as schoolmaster to the 'henchmen' are given in Beatrice White's edition of the *Vulgaria*.

It remains to narrate the issue of the grammatical war. In about 1540 Henry VIII, to avoid the hurt caused by diversity of grammars and in the changing of schoolmasters, appointed 'sundry learned men', among them Dr Richard Cox, Bishop of Ely, to judge between the various rival grammars; and Lily won the day. Thereafter his was by law the only Latin Grammar that could be taught in schools. Into the evasions of the rule, the additions, supplements, alterations, construings of the Latin parts, and what not, that ensued for centuries there is no need to go here.[1]

CURRICULUM AND MANNER OF LIFE

Of the curriculum of the School no exact account exists, but it can be reconstructed with a fair amount of probability from various evidence. At Bruton Grammar School in 1519 it was laid down that all scholars 'were to be taught freely grammar after the form of

[1] For the history of these events, see John Ward's preface to Lily's Grammar, and Henry VIII's Proclamation (quoted in White, p. xxxviii).

Magdalen College, Oxford, or St Paul's School,
London, and not songs or petite learning or English
Reading, but to be made perfect Latin men'.[1] This
tells us, not only what we know already, that Magdalen
School was a Grammar School and not a Song or
Elementary School; but also that among grammar
schools which turned out 'perfect Latin men' there
were probably two types, that of Magdalen and that
of St Paul's. The difference between the two types
must have been in the curriculum and probably lay
in the authors read.

Colet, the refounder of St Paul's, in spite of the
famous statute of 1518 in which he says that 'fylthy-
nesse and all such abusyon which the later blynde
worlde brought in, which more ratheyr may be callid
blotterature thenne litterature I utterly abbanysh and
exclude oute of this scole', wanted his school to study
'goode auctors such as have the veray Romayne
eliquence joyned with wisdome, specially Cristyn
auctours that wrote theyre wysdome with clene and
chast laten other in verse or prose'. Accordingly his
list of authors starts with the catechism he wrote himself and ends with the fifteenth-century eclogues of
Baptista Mantuanus, ignoring the classical writers
whose study was the peculiar aim of the Renaissance.[2]

Three other great schools whose curriculum at the
same time is known, Eton, Winchester, and Wolsey's
school at Ipswich, are of a very different type; and the
table below, giving the authors read in the order they
were approached, shows by the closeness of the
resemblances between the schools that there was what
may be called a normal course.

[1] *Schools Inquiry Commission Report*, 1868, p. 121.
[2] *S.M.E.*, pp. 279, 280.

Ipswich	Eton	Winchester
Cato's *Moralia* and Lily's *Carmen* *Monitorium*	Cato	Cato
Aesop	Erasmus	Aesop
Terence	Terence	Lucian
		Terence
Virgil	Virgil	Virgil
Cicero's letters	..	Cicero's letters
Sallust or Caesar	Horace	Sallust
Horace	Ovid	Ovid
Ovid	Cicero	Horace

The close connexion of Magdalen with all the three[1] leaves no doubt which type Magdalen School would belong to, and the Bruton statute confirms that it was of the opposite type to St Paul's.

The authors read at Magdalen, then, may be taken to have been very similar to those that Wolsey laid down for Ipswich. But even among the schools of the 'humane' as opposed to the 'Christian' type there were differences, in particular the rivalry between the various grammars. Of these the two most important were that designed for St Paul's by Colet, Erasmus, and Lily, which went by the name of Lily's and that originated at Magdalen by Anwykyll, Holt, and Stanbridge, and elaborated by Whittinton, which was usually called 'Stanbridge Grammar'. Lily had been one of the Demies brought up as teachers in the College School, but his grammar was associated more closely with St Paul's than with Magdalen, and it might have been expected that Magdalen would cling to Stanbridge grammar. There are reasons, however, for thinking that it was not long before Lily's was adopted.

[1] Waynflete, founder of Magdalen, had been Headmaster of Winchester and Headmaster and Provost of Eton; Stanbridge, the most famous, academically, of the Magdalen schoolmasters, was a Wykehamist; Wolsey, who drew up the curriculum for his school at Ipswich, had learnt Grammar, probably, and schoolmastering, certainly, at Magdalen School.

The schools at Reading and Manchester are ordered to study Stanbridge Grammar, as taught at Banbury School,[1] and, though both John and, conceivably, Thomas Stanbridge[2] had some connexion with Banbury, it is inconceivable that Banbury rather than Magdalen (where John made his grammar and Thomas ended his days teaching) should have been mentioned as the home *par excellence* of Stanbridge Grammar, unless by 1515, the date of the original Manchester statute,[3] Stanbridge Grammar had ceased to be taught at Magdalen.[4] Lily was winning the day —Eton changed from Whittinton to Lily between 1528 and 1530—and Wolsey appoints him to be used from the Third to the Sixth Form at Ipswich; and Wolsey's influence would have been enough to effect the change in the college he loved and dominated.

The grammar studied and authors read at Magdalen, then, were probably much the same as those that Wolsey ordains for Ipswich. In the First Form the boys learned the eight parts of speech and the pronunciation of Latin (very likely in Stanbridge: Wolsey mentions no book, but Winchester and Eton used him, being written in English, and therefore suited to beginners). In the Second they learn to speak Latin and do easy sentences into Latin and write them out fair; for reading Lily's 'Carmen monitorium', i.e. the *De Moribus*, and Cato's *Moralia* are recommended. In

---

[1] See, e.g., *S.M.E.*, p. 271; Beesley's *History of Banbury*, p. 196. The statutes of Manchester Grammar School ordain that the High Master shall be 'able to teche Childeryn Gramyer after the scole, use, maner and forme of the scole of Banbury in Oxford schyre, nowe there taught, wiche is called Stanbryge gramyer'.

[2] But see pp. 67–9 for reasons to doubt if Thomas had anything to do with Banbury at all.   [3] *S.M.E.*, p. 297.

[4] Thomas Pope, the founder of Reading, was taught at Banbury, but Oldham, the founder of Manchester, was not.

the Third Form Aesop and Terence are read and Lily's Nouns studied: in the Fourth, Virgil and Lily's Principal Parts of Verbs. The Fifth are to read select letters of Cicero; the Sixth Form 'seems to call for some history, whether Sallust or Caesar'. In the Seventh the boys read Horace's *Epistles* or Ovid's *Metamorphoses* or *Fasti*; they compose verses or letters, practising the turning of verse into prose and back again into verse, and learn by heart, just before going to sleep, passages to be said next day. In the Eighth Class they study the science of Grammar proper in Donatus or Valla[1] and deal with some set book thoroughly. Letters and compositions are to be practised.

The hand of the skilled schoolmaster shows itself at various points in Wolsey's recommendations. He recognizes the temptation to concentrate on the more advanced boys ('least of all is it right to rob this age—the First Form—of your full attention'). Accuracy and neatness in writing out exercises, the ease of Aesop and the usefulness of Terence (as an aid to conversation), the necessity of reading Virgil *voce bene sonora* to bring out the majesty of his poetry, the advantage of learning by heart last thing at night—all are noted and commended to the masters. The emphasis on literature is obvious, and even more striking is the kindly and sympathetic approach to the boy, very different from that which made the name 'schoolmaster' a word of terror in subsequent centuries. The English sentences that the Second Form turn into Latin are to be 'not silly or pointless, but with a clear or well-phrased meaning

[1] Wolsey cuts down the study of grammar in the lower forms to the minimum possible; and it is interesting to find this practice recommended once more by the most modern authorites, e.g. the section on teaching Latin in the 1938 Report of the Consultative Committee on Secondary Education.

which a boy's mind might sympathise with'; the whole
day is not to be spent grinding at grammar; the
teacher is warned not to deal with the *tenera pubes* by
severe beatings, threats, or tyranny; and 'from time to
time the mind must be relaxed; play is to be admitted
but gentle and worthy of letters. Pleasure must be
mixed with study in such a way that the boy may think
of the game rather than the labour of learning. Care
must be taken that the pupil's minds are not crushed
by excessive strain or wearied with too long reading.'

Much like the Ipswich curriculum must that of
Magdalen have been by about 1510. To begin with it
was, no doubt, intermediate between this and the
parsing and grammar-grinding of medieval days.
Wolsey's recommendations to Ipswich were, doubtless,
due partly to his own study and interest in teaching;
but his scheme must have been founded on his schoolboy and schoolmaster memories, and, when we see
him stressing the usefulness of Terence, we may guess
that he is thinking of Anwykyll's *Terentii Vulgaria*
which he found Magdalen School studying when he
became Master there, and which he had probably
studied there himself, when a boy.

Greek, so far as we know, was not a regular part of
the curriculum at first, but as will be seen later (page
76) was added to it at the order of Cromwell's Visitors
in 1535. Even before this, however, the Master was
often capable of teaching Greek and, no doubt, did
teach it to those who wished. The epitaph of Stokesley
(Usher 1498) makes mention of his knowledge of
Greek;[1] and it is significant that Edward Wotton, who
was at Magdalen School from 1503 to about 1513,

---

[1] 'Huic et Graecorum palma parata fuit.' Quoted by Bloxam, iii. 22.
The epitaph is wrongly credited to Scarbott (Master, 1494–8) by Foster
Watson, p. 240.

CARDINAL WOLSEY

From the portrait in Big School, a copy of the portrait by Holbein at Christ Church

was made Socio Compar of Corpus Christi in 1520, and 'read the Greek lecture there for some time' before travelling abroad and returning to be Greek Reader of that College.[1]

The time-table was, no doubt, similar to that of the University and most schools of the day: early school from 6 to 9, breakfast, school from 9.45 to 11, dinner, school from 1 to 5; and every day, until the Reformation abolished many customs good and bad, school ended with prayer to God for the souls of the Founder and all other benefactors and the Founder's parents and all the faithful departed.[2]

Something of that kind would the hours be; they seem hard, but in Elizabeth's day, and probably earlier, at Eton at any rate, there were only four or five days' work in the week, and few weeks went by without a whole- or half-holiday; for 'every greater feast-day was a whole holiday, and on every eve of the "greater doubles", feasts on which double rations were enjoyed, there was a partial holiday, no work being done after dinner at 11 a.m.'[3]

These practices may not have been to the letter those of Magdalen, but the boys must have had numerous holidays on saints' days, and there were frequent occasions which helped to diversify the routine of the schoolboy's life. Among these Maundy Thursday may be mentioned, when the President of the College reminded himself and the world that he was but a man by washing the feet of seven Choristers. The Informator Choristarum, doubtless, was responsible for selecting the most suitable candidates for the honour. Another festivity was provided by the celebrations connected with the Boy-Bishop. Frequent charges for gloves for the Boy-Bishop on St Nicholas' Day

[1] *Athenae*, i. 94.   [2] *Statutes*, p. 77.   [3] *S.M.E.*, p. 307.

(December 6th) appear in the early account books, and from what is known of the procedure elsewhere we may deduce with Bloxam[1] that the Bishop, one of the Choristers, and his fellows sang the first vespers of their patron saint, and afterwards

'partook of a *convivium* prepared by the College at which there seems to have been a great consumption of apples, pears and even wine. We may fancy also the Procession of the Boy-Bishop and his youthful band, arrayed in copes and bearing burning tapers, moving solemnly round the Cloisters, while the *Centum Quadraginta Quattuor* is sweetly chanted, and then passing with the Banner of St Nicholas through the western door of the Chapel to one of the six altars in the nave, perchance that dedicated to the Holy Innocents, when the censing commences; and then, the antiphon and other functions ended, the Bishop, standing on the steps of the altar, wearing cope and mitre, and holding his pastoral staff in his left hand, gives his solemn benediction to all present, and while he makes the sign of the cross over all the kneeling crowd, sings aloud,

"Crucis signo vos consigno: vestra sit tuitio,
Qui nos emit et redemit suae carnis pretio." '

The original idea of the Boy-Bishop celebrations seems to have been to remind men of the purity and sanctity of children; but by 1480 it seems to have been generally abused and made the occasion of ribaldry and jollification. The Boy-Bishop, together with the foot-washing on Maunday Thursday, disappeared at the Reformation, appeared again under Mary, and vanished for ever when Elizabeth came to the throne.

Another celebration, that of singing on top of Magdalen Tower to greet the dawn on May 1st, has lasted with variations to the present day. Originally a secular concert was held, at which, in Wood's words, 'the

---

[1] See Bloxam, i, pp. vi, vii, for the Boy-Bishop and the washing of the feet of the Choristers.

choral ministers of this House do . . . salute Flora every year on the first of May at four in the morning with vocal music of several parts'.[1] But late in the eighteenth century a change was made; one year, the weather being particularly bad, the Choir ascended the Tower an hour late and scrambled through a hymn which they all knew by heart, the 'Te Deum Patrem' by Dr Thomas Smith (Fellow 1665-92), set to music by Benjamin Rogers (Organist 1664-86). This procedure, to the greatly increased comfort of the Choir, has been followed ever since, except that it is now taken more seriously than it was on that first wet day, and the legend has arisen that the celebration was always religious, and used to be a requiem mass for Henry VII. Wilson suggests that its real origin was in a kind of inauguration ceremony on the completion of the Tower.[2]

Another custom that prevailed at many medieval schools was that of 'barring out'. Once a year as a rule, but the date or dates varied, the boys used to claim the right to bar themselves in and the Master out of the School until they were given a holiday. No doubt the reception the barring out met with hung on the temper, mild or fierce, conscientious or lazy, of the Master. That the custom prevailed at Magdalen in the fifteenth century one may tentatively deduce from the account we possess of barring out in the eighteen-thirties.[3] By far the most likely explanation of the existence of this almost obsolete custom in the nineteenth century is that it had never died out.

Traces of other amusements can be gathered from the statutes and from casual references in College documents. Hares, hounds, ferrets, hawks, and song-

[1] *Colleges and Halls*, p. 350.
[2] Wilson, pp. 50–3.   [3] See below, pp. 141f.

E

birds are forbidden to 'Scholars and Fellows', as are dice, cards, and every 'noxious, inordinate, and unlawful game'. 'Scholars and Fellows' for our purposes means 'Demies'; and even if we make the bold assumption thay they all avoided the forbidden amusements we may guess that the freer members of the School practised them to whatever extent their purses allowed. Even the Demies were forbidden to throw or shoot stones, arrows, balls, and logs only if they were likely to injure the College buildings; the frequent notices in the College accounts for the repairs to windows in the School suggests that some of the pupils did not consider themselves bound even by this modified prohibition. In 1509 King Henry VII, who is said to have been troubled on his death-bed by pangs of conscience for the close-fistedness he had displayed during his lifetime, gave the College a she-bear.[1] An embarrassing gift, but no doubt the School was given leave to attend the baitings. In 1510 seventeen pence were spent on food, &c., for the boys taking part in the play on Easter Day;[2] and in 1519 the Master of the Choristers received 2s. 6d. for 'the dyeing and making of the tunic of him who played the part of Christ, and for the wigs of the women'.[3] It was Choristers rather than schoolboys, no doubt, who took part in these plays, but the schoolboys would attend them.

The *Fifteenth Century School Book* gives a varied and clear picture of some of the schoolboy's amusements, which amplifies what has been deduced above from College records. A reference to play-acting is discussed in connexion with the account of Thomas More's attendance (page 60); and a predecessor of Henry VII's bear is mentioned.

[1] Macray, i. 64.   [2] Ibid. i. 65.   [3] Ibid. i. 71.

All the young folks almost of this town did run yesterday to the castle to see a bear baited with fierce dogs within the walls. It was greatly to be wondered, for he did defend himself so with his craftiness and his wiliness from the cruel dogs methought he set not a whit by their woodness (madness) nor by their fierceness.

And there are other open-air amusements:

Put off shortly that long heavy gown and have a lighter, and let us go to Headington grove and there we shall have a hare start. Why standest thou still? See how the weather looketh up lustily against our journey.

Bend your bow and shoot with me; let us prove whether of us be the better archer. I can tell where is a pair of butts made with new turves. Shall we go thither?

This day, early in the morning, about three of the clock, mine host and his neighbours went to the wood to kill the wild boar that men say is there, they with their curs and mastiffs and he with his greyhounds and spaniels. I pray God prosper that they go about, and tomorrow I will tell you how they sped. . . .

Yesterday I promised that I would tell you how the hunters did speed. Hearken a little and I will. As soon as they were come to the wood and had set on their dogs for to take the boar, straightways every one of them fought so sore with another that it was very hard for the masters to depart them.

There are similar passages about fishing, liming birds, maying, competitions in shooting and running, dancing, orchard-robbing, country walks, and even

Go into the garden and gather some flowers to set in our window.

Out of school the manner of life of the different classes of pupil would vary. The Demies and Choristers would be subject to the discipline of the College. They had to speak nothing but Latin, and they were forbidden to linger in Hall after meals, by the fire, except when the fire was kept going 'through reverence for God and his Mother or some other Saint', when they could amuse themselves in a sober way with songs, poems, chronicles, and marvels. Every one had to be in the College by eight at night in winter and by nine in summer; and, as they rose at five, the boys were probably abed early. Waynflete left minute instructions about beds; in each room there were two principal beds and one or two 'trookyll beddys'; Fellows slept in the principal beds and exercised authority over the boys who slept in the same room; any one over fifteen years of age had a bed to himself. The juniors in each room were no doubt expected to 'fag' for their elders; and 'the Choristers waited in Hall, a custom which was retained until 1802, and continued as a form at the Gaudy for many years after that date'.[1] Servants in College were few and the College accounts show frequent payments to *scolastici* or *pauperes scolares*, both of which terms probably mean members of the School, for such odd jobs as carrying logs or cleaning out the President's house.[2]

Other members of the school would live with their parents in the town or in the Hall or in other houses under 'creansers'—housemasters so to speak—to whom the *Fifteenth Century School Book* makes several references.

They do wisely that send no children to the university but they put them under Creansers to have the rule of them and of their money. For if they were not so ordained, they should waste all their money at dice and cards in Christmas time.

John, methinketh there is no man more ungentle neither more uncourteous to me than thou art, for alway thou complainest upon me without a cause to my Creanser.

The book brings vividly before the reader a host of

[1] Wilson, pp. 43, 44.　　　　　　[2] Macray, i. 62, 66, 68.

other elements in the boys' lives. Passages about their eating and drinking imply a surprisingly varied menu. A bridal where 'after our frumenty we were served with goose, capon, peacock, crane, swan and such other delicates that longeth to a good feast' was no doubt a special occasion. But some other passages imply a surprisingly 'choosy' outlook.

I have no delight in beef and mutton and daily meats. I would once have a partridge set before us, or some other such, and in especial little small birds that I love passingly well.

Thou will not believe how weary I am of fish, and how much I desire that flesh were come in again. For I have eat none other but salt fish this lent, and it hath engendered so much flewm within me that it stoppeth my pipes that I can unneth (scarcely) speak neither breathe.

Excess in drink was evidently possible though not recommended.

Meseemeth thou hast drunk enough, Thomas, when neither thy tongue neither thy feet will serve thee.

As I haunted ale houses and wine taverns, I have spent all the money that I had in my purse.

Books are important but not impossibly rare.

As I was cheaping of a book, there came one that proffered more than I and bought it out of my hands.

My master sent me to enquire a certain man of whom I should ask the keys of the library to be brought unto him and I could not find him nowhere. I came again to my master and then I missed my Latin book, but I cannot tell whether I lost him running or left him in the tavern.

Methinketh thou lackest many things that is need for a good scholar to have: first, a pennar (pen-case) and an ink-horn, and then books, and yet furthermore, the which is first and chief and passeth all precepts of masters and all other doctrine, as exercise of Latin tongue and diligence.

I may blame thee, William, for thine unkindness that thou hast kept my book so long.

Some of the classroom discipline is in the hands of a senior pupil or monitor called 'custos', but it seems to have been imperfect even under the master.

It is a noble sport for me to hear the fasing (swaggering) and brawling of these boys when they shall be accused of custos and to see how subtle every man is in defending himself.

As soon as I am come into the school this fellow goeth to make water and he goeth out to the common draft. Soon after another asketh licence that he may go drink. Another calleth upon me that he may have licence to go home. These and such other leyth my scholars (my scholars lie?) for excuse oftentimes that they may be out of the way.

One of the most touching pieces in the book is a long soliloquy by a twelve-year-old new boy.

The world waxeth worse every day, and all is turned to upside down, contrary to the old guise, for all that was to me a pleasure when I was a child, from three year old to ten (for now I go upon the twelfth year), while I was under my father and mother's keeping, be turned now to torments and pain. For then I was wont to lie still abed till it was forth days, delighting myself in sleep and ease. The sun sent in his beams at the windows that gave me light instead of a candle. O, what a sport it was every morning when the sun was up to take my lusty pleasure between the sheets, to behold the roof, the beams and rafters of my chamber, and look on the cloths the chamber was hanged with! There durst no man but he were mad awake me out of my sleep upon his own head while me list to sleep. At my will I arose with entreaties, and when the appetite of rest went his way by his own accord, then I awoke and called upon whom me list to lay my gear ready to me. My breakfast was brought to my bed's side as oft as me list to call therefor, and so many times I was first fed or I were clad. So I had many pleasures more besides these, whereof some be forgotten, some I do remember well, but I have no leisure to rehearse them now.

But now the world runneth upon another wheel, for now at five of the clock by the moonlight I must go to my book and let sleep and sloth alone. And if our master hap to awake us, he bringeth a rod stead of a candle. Now I leave pleasures that I had sometime; here is nought else preferred but monishing and stripes, Breakfasts that were sometime brought at my bidding is driven out of country and never shall come again. I would tell more of my misfortunes, but though I have leisure to say, yet I have no pleasure, for the rehearse of them maketh my mind more heavy.

A sad little boy, who will read Ovid among the Goths with sympathy when he gets so far in his Latin; but besides a schoolmaster who is not unaware of his sorrows he has other, everlasting consolations.

Upon a fair, clear night, the sky garnished with stars out of number shining goodly, which and ye take heed ye may see them twinkle as it were a candle or a taper burning, and among them the moon with her full light goeth forth by little and little, gliding softly; be not these pleasant things?

CHAPTER III

THE HISTORY OF THE SCHOOL, ITS MASTERS & PUPILS DOWN TO 1564

Claymond, Lily, John Stanbridge, Thomas More, Whittinton, Scarbott, Stokesley, Wolsey, Brynknell—Strife in the College—Tyndale, Wotton—Migrations: Brackley—Hooker—The Stanbridge Problem—Parkhurst, Bickley, Robertson —Cromwell and the Reformation: Sherrey, Harley, Bentham, Piers, Humfrey Whythorne—Cooper, Camden: the Marprelate Controversy: the Attempted Suppression of the School

CLAYMOND, LILY, JOHN STANBRIDGE, THOMAS MORE, WHITTINTON, SCARBOTT, STOKESLEY, WOLSEY, BRYNKNELL

SOMETHING has already been said about Anwykyll, the first Master known. As to his pupils, though we cannot be certain of some of them, it is probable that Cardinal Wolsey, William Lily, and John Claymond were the most famous.

Where Wolsey got his grammar learning is not certainly known. Wilson[1] suggests that he became a Probation Fellow in 1491 or 1492; and it is a likely deduction of Chandler[2] that Wolsey, like Lily, was one of those Demies selected in accordance with the statutes[3] to spend extra time in the School that they might subsequently become grammar-teachers. Of Wolsey's mastership of the School and his later promotion more will be said later.

Claymond, says Wood,[4] 'when a boy, was sent to Oxford, where, after he had completed his grammar learning in the school near to Magdalen College great gate (being then within and not without the said gate) he was made demy first, and in 1488 perpetual fellow of that College'. He became Demy in 1484, and if

[1] p. 49.   [2] p. 274.   [3] p. 22.   [4] *Athenae*, i. 47.

Wood's account is to be believed he must have been a member of the School at least since 1480, when the Schoolroom outside the Great Gate was built. Claymond became President of Magdalen in 1507, and in 1516 was selected by Bishop Fox to be the first President of his new college of Corpus Christi. He appears to have been not only one of the wealthiest Heads of Houses, but also one of the best renowned for piety, good works, and learning. 'He was the friend of Erasmus and More, and was in correspondence with other noted scholars of his time, both in England and abroad',[1] and 'even the "martyrologist", Foxe, when he mentions him, is careful to say that he does so "for reverence and learning's sake", and forbears to scoff at an instance of the devotion which he practised.'[2] We have already seen that Claymond was responsible for equipping the old Schoolroom in the *aula bassa* with beds for the poor.[3]

William Lily entered Magdalen as a Demy in 1486, aged eighteen, and, no doubt having been trained as a schoolmaster, went to the East, where he visited Jerusalem and perfected himself in Greek and Latin at Rhodes and Rome. After his return he settled in London, and in 1510 was made by Colet the first High Master of the reconstituted St Paul's School. His grammatical writings have been discussed above.

John Stanbridge, a Wykehamist who became Fellow of New College in 1481, was first Usher and

---

[1] Wilson, p. 62.

[2] Ibid., p. 61. Foxe relates that, when a false alarm of fire was raised at St Mary's Church, all disgraced themselves except Claymond 'and a few other aged persons with him, who for their age and weakness durst not thrust themselves into the throng among the rest, but kneeled down quietly before the high altar, committing themselves and their lives unto the Sacrament'.

[3] p. 14.

then successor to Anwykyll. His grammatical works and those of his pupil Whittinton have already been described. Stanbridge was Master from 1488 to 1494, Holt, the grammarian, being his Usher for a time. In 1501 Stanbridge became Master of the Hospital of St John at Banbury.[1]

'This John Stanbridge', says Wood,[2] 'was a right worthy lover of his faculty, and an indefatigable man in teaching and writing, and, as it may appear by those things which he has published, very grateful to the muses and public concerns. The last of which he has consulted more than his own private interest; and when in his old age he should have withdrawn himself from his profession, which is esteemed by the generality a drudgery, and have lived upon what he had gotten in his younger days, he refused it and lived poor and bare to the last, yet with a juvenile and cheerful spirit.'

'A gracious picture', comments Beatrice White;[3] but probably not an entirely authentic one; for Wood in some respects appears to confuse John with his relative (?) Thomas Stanbridge.[4] John may have gone on teaching in the school attached to the Hospital at Banbury,[4] but, far from living 'poor and bare', he died in 1510, possessed not only of his Hospital, worth £16. 13s. 4d. per annum in 1534,[5] but also of the Rectory of Winwick and a Prebend of Lincoln Cathedral.

That Thomas More, Henry VIII's Chancellor and victim, later to be canonized as a saint in the Roman Church, attended the school in the time of Stanbridge and Holt, is, I think, almost certain; and as this has only lately been realized it may be desirable to give evidence for so important a matter. The pre-eminence

[1] See Bloxam, iii. 12.   [2] *Athenae*, i. 39.   [3] *Vulgaria*, p. xvii.
[4] For a discussion of Wood's confusion of the two Stanbridges, and of the school at Banbury, see below, pp. 69 ff.
[5] Beesley's *History of Banbury*, p. 197.

SIR THOMAS MORE

From the Portrait by Holbein. Reproduced by gracious permission of H.M. The Queen

of the School in the 1490's, when More was at Oxford, was such that it would be surprising if a passionate enthusiast for the new education, such as More later showed himself to be, had not taken the opportunity of studying under men like Stanbridge and Holt; and a definite link can be seen in the fact that More's earliest extant letter is one written to John Holt in 1501. The letter itself contains a passage that might well have been written to a former teacher: 'How am I getting on with my education (in bonis artibus)? you say. Excellently! I have dropped Latin in favour of Greek, with such effect that I have forgotten the former and not acquired the latter.' Holt dedicated his Latin Grammar to Cardinal Morton (who had sent More to Oxford to perfect his Latin) and the book contains epigrams composed to Holt's honour by More; so that it is surely reasonable to suppose that More is the link between Morton and Holt; in other words that Holt taught More Latin at Oxford.

A correspondence in *The Times Literary Supplement* of December 1953 and the following January had some relevance in this connexion. It is generally believed that More was taught, before he came to Oxford, by Nicholas Holt (no relation of John Holt) at St Anthony's School in London. The correspondence made it clear that this belief really rests entirely on the statement to that effect in Stapleton's *Tres Thomae*, which was written long after More's death and is far from reliable; and I have ventured to suggest that there has been a confusion between Nicholas and John Holt.[1] Even if this suggestion is not correct, of course, the reasons given above for believing More to have been taught by John Holt at Oxford are not affected.

A similar conclusion, based on further evidence, is

[1] *The Times Literary Supplement*, Jan. 1st, 1954.

reached by Professor William Nelson, in his introduction to *A Fifteenth Century School Book*. He writes,

'At about the time that the Magdalen *vulgaria* was being compiled, Thomas More was studying grammar—that is, humane letters—at the University . . . since Waynflete's statutes specifically provided free tuition in grammar for Oxford students of whatever college, More certainly had the opportunity of studying there. The number of More's friends and acquaintances who studied or taught at Magdalen during the last years of the fifteenth century is remarkable. The list includes Grocyn, Colet (probably), Holt, Wolsey, Whittinton, Claymond, Stokesley, Lily and Lee. The last two, both scholarship boys at the School, had been his friends since his early youth, as More himself tells us, and it was before 1499 that the *adolescentulus* More had contributed his poems to Holt's Latin Grammar. It is therefore not unreasonable to suppose that young More may have been set exercises in translation from the very *vulgaria* which we have before us, or from one like it.'

Professor Nelson's introduction raises a further interesting point:[1]

'A curious detail offers a link between Thomas More and the Magdalen *vulgaria*. Among the exercises is a bit of dramatic criticism which may be the earliest example of the genre in English:

I remember not that I ever saw a play (*ludicrum*) that more delighted me than yesterday's. And albeit chief praise be to the doer (*auctor*) thereof, yet are none of the players to be disappointed of their praise. For every man played so his parts that (except him that played King Solomon) it is hard to say whom a man may praise before other.

More's earliest extant letter, written to the Grammarian Holt in 1501 . . . begins, "I am sending you everything you asked for except for the parts which I added to the comedy

[1] pp. xxvi–xxix.

of Solomon; I cannot send them to you because I do not have them in my possession". Considering the rarity of "comedies" at this time, I find it difficult to believe these are two different comedies of Solomon. . . . Erasmus tells us that Thomas More wrote many comedies in his youth. The letters I have quoted and the enthusiastic comment on the comedy of King Solomon in the *vulgaria* exercises suggest that interest in such plays was strong at Magdalen. It is tempting to conclude that More's comedies were written for performance by the schoolboys, and that the exceptionally delightful *King Solomon* ("chief praise be to the doer") was one of them.'

Thus we can now think of More, the future Chancellor and martyr, sent by his patron Cardinal Morton to Oxford about 1492, not only studying under Holt and Stanbridge but also contributing in a practical way to those dramatic productions which then as now combined entertainment with education for the boys of the School.

Among Stanbridge's other eminent pupils were Robert Whittinton, the grammarian, of whom enough has been said above,[1] and John Longland.[2] Longland became a Demy in 1493, and after being Principal of Magdalen Hall from 1505 to 1507, he rose in the Church to be Bishop of Lincoln in 1521. He was apparently intimate with Wolsey—they were Fellows of Magdalen together—and 'in 1528, or thereabouts, he was the first man of account that, by the persuasions

---

[1] Wood (*Athenae*, i. 55) says, 'Robert Whittinton was . . . educated partly in grammaticals under John Stanbridge in the school joining to the common gate of Magdalen College; and afterwards made a considerable progress in logicals and philosophicals, but in what College or Hall it appears not.' The passage is interesting; Wood is puzzled at not being able to find a college or hall for Whittinton, when clearly in Stanbridge's day the School carried its pupils so far that for a grammar teacher further education at the University was unnecessary.

[2] Bloxam, iv. 26 ff.

of Cardinal Wolsey, mentioned a divorce to the king to be between him and his Queen Katharine'.[1] Being the chief commissioner in this matter of the divorce, Longland apparently incurred a good deal of odium; but he was elected Chancellor of Oxford in 1532, and in 1534 his name heads the unanimous answer which the University made to the King's question, 'That the Bishop of Rome had no greater jurisdiction given him by God in Holy Writ in this realm of England than any other foreign Bishop'.

Andrew Scarbott, Stanbridge's successor, ruled from 1494 to 1498. Little is known of him, but he has the credit of having taught not only Longland but also Edward Lee. Lee became a Demy in 1495 but in 1502/3 migrated to Cambridge,[2] and having become Chaplain to Henry VIII, was sent by him on several important embassies to the Continent, being rewarded with many prebends, the Archdeaconry of Colchester, and finally in 1531, the Archbishopric of York. He died in 1544.

From the retirement of Holt in 1495 several obscure Ushers worked for short periods; in 1498 both Master and Usher were men of note, though they ruled only for a short time and probably did not overlap. In the beginning of the year the Usher for one month was John Stokesley, and for the last two terms of the year (before and after Christmas, the year then ending in March) the Master was Wolsey.

Stokesley was a man of great ability and was Vice-President of the College during the days of confusion that marred the last part of Mayew's Presidency. At the visitation which Bishop Fox held in 1507 to investigate the trouble, Stokesley was accused by the rival faction of numerous crimes and misdemeanours,

[1] Wood, *Athenae*, i. 161.　　　　　　　　　　[2] Bloxam, iv. 35 ff.

ranging from disobedience to the President to adultery with the wife of the Organist and baptizing a cat in order to discover a treasure by magic. The evidence against him, however, was mostly reminiscent of 'what the soldier said', and more suggestive of prurience and pettiness on the part of his accusers than of guilt in Stokesley; such, at any rate, was the view taken by the Visitor's Commissary. Like Lee, who had probably been his pupil, Stokesley became one of Henry VIII's trusted agents and ambassadors, and was rewarded in 1520 with the Bishopric of London. He was not popular with the Puritans, with whom he had a reputation for burning heretics. Foxe[1] credits him with thirty-one, but the disingenuous Lawrence Humphrey swells this to 'over three hundred'.[2] Stokesley was a staunch Catholic and 'being much harassed by Cromwell and others on a frivolous suspicion of not having aided the King's attempts in abolishing the Pope's Supremacy, and the destruction of the Monasteries, he died miserably, being, as it appeared, almost worn out with grief'.[3]

Wolsey, as we have seen, had probably attended the School as Demy under Anwykyll. By 1497, the first year in which his name appears in any surviving College books, he was about fourteenth in the list of Fellows, and next year he was appointed Master. It was this appointment which led to his future greatness, for in the School at this time were three sons of the Marquess of Dorset, a step-son of Edward IV. 'It pleased the said Marquess', says Cavendish,[4] 'against a Christmas season to send as well for the schoolmaster as for his children home for their recreation in that

---

[1] *Acts and Monuments*, iii. 104.   [2] *Vita Juelli*, p. 268.
[3] Letter from Richard Hills to Henry Bullinger, *Orig. letters* (Parker Soc.), i. 231.   [4] *Life of Wolsey*.

pleasant and honourable feast.' The immediate result was a living for Wolsey, and, when Henry VII died an introduction to Henry VIII; for one of Wolsey's pupils had by then become Marquess of Dorset and had been very intimate with Henry VIII as Prince. Thereafter Wolsey's rise was rapid, but, having neither space nor need to go into his later career and ultimate fall, I may sum it up in the words of Erasmus, which are quoted on the Cardinal's picture in the present Schoolroom: 'Ex ludimagistro subvectus est ad regnum, nam plane regnabat verius quam ipse rex.'

William Bothewood was Master for a few weeks in 1499 after Wolsey's retirement, and was himself succeeded by Richard Jackson. Edward Martyn, one of the Demies trained for teaching, was Usher for three terms in 1498,[1] and was succeeded by John Goldyffe, who was later to be Headmaster of Eton.

The rapidity of the changes and the fact that most of these teachers (Wolsey, Stokesley, Jackson, Martyn) were already Fellows of the College is noticeable. The College was finding the School an expense, and, in Jackson's last year (1501), succeeded in inducing the Bishop of Worcester to appropriate part of the revenues of the Rectory of Slymbridge to Magdalen. The petition of the President and Fellows urged

'that their College consisted of seventy Scholars, continually studying in divers faculties, theology, civil law, and philosophy; also of four stipendiary Priests, eight Clerks, and sixteen Choristers; and especially one suitable Master or Instructor in Grammar, appointed and deputed within the precinct of the College itself, who, at the cost and expense of the same College, at all future times, ought to rule the Grammar School, and is bound to teach, instruct and inform gratis all boys and every other person wishing to learn; and

[1] The year was then divided into four terms.

that in consequence the ordinary and extraordinary charges of the College could scarcely be conveniently supported.'[1]

By an arrangement soon made, £10 was agreed on as the sum payable in lieu of tithes; and it is still paid.

From these facts and from the obviously outstanding ability of many of the teachers one may deduce that the College at the time took its duties towards the School seriously, and was genuinely finding it difficult to make its revenues cover all that Waynflete had meant them to. One may also deduce that most of the Fellows appointed, like Antony Wood and 'the generality', esteemed the job a drudgery, and preferred 'research' and the chance of a living to teaching and £5 or £10 per annum.

Be that as it may, the £10 from Slymbridge enabled the College to appoint an excellent successor to Jackson. This was Thomas Brynknell (1502-8), of Lincoln College, already B.D., and, says Wood,[2] 'a person of great literature and a most skilful interpreter of Sacred Writ'. It was probably as Master of the School that Brynknell became known to Wolsey; 'such respect had the Cardinal for him that by his means he was selected by the King as the most considerable person to write against Luther'. This was in 1521, when Brynknell was appointed Reader of the Cardinal's newly founded Divinity Lecture. He had succeeded John Stanbridge as Master of the Hospital at Banbury in 1511 and held this post with others till his death in about 1539.

STRIFE IN THE COLLEGE

Obviously an extremely able man, great credit is due to him for the skilful way in which he seems to

---

[1] Quoted from Bloxam, iii. 69, the Latin being translated.
[2] *Athenae*, i. 29.

F

have kept the School clear of the troubles that affected most of the College in the last years of President Mayew. Allusion has already been made to the strife between the parties of Mayew and Stokesley (p. 62); the main question at issue was whether Mayew was within his rights in retaining the Presidency after he had become Bishop of Hereford; but at the visitation ordered by Bishop Fox in 1507, when, in accordance with medieval custom, each Fellow was invited to tell all he knew about every one else, charges of perjury, keeping ferrets, sleeping in Chapel, adultery, playing cards, in fact everything, were used as weapons. It is noteworthy that in Macray's long analysis of the evidence the only thing that could conceivably be construed as reflecting on the School is a criticism of the Choristers' manners, and even that apparently refers to the little boys (it is the Organist rather than the Master who is blamed).[1]

TYNDALE, WOTTON

It was probably under Brynknell that William Tyndale, the translator of the Bible, was at Magdalen School, as he took his B.A. in 1512; but the early dates of his life are very uncertain. He was a member of Magdalen Hall, and was, according to Foxe, who lived very little later, 'brought up from a childe in the Universitie of Oxford, where he, by long continuance, grew and encreased as well in the knowledge of tongues and other liberall artes, as especially in the knowledge of Scriptures, whereunto his mind was singularly addicted, insomuch that hee, living in Magdalen Hall, read privelye to certain studentes, and fellowes of Magdalene College, some parcell of

---

[1] Macray, i. 35 ff.

Divinity, instructing them in the knowledge and trueth of the Scriptures'.[1]

It was, no doubt, as a B.A. that Tyndale indulged in these heretical Bible-readings, and Brynknell, the orthodox opponent of Luther, would have been the last to claim any responsibility for them, or for Tyndale's theology in general; but he may fairly be given some of the credit for Tyndale's 'knowledge of the tongues', which he afterwards put to such good use.

Tyndale, after taking his M.A., migrated to Cambridge, and then, after some years' work in Gloucestershire, which gave him a low opinion of the English clergy, left England to spend the rest of his life in his great work of translating the Bible. In spite of the charm and power of his translation, certain passages were tendentious and heretical;[2] and in 1535 Tyndale was betrayed to the Emperor as a heretic, and burnt the year after. 'Tyndale is the man to whom, above all other men, the literary merit of the English Bible is due, because he impressed upon his translation his own character of simplicity, strength and truth.'[3]

Another eminent pupil of Brynknell's was Edward Wotton, a man of remarkable and versatile learning. Chorister in 1503, Demy in 1506, and Fellow in 1516, he was not only famous as a physician, and published a book *De differentiis animalium*, but was singled out by Bishop Fox and made 'socio compar' of his College of Corpus Christi, apparently for his knowledge of Greek. At any rate, he 'read the Greek lecture there for

---

[1] Preface to Foxe's edition of Tyndale's *Works*, 1573.

[2] But that Tyndale's aim was, genuinely, not to spread heresy, but to give every Englishman a chance to read the Bible is proved by his offer to Henry VIII to write no more if Henry would sanction a translation of any sort, 'be it the translation of what person soever shall please his Majesty'.

[3] R. W. Chambers, *Man's Unconquerable Mind*, p. 192.

some time' and, returning from a tour of Italy in the course of which he became Doctor of Physic at Padua, 'he was settled Greek Reader of his College'. He died in 1555.

MIGRATIONS: BRACKLEY

Throughout these early years of School and College, migrations from Oxford owing to plague were frequent, the numbers of the College that left and the place of resort varying. Migrations took place in eleven years between 1485 and 1507, and in 1507, the only occasion when exact figures are available, 'during six weeks in the summer and six weeks of the term beginning in November the residents in College seem to have consisted only of about a dozen Fellows, the four Chaplains, seven Clerks and a few Choristers and servants. The rest of the body were quartered apparently for the most part at Witney, but in part at Brackley, Thame, Burford, and elsewhere.'[1] Other places to which we find members migrating at different times are Wallingford, Wallington, Aynho, Brailes, and Highworth.[2] To many members of the School these removals must have formed a pleasant holiday, but such had not been the Founder's intention. Waynflete had selected Brackley as the place for migration with the idea that the Hospital there should be a refuge in which the School's work could be continued; and before long it became Magdalen College School, Brackley, which still flourishes. Even before Brackley became a separate school Magdalen School must have continued to function wherever a quorum of pupils and teachers was gathered.[3]

[1] Wilson, p. 62.   [2] Macray, i, details under the various years.
[3] The *Victoria County History*, *Northants.*, ii. 231, suggests that the Chantry of the Hospital at Brackley was turned into a school to save it

HOOKER

Of the Masters between Brynknell's retirement in 1508 and Thomas Stanbridge's appointment in 1517, and of the Ushers at this time little is known beyond the names; but that the School was in a flourishing condition is shown by the statutes of Corpus Christi College. The Founder of Corpus, Bishop Fox, was, as Bishop of Winchester, Visitor of Magdalen College and School, and was therefore in a position to know all about both; he gave the new college a very close connexion with Magdalen, and among other things, ordered its choristers to attend the Grammar lectures at Magdalen School. The custom lasted till about 1600, and through it Magdalen School can probably count Richard Hooker among its old boys.[1]

The fact that in 1513 there were two Ushers suggests that the numbers of the School were too great for a Master and one Usher to deal with. Maurice Byrchenshaw, the second Usher, when appointed, had just been admitted to one of those rare degrees in Grammar of which Whittinton had been so proud.

'Maurice Byrchenshaw, a Scholar of Rhetorick, who had spent forteen years in that and Grammar, supplicated that he might be admitted ad informandum et docendum in eadem facultate, which being granted, he was admitted Bachelor in that faculty, but with this condition, that he compose one hundred verses de nobilitate Universitatis, and that he should not at any time teach his scholars Ovid "de arte amandi", or Pamphilus "de amore".'[2]

THE STANBRIDGE PROBLEM

The history of Thomas Stanbridge and his relation-

from extinction under the Chantries Act. But teaching had gone on there before, at least from 1548. Waynflete bought the Hospital in 1484.

[1] See the *History of Corpus Christi College*, by Fowler (O.H.S.), pp. 48, 148, 239.   [2] Wood's *Annals*, ii, pt. ii, p. 721.

ship to John Stanbridge have long been a puzzle. Bloxam gives an imposing list of authorities for the statement that Thomas Stanbridge taught at Banbury before becoming Master of Magdalen School, but all of them spring from one ancestor, Wood.[1] Wood undoubtedly thought that Thomas taught at Banbury, but there is good reason to think him, for once, mistaken. It is fairly certain that the Master of the Hospital at Banbury was normally Master of the school attached thereto; all the Masters of the Hospital we know of were schoolmasters by profession —John Stanbridge was Master of the Hospital from 1501 to 1510; Brynknell succeeded him from 1511 to about 1539, and is described as 'schoolmaster in Banbury'[2] in 1539; his successor, Nicholas Cartwright, is called schoolmaster by Edward VI's commissioners.[3] Thus the facts are that John Stanbridge taught at Banbury from 1501 to 1510, and Thomas at Magdalen from 1517 to 1522. The difficulties in Wood's story are that he says nothing of Thomas teaching anywhere except at Banbury, and nothing of John teaching anywhere except at Magdalen. If this were all we might, with Bloxam, assume that Thomas had taught at Banbury before coming to Magdalen, or, with Leach,[4] suggest that John Stanbridge 'was succeeded,

---

[1] Beesley's *History of Banbury* is admittedly derived from Warton's *Life of Sir Thomas Pope*, and Warton derives from Wood. The references Warton gives are to Wood's life of Oldham (*Athenae*, ii. 658) and some MS. notes in the Bodleian (now catalogued as MS. Wood D 11). These only indicate that 'Stanbridge Grammar' was taught at Banbury School. Wood elsewhere amplifies this by saying that Thomas Stanbridge taught at Banbury the Grammar composed by John Stanbridge; and Warton, from this and from Pope's statement that he had been taught at Banbury, deduced that Pope had been taught by Thomas Stanbridge. (See Warton's *Life of Sir Thomas Pope*, edition of 1772, p. 5.)

[2] Foxe's *Acts and Monuments*, i. 209.

[3] Leach, *E.S.R.*, p. 27.   [4] Ib.

so it is said, as schoolmaster, though not as master of the hospital by his "brother or near relative" Thomas Stanbridge'; but as Wood says distinctly:[1] 'Thomas Stanbridge took the degree of M.A. *in* 1518, *being then* a noted schoolmaster of Banbury in Oxfordshire',[2] although in 1518 Thomas was not at Banbury but at Magdalen School, and as he speaks of Robertson as Master of Magdalen School in 1526 'in the place of *John* Stanbridge', who retired in 1494, instead of 'in place of Thomas' who died in 1522, we may surely take it that Wood has quite confused the two Stanbridges, and that it is therefore better to disregard his statement altogether than to manufacture unsatisfactory explanations for it.

Thomas Stanbridge, then, never taught at Banbury but was Master of Magdalen School from 1517 to 1522. We cannot be certain if Wood, so far at sea about the Stanbridges, was right in thinking Thomas a brother or near relative of John. As far as can be told he was not so skilful a schoolmaster; when Fox held another visitation of the College in 1520 the School did not escape unscathed as it had under Brynknell. The President, Hygden, had given offence to various people owing to his strictness, and among various complaints against him, most of them rather vague, it was alleged that he 'is negligent with regard to the teacher of the boys in grammar, because there is no order in teaching, but the whole day is wasted in trifles, in that no authors are read'. The President replied 'that he was not to be blamed, for he did his best that those things were taught which were before his time, and he thought them useful, and the Schoolmaster said the same'. The Visitor 'warned the Teacher in the Grammar School,

[1] *Athenae*, i. 40.
[2] Bloxam, quoting this passage, silently omits the words 'of Banbury'.

as shown up in the visitation, to apply a more exact diligence to the education of his scholars in good letters for the future'.[1] The admonition suggests that the complaints were not unfounded; but the School continued popular, for it was in 1518 that a new wing was added to it.

From Stanbridge's time to the appointment of Thomas Robertson (his names are sometimes given as Robert and Robinson) various obscure Masters and Ushers held sway. Robertson, Master from 1526 to 1534, has won more fame perhaps as a Grammarian than for his other labours. He made various additions to Lily's Latin Grammar[2] and his work in this field, thanks to the monopoly given to Lily's Grammar by Henry VIII, became familiar to English schoolboys for three hundred years. But in his day Robertson was probably more famous as a theologian, his views being Catholic but enlightened. In 1525 Wood[3] notes him for a 'great oppugner and vilifier of the Questionists [or scholastic theologians] in the University', and this reforming tendency may explain the Protestant views of his famous pupils, three of whom became bishops under Elizabeth.

PARKHURST, BICKLEY, ROBERTSON

John Parkhurst entered Magdalen College School as a boy and later became a Fellow of Merton. In 1543 he became Chaplain to Queen Catharine Parr; he was intimate with Bishop Jewell and Coverdale, and his Puritan views were strengthened during his exile at Zurich in Mary's reign. He became Bishop of Norwich

---

[1] Quoted in Bloxam, iii. 79, the Latin being here translated.

[2] Rules for Heteroclites, Supplement of Defective Verbs, Annotations on Lily's Rules for the Genders of Nouns, and Praeterperfect Tenses and Supines of Verbs.   [3] *Athenae*, i. 320.

under Elizabeth in 1560; and both then and in his earlier life he was noted for his generosity and his fertility in Latin epigrams. Here are those on his old teacher, Robertson, and his old School:

DE THOMA ROBERTSONO, OLIM PRAECEPTORE SUO

Multi grammaticen illustravere libellis
    Ex quibus est isdem gloria parta viris.
Nemo Robertsono tamen hanc felicius unquam
    Tractavit, nemo dextcritate pari.
Hoc gaudere potes populosa Britannia alumno,
    Hunc licet invideant caetera regna tibi.[1]

AD GYMNASIUM MAGDALENENSE

O Praeclara domus! musarum candida sedes,
    Per quam sunt multis semina sparsa locis:
Dulcia Divini nimirum semina verbi,
    Quae possunt homines sola beare pios.
Salveto! servet te Christus, servet alumnos,
    Quos gremio nutris officiosa tuo.
Me quoque nutrieras olim, cum parvulus essem,
    Nunc factus juvenis sum memor usque tui.
Si mihi suppeterent vires, tibi grata referrem
    Munera: cum nequeam, sit voluisse satis.[2]

A prose rendering—and there is more piety than poetry about them—runs:

'Of Thomas Robertson, once the author's teacher. Many have illustrated Grammar with books from which they got glory; but no one ever handled the matter with more felicity than Robertson, or more dexterously. Populous Britain, you may rejoice in this scion; other realms may envy you him.'

'To Magdalen School'

'O goodly House! Bright seat of the muses, through which

[1] *Ludicra sive Epigrammata Juvenilia* (ed. 1573), p. 28.
[2] Ib., p. 77.

seeds have been sown in many places: sweet seeds, to wit, of God's word, which alone are able to make good men happy. Hail! May Christ preserve you and your pupils, whom you rear with loving care in your bosom. Me too you once reared, when I was a little boy; now, grown up, I am ever mindful of you. If I had strength I would repay your pleasant gifts; since I cannot, may the wish be enough.'

Thomas Cooper, Bishop successively of Lincoln and Winchester, may be more properly described when we consider his mastership of Magdalen School. Thomas Bickley, who, like Cooper, entered Magdalen as a Chorister in 1531, was an extreme Protestant.

'In the first of Edward the Sixth', says Fuller,[1] 'his detestation of superstition may rather be commended than his discretion in expressing it, when (before the publique abolition of Popery) at Evening Prayer he brake the consecrated Host with his hands, and stamped it under his feet, in the Colledge Chappel.'

We are not surprised to find that Bickley, after holding many offices in the College in the reign of Edward VI,

'about that time showing himself a very forward person for reformation, and therefore looked upon as an impudent and pragmatical man by the Roman Catholic party, nay and by some also of his own, he was forced to leave the College in the beginning of Queen Mary's reign, being then Bachelor of Divinity.'[2]

After Elizabeth's accession he returned from France, where he had taken refuge, and became successively Chaplain to Archbishop Parker, Warden of Merton, and Bishop of Chichester. Dying in 1596, he left £40 to Magdalen College for the ceiling and paving of the College School.[3]

---

[1] *Worthies*, p. 129.
[2] Wood's *Athenae*, i. 776.
[3] Wood's *Athenae*, i. 776.

Robertson, in the reign of Henry VIII, held numerous preferments and in 1537 was one of the divines who signed the Preface to the 'Bishops' Book', the second of the three attempts in Henry's reign to outline the position of the Church of England. In 1540 he was one of the Members of Convocation to consider the validity of Henry's marriage with Anne of Cleves, and one of the Commission appointed in that year to deliberate on certain matters of religious controversy.[1] He assisted in drawing up Edward VI's first Prayer Book in 1548, but he disliked it when finished,[2] and it is not surprising that his activities and preferments both cease in the later days of Edward VI, when Calvinist 'gospellers' poured into the country, and official doctrine became more and more Puritan. In 1557 Mary made him Dean of Durham, and in 1559 Elizabeth ejected him. The last we hear of him is in 1561, when he appears in a list of 'certain evil disposed persons, of whom complaint had been made, who lurk so secretly that process cannot be served on them'.[3]

CROMWELL AND THE REFORMATION

The confiscations and reformations of Henry VIII and his agent Cromwell were reaching more and more widely when Richard Sherrey (or Shirrey) took over the School from Robertson in 1534. By that time Henry's first marriage was annulled and Oxford University had recognized him as Head of the Church. The dissolution of the smaller monasteries was in the air, and Oxford colleges were concerned to put their house in order lest they should follow the same way.

[1] Strype's *Cranmer*, pp. 110, 113, *Memorials*, 1, i, pp. 553, 558.
[2] Ib., 11. i, p. 134.
[3] Strype's *Annals*, 1. i, pp. 415, 416.

We find in 1534 various entries in the College accounts for desks, windows, stone, etc., for repairing the School and neighbouring walls.[1] But, in spite of the popular picture of Cromwell and his agents as greedy blood-hounds thirsting for spoil, at Oxford their main concern seems to have been to stamp out the old scholastic learning, and Magdalen received honourable mention for, among other things, the Latin Lecture in the Grammar School. Layton, one of the Visitors, wrote to Cromwell of their proceedings at Magdalen:

'Pleasit your goodnes to be advertisyde that in Magdalen College we fownde stablisshede one Lecture of Divinitie, two of Philosophie—one Morale, another Naturale—and one of Latin tonge, well kept and diligently frequentede. To this we have adjonede a Lecture in the Greke, that is, the Grammer in Greke perpetually to be rede there, and all the yewthe therunto to have confluence for ther principulles.'

Latin and Greek Lectures were also established at All Souls, Corpus, New College, Merton, and Queen's; and the other colleges, which were not wealthy enough to run lectures of their own, were ordered to send their members to one of these.[2] By 'Lecture' is meant a regular course of teaching. It appears that owing to the confusion of the times the Greek Lecture at Magdalen was not given till 1540;[3] and, though members of the School no doubt attended it then, it was not until 1569 that the teaching of Greek became a regular part of the Grammar Master's duties.

After the visitation further building in connexion with the School took place, but what this was is not known.[4]

[1] Bloxam, iii. 90.
[2] Wright's Letters relating to the Suppression of the Monasteries, p. 70, quoted in Bloxam, iii. 90.   [3] Wilson, p. 78.
[4] See the extracts from the accounts printed by Bloxam (iii. 91).

SHERREY, HARLEY, BENTHAM, PIERS, HUMFREY

Sherrey was obviously a competent teacher and interested in his profession, as the subjects of some of his books show—'A treatise of Schemes and Tropes, gathered out of the best Grammarians and Orators', 'A Declaration showing that Children should from their infancy be gently brought up in learning (translated from the Latin of Erasmus)', and 'A Treatise of the figures of Grammar and Rhetorike profitable for al that be studious of eloquence, and in especiall for suche as in Grammer Scholes doe reade most eloquent poetes and oratours: whereunto is joyned the oration which Cicero made to Cesar, geving thankes unto him for pardonyng and restoring again of that noble man Marcus Marcellus.'

To Sherrey must be given much of the credit for the education of Bickley and Cooper, and he can claim to have reared up yet another bishop, Thomas Bentham, who became Bishop of Lichfield in 1560. Bentham had been ejected from the College under Mary, and, after fleeing to Switzerland, returned and organised secret meetings for Protestant worship in London, being the only 'gospeller' to brave the fires.[1] Henry Bull, who entered the School as a Demy in 1537, was another doughty Protestant of the time, who helped Bentham to outrage the feelings of the Catholics in the first year of Edward VI. Wood records that 'Henry Bull did, about that time, with the help of Thomas Bentham, openly in the choir snatch the censer out of the priest's hand, who was about to offer incense therein'.

Sherrey's Ushers were Ralph Smallpage (1535–7), John Heron (1537–9), and Robert Dighton (1539–40). Not much can be said about Smallpage and Dighton,

---

[1] *Zurich Letters*, first series, p. 7, quoted Bloxam, iv. 73.

except that Dighton was Lecturer in Natural Philosophy from 1542 to his death in 1546. More is known of Heron; he became M.A. in 1544, 'at which time he was in great esteem for his singular skill in the Latin tongue',[1] and, after retiring from his Usher's post, he went into Kent, where, if it was not another of the same name, he appears to have been 'tampering much with necromancy, to the great affrightment of his neighbours'.[1] By 1552, at any rate, he was Master of the King's School, Rochester, appealing to Cecil for a Prebend in Rochester Cathedral. Strype[2] has a long story of Heron's stimulating the diligence of his pupils in 1552 with the example of Edward VI. A parent was in the habit of writing to his son long accounts of the young king's industry, and Heron 'incontinently caused them that were written in English to be turned into Latin by his scholars, and such as were written in Latin to be Englished, . . . declaring plainly that in his opinion the virtuous example of that worthy and good young king wrought more in the heads of his unwilling scholars . . . than all his travail among them in one year past before.'

Godall succeeded Sherrey from 1541 to 1542, when he gave place to a more famous schoolmaster, in the person of John Harley. No better résumé of his career could be given than that of Fuller,[3] who after mentioning that Harley was 'bred first Fellow, then Schoolmaster in Magdalen' goes on:

'in the dangerous days of King Henry VIII he was an hearty but concealed Protestant. In the first week of the reign of King Edward the Sixth while most men's minds stood at a gaze (it being dead water with them which way the tide would turn) Master Harley, in the Parish Church of St

---

[1] Wood's *Athenae*, i. 188.
[2] *Ecclesiastical Memorials*, ii. ii. 49.   [3] *Worthies*, p. 128.

Peter's in Oxford and a solemn Lent sermon, publiquely preached Antipapal doctrine and powerfully pressed justification by faith alone, whereupon the over-officious Vice-Chancellor hurried him up to London for an Heretick, there to answer for his contempt. But the case was soon altered, Harley was acquitted, commended, preferred to be tutor to the sons of John, Earl of Warwick, afterwards Duke of Northumberland. He was thence made Bishop of Hereford. . . . Doctor Laurence Humphred, Harley his scholar in Magdalen College, hath consecrated this Distick to the memory of his Master, though the Muses, in my mind, looked very solemnly, without the least smile at the making thereof,

"Flos domui Harlaeus, socius ludique magister,
Celsus deinde throno, celsior inde polo." '

Warwick, of whose children Harley became tutor in 1548, was the extreme Protestant Protector in the last part of Edward VI's reign.

In spite of Harley's obviously Protestant sympathies they were not extreme enough for a cabal that tried to oust Owen Oglethorpe from his Presidency of Magdalen in 1551. They put up two candidates in succession, neither of them statutably qualified, William Turner and Walter Haddon, Haddon being finally elected. Harley was at one time proposed for a candidate, and Bloxam[1] quotes an interesting letter from one of the cabal to Turner.

'Some fear lest Mr Harley should be preferred. God forbid it. He is my friend, and yet shall he never have my good will; for he is idle, and not so ripe in God's truth; and, which is worst of all, not much passing, as I think, how religion goeth forward, so that he hath the pelth of the world. To conclude, for God's love, Mr Turner, stick to it lustily, as we do and will to you. We had rather keep Mr President than receive Mr Harley. Regard you the

[1] iii. 101 (letter dated 20 Jan. 1551/2: State Paper Office, Domestic, Edward VI, vol. xiii, No. 4).

state of our College, how it is provided to set forth learning, and that to the glory of God. God continue the King's favour towards you in this matter, also the rest of your friends. You shall have our daily prayers, but this know you that, if it come to election, they will choose Harley, for the Papists can away with him well enough. To make an end, only our noble King's letters must strike the stroke, whom the Lord preserve for ever and ever.'

The writer does not commend himself by his obvious desire to contravene the statutes and get the vote of the College quashed by royal interference. The root of his objection to Harley seems to lie in the latter's tolerance; the accusation that he cared more for money than religion is sufficiently refuted by Harley's courage at the opening of Edward's reign, and by his end. Deprived of his bishopric by Mary, for being married, he 'did go at length from place to place in an obscure condition to console the poor remnant of Protestants and confirm them in their belief, but died soon after in his wandering to and fro in England'.[1]

Bentham was probably Harley's pupil for a time, and he also taught William Overton and John Piers. Thus, within some twelve years, Magdalen School numbered among its pupils one Archbishop and five Bishops to be, to say nothing of Harley himself. William Overton, who entered the School as a Demy in 1541, became Fellow in 1550, resigned on the accession of Mary, and returned under Elizabeth, becoming Bishop of Lichfield and Coventry in 1579.

John Piers became Demy in 1542 and Fellow in 1545, and being made Rector of Quainton, according to Wood[2] 'by keeping rustical company', he was 'in great hazard to have lost all his excellent gifts that came after to be well esteemed and rewarded in him',

---

[1] Wood's *Athenae*, ii. 768.   [2] Ib., i. 713.

for he acquired the habit of sitting 'tippling in a blind alehouse with some of his neighbours'. However, he got the better of this, and, after being Master of Balliol and Dean of Christ Church, he became successively Bishop of Rochester, Bishop of Salisbury, and Archbishop of York.

Other famous pupils of Harley were Lawrence Humfrey, the Puritanical President of Magdalen, Thomas Whythorne, whose autobiography has been referred to already (pp. 22 ff), and Julins Palmer. Palmer, strangely enough, was a Catholic, and is said to have been expelled from Magdalen for his 'Popish pranks',[1] but his heart was turned by the sight of the burning of Latimer and Ridley at Oxford in 1555, and he himself, becoming a Protestant, was burned a year later.

Thomas Whythorne, as we have seen, entered the Song School in about 1537 and the Grammar School in 1544, the year in which he became a Demy. Dr Burney, the eighteenth-century historian of music, thought little of him as a composer, but he was a pioneer among Elizabethan song-writers. His 'Songes of three, fower and five partes', published in 1571, are (apart from an early song-book printed by Wynkyn de Worde) the first printed in England. His autobiography, like his songs, was a pioneer work; and should prove, when published, an interesting as well as a valuable historical document.

Lawrence Humfrey was Harley's pupil while a Demy at Magdalen between 1547 and 1549, when he became a Fellow. Under Queen Mary he was given leave to go abroad and remained in Switzerland until Elizabeth's accession. Returning then to Oxford he became Professor of Divinity, President of Magdalen,

[1] Foxe, *Acts and Monuments.*

G

and in every year from 1571 to 1575 Vice-Chancellor. Intellectually he was probably the leading figure in the Oxford of his day, but owing to his Puritanical leanings he never rose as high in the Church as he might have done. Only with the greatest difficulty could Cooper as Visitor persuade him to allow surplices in the Chapel; and even when Elizabeth visited Oxford in 1566 Humfrey wore his doctor's robes only under protest, drawing from the Queen the remark, 'Methinks this gown and habit becomes you very well and I marvel you are so straitlaced on this point—but I come not now to chide.' For all his ability, Humfrey was not a successful governor, and, as we shall see, the School, like the rest of the College, fell into a bad way during his Presidency. The charges of corruption made by his opponents, apparently with some truth, are hardly excused by the plea that the first married President had heavier expenses than his predecessors.[1]

One of Harley's Ushers, John Slade (1546–8), succeeded him as Master in 1548, and in 1550 obtained leave to go to Bruton, in Somerset, *ad aperiendum ludum grammaticalem*. The phrase 'to open a grammar school' is at first sight surprising, for Bruton had been founded long before then; but the endowment had been seized at the dissolution of Bruton Abbey in 1539, and the school had lapsed. The endowment, however, was restored under Edward VI and Slade became the first Master of the King's School, remaining till 1553.[2]

COOPER, CAMDEN: THE MARPRELATE CONTROVERSY

Thomas Cooper, whom we have met as a pupil of Robertson, became Master in 1549, and, except for a short interval (1557–8), remained Master till 1567,

---

[1] See Wilson, chapter ix.
[2] I owe this information to Mr T. D. Tremlett of Bruton.

when he resigned, apparently to become tutor to Sir Philip Sidney.[1] The son of a poor tailor in Cat Street, Oxford, Cooper entered Magdalen as a Chorister in 1531, and became Fellow in 1539, resigning in 1546.

'The course of his life in Oxford was commendable and in some sort saint-like; if it be saint-like to live unreproveable, to bear a cross patiently and to forgive great injuries freely, this man's example was without pattern. The truth is, he, being little acquainted with the world of men, did unhappily marry an Oxford woman who proved too light for his gravity and in the end became so notorious for her ill living that the libels that then came forth did sound out her infamy, especially that made by Tho. Bulkley of All Souls, which tells us that a certain person (Tho. Day, Canon of Christ Church, sometime Fellow of All Souls) did so much frequent her company that at length he was bound in a bond of £100 not to come near her.'[2]

Cooper took up the non-controversial study and practice of medicine under Mary, and during the last years of her reign even resigned the mastership of the School, to resume it in 1559. Accumulating the degrees of B.D. and D.D. in 1567, he gave up schoolmastering and became in succession Dean of Christ Church, Dean of Gloucester, Bishop of Lincoln, and Bishop of Winchester (1584).

Before he became Master, Cooper had published his famous *English and Latin Dictionary*, a revised edition of Sir Thomas Elyot's, and an *Epitome of Chronicles*, a world history brought down to the time of Edward VI; and both these works he republished in the course of his life, taking the opportunity in 1560 of bringing the *Chronicle* up to date. His learning in Latin earned him in 1566 the honour of writing and conveying to Queen

---

[1] *Parker's Correspondence*, p. 316, cf. Bloxam, iii. 117.
[2] *Athenae*, i. 265.

Elizabeth the invitation of the University to visit Oxford.

William Camden, the famous antiquary and author of *Britannia*, who was later Headmaster of Westminster and wrote the *Westminster Greek Grammar*, was Cooper's pupil, and may have owed some of his historical enthusiasm to that of his teacher; he is said to have started writing *Britannia* at school. Lord Edward and Lord John Russell, sons of the Earl of Bedford, and Robert Temple, who all wrote complimentary verses to Queen Elizabeth on her visit to Oxford, were all, probably, taught by Cooper at the School.[1] But perhaps the greatest of Cooper's pupils was Richard Hooker, the author of the *Ecclesiastical Polity*. It is probable that he came up to Corpus Christi College as a Chorister in 1567, and was taught by Cooper in accordance with Bishop Fox's statute referred to above (p. 69); but as Cooper retired in that year, some of the credit for Hooker's latinity may be due to Cooper's successor, Nicholas Balguay.

Bishop Cooper earns a place in the history of English literature for his share in the Marprelate controversy. Who Martin Marprelate really was is still a matter for dispute, but he has the distinction of being the first English prose satirist, and his somewhat ribald attacks on episcopacy and bishops, with their quaint mixture of personalities and reasoned theology, are still amusing to read. The Bishop of London, who played bowls on Sunday, and swore 'by my faith', suffered most from Martin's abuse,[2] Cooper being accused only of such theological misdemeanours as underestimating the

[1] Nichols's *Progress of Queen Elizabeth*, vol. i, 1566.

[2] The following may serve as a sample of Martin's style: 'Therefore our Lord Bishops,—what sayest thou, man?—our Lord Bishops (I say) as John of Canterbury, Thomas of Winchester (I will spare John of London for this time, for it may be he is at bowls and it is pity to trouble

WILLIAM CAMDEN

From the portrait in Big School: painter unknown

value of preaching as a means of salvation; but Cooper, as the most learned of the Bishops, presumably, stepped into the lists on behalf of all. His *An admonition to the People of England, wherein are answered not only the slanderous untruths reproachfully uttered by Martin, the Libeller, but also many other crimes by some of his brood, objected generally against all Bishops, and the chief of the Clergy, purposely to deface and discredit the present slate of the Church* was anonymous except for the initials T. C.; but Martin Marprelate had no difficulty in piercing the disguise, and responded with *Hay any work for Cooper; or a briefe Pistle directed by waye of an publication to the reverende Byshopps, counselling them, if they will needs be barrelled up for feare of smelling in the nostrils of her Majestie and the State, that they would use the advice of reverend Martin for the providing of their Cooper. Because the reverend T. C. (by which misticall letters is understood eyther the bouncing parson of Eastmeane, or Tom Coakes his Chaplaine) hath shewed himself in his late Admonition to the people of England to be an unskilful and a deceytfull tubtrimmer.* Whatever the respective merits of the two works may have been, the majesty of the Law soon stepped in on Cooper's side and Martin Marprelate's work was declared treasonable.

THE ATTEMPTED SUPPRESSION OF THE SCHOOL

But from our point of view Cooper's greatest moment came early in his tenure of the mastership, when he and the College, and indeed the City of Oxford as well, successfully resisted an attempt to suppress the School.

As we have seen, the School had successfully sur-

my good brother lest he should swear too bad) my reverend prelate of Lichfield, with the rest of that rabble, are petty Antichrists, petty popes, proud prelates, intolerable withstanders of reformation, enemies of the gospel, and most wretched covetous priests.' For the whole business, see the *Cambridge History of English Literature*, iii. 374 ff.

vived the whips of Henry VIII, but it had a narrower escape from the scorpions of Edward VI. Of these the chief was Dr Cox, Dean of Christ Church, and the most active of the Visitors appointed in 1549 to put the University in order. Early in 1550 he brought to Oxford certain injunctions signed by twelve of the King's Council (Edward VI was, of course, a minor), forbidding Magdalen to spend any of its money on grammar teaching, or on the upkeep of Chaplains, Clerks, and Choristers, and ordering that no Fellow should retain his place more than twenty years unless a Public Reader, and that one Fellow should always be an Irishman. Similar orders were given to All Souls.

Why any one wanted the School suppressed has never been explained. The Puritan Council may have been acting honestly, if mistakenly, according to its lights, supposing the grammarians at Magdalen to be either pseudo-grammarians introduced into the College to minister to the idleness of the Fellows,[1] or backward undergraduates who ought to be superannuated —they seem to have been surprised to learn of the size and nature of the School—but Cox, the real author of the injunctions, must have known better.[2] Wood insinuates dark things.[3] 'What advantage', he says, 'Cox could get by annulling the said school of Magdalen, unless he was set on by some of the Society,[4] I know not.' The Fellows are absolved from this charge by their unanimous protest, but Wood's implied view

---

[1] The original terms of reference of the Visitors empowered them, in the whole University, to convert money spent on *pueros grammaticales* to more advanced studies (Wood).

[2] The success of the appeal shows that the Council had signed the injunctions only under a misapprehension.

[3] *Annals*, 1549, where the whole story of the injunctions is given.

[4] i.e. the College.

of Cox's character is not so easily refuted. Something Cox must have hoped for; but what? It is the more difficult to explain in that the School had recently produced three such redoubtable champions of the Puritan cause as Bickley, Bull, and Bentham.

The other injunctions are not quite so strange. The attempt to suppress the Choir needs no explanation— to Puritans money spent on elaborate music was sinful waste; and it might be maintained, not without plausibility, that the limitation of Fellowships to twenty years would not only prevent Fellows from sinking into an idle, if academic, rut, but would also tend to spread the fertilizing influence of Oxford learning about the country; the intrusion of Irishmen was unstatutable, but not obviously outrageous.

When the injunctions were received the President and Fellows unanimously resolved to oppose them as 'fatal to the foundation of their College, breaking up and dispersing the society of the Scholars, thrusting out sixty, more or less'.[1] A petition was sent to the Council which, with regard to the Choir, stated that of the number (about thirty) affected by the injunction, sixteen were Choristers, 'which, after they have lerned there songe, go to the Grammer Schole, the rest of the xxx applie them selfes to the liberall sciences and divinitie'. With regard to the School, the petition ran:

'Whereby the Founder appoynted xxx poore Scholars, called demies, for the mayntenance of the societie, so they were xii yeres olde, and coulde competently reade latine,

---

[1] Coll. Magd. Reg. 3, fol. 17*b*, ap. Bloxam, iii. 110: 'Collegii sui fundationis exitiales, Ludum Grammaticalem adeo celebrem dissolventes, caetum Scholarium dirimentes ac discerpentes, sexaginta plus minus detrudentes . . .'. (The '60 more or less' include the thirty of the choir, sixteen of them Choristers, the remaining thirty being the thirty Demies; so that of the sixty some forty odd would probably be attending the School.)

whom he wolde have taught in his grammer Schole, chefly founded for that cause, untyll they sholde be able to go to logyke by the iudgemente of the President, the Scholemaister, and a deane; and whereas the said Schole is to Magdalen College, as Eaton Schole is to the Kinges College in Cambridge, and the Schole at Winchester to the New College in Oxforde, that is to say, as a Norisshe to trayne up their youth in vertue and lerninge, whereby as well th other Colleges of th Universitie receyve singular commoditie and proffit, and the hole countrie; and the said College dothe maintein there Societie with soche, whose maners, education, and lerninge they dayly see and have experiment of; if this injunction be utterly executed, then shall the sayd College be forclosed from the most principale treasure they or th Universitie have.'[1]

The College also begged the assistance of Archbishop Cranmer[2] in their fight, and, the news of the School's danger spreading abroad, the Mayor and Council also sent an appeal to the King, saying that they had always had by means of the colleges 'singularie treasure, help, and commoditie, for the education of theyre sonnes', being mostly unable to educate their children in good learning 'without the ayd and help of the Colledges trayning our children in good letters, some being called Schollers of the Howses, and some called Quiristers, and yet learning their Grammar'.

'Your said Commissioners', the petition ran, '. . . have . . . decreed . . . that none should be found in Grammar, or remayne Quirister within your said Universitie at the chardges of anye Colledge, whereby there be in danger of

---

[1] Archbishop Parker's MSS., C.C. Coll., Cambs., No. cxxvii, 25. The passages given here are quoted by Bloxam (ii, p. xlviii and iii. 101) with spelling modernized. Mr J. R. T. Bury, Librarian of Corpus Christi College, has very kindly restored for me the original spelling, and made one or two slight corrections.

[2] The Latin appeal, probably composed by Cooper, is quoted in Bloxam, ii. 305.

casting out of some Colledge thirtie, some other XL or L, some other more or fewer, and the most part of them children of your said poore Oratours, haveing of the said Colledges meate, drinke, cloth and lodginge, and were verie well brought up in learninge in the common Grammar Schoole at the Colledge of St Marie Magdalen, and soe went forward and attayned to Logicke etc. . . . which thynge hathe allwayes heretofor binn a great succoure unto your sayde poore Oratours, and now an utter undoeinge to the heavie discomfort of us and our posteritye, and diminishing of your Universitie, and the decaying thereof, unless it may please your Highness of your passing clemencie to call backe the sayd Injunction, as well for the continuance of this only School of all the Shire, as for the bringing up of our children and our posterities as is aforesaid . . .'.[1]

Whether the threat to the School was due to a genuine misunderstanding or not, the petitions were successful; and, after the customary delay had taken place, 'both parties were kindly received, heard, and dismissed with accomplishment of their desire'.

[1] The whole petition is found in Wood's *Annals*, vol. ii, p. 102.

CHAPTER IV

THE SCHOOL, 1564-1703

Loss of Pre-eminence: Finance—History of the University—Leicester's Settlement—Abandonment of the Founder's Aims—The Pupils—School Life

LOSS OF PRE-EMINENCE: FINANCE

THE reasons for the choice of period that this chapter covers will appear in due course. It is a period in which the School was, on the whole, prosperous, but no longer enjoyed the pre-eminence of its early days among the schools of England. This loss of pre-eminence was, to some extent, the actual result of the labours of the masters and pupils of the School itself. They had been largely responsible for setting the standards of education which lasted with very little change for centuries; and it was inevitable that schools throughout the country as a whole should gradually arrive at the same level.

Another important factor was finance.

Endowed schools in England of any age fall roughly into two classes: those with an endowment of land, and those with an endowment of money. The first class have, as a rule, been little affected by the fall in the value of money; often the land has become more valuable, owing to industrial development or the spread of big towns like London. But schools with a fixed income have generally been entirely ruined. Before, say, 1540 the value of money had not altered for centuries. Numerous founders of schools, like Waynflete, allotted perhaps £10 to their schoolmasters, a handsome salary in the fifteenth century: but by the end of the seventeenth century prices were five or six times as high and salaries on the fifteenth-century scale were quite impossible. Magdalen College School was not quite so hard hit as some, for the College revenues were rising so as to keep pace with the fall in the value of money, but the Master's and Usher's share in the increase was precarious. From 1597 onwards the custom prevailed of dividing the surplus revenues of the College among the President and Fellows: at times the Master was a Fellow and so received a share, at times he seems to have received a share even when not a Fellow;[1] but on the whole the Master's and Usher's case was dealt with by increases of salary on various pretexts and occasions. In discussing these, it must be remembered that all this time the Master and Usher received an allowance for commons and dress equal to that of the Fellows. This rose with the rise in prices, though it probably did not keep pace with it. Apart from these allowances, the payments to the Master rose from the original £10 to £27. 6s. 8d. by the end of the seventeenth century, while that to the Usher rose from £5 to £12.[2] When it is remembered that the cost of living was multiplied in this period by 5 or 6 and the average wage paid to skilled labourers by nearly 4, it is clear that the Master and Usher had, financially speaking, lost a good deal of ground.[3]

[1] Macray, iii. 32 ff.; Bloxam, iii. 216

[2] The additions were as follows:

	To the Master	To the Usher
Original salary	£10	£5
1560: 'access.' or 'augment.' . . .	£3. 10s.	..
soon altered to	£3. 6s. 8d.	..
1569: for the 'Greek Lecture' . . .	£2	..
1582	..	'increment' £2
1589: 'increment.'	£2	..
1665: 'augment.' at Visitor's command .	£10	£5
Total .	£27. 6s. 8d.	£12

[3] Thorold Rogers's *Political Economy* gives elaborate statistics pointing to these results. The average wage of the skilled labourer rose from 3s. to 11s. a week, i.e. from £7. 10s. to £27. 10s. per annum.

HISTORY OF THE UNIVERSITY

But if these changes are to be fully understood, a brief summary must be given of the University history that forms their background. Between medieval Oxford and Oxford of the eighteenth century, the Oxford of Wycliffe and that of Gibbon, there was an almost ludicrous difference. Both have now passed away—medieval Oxford with its horde of often hungry, often frozen students, barbarously uncultured, perhaps, but alert in mind, some eager to rise in the workaday world by the only ladder of those days, some disinterested students of theology, all burningly alive—and that eighteenth-century Oxford, easier for us to imagine, though fundamentally more different from the Oxford of today, where religion was a convention, enthusiasm an offence, poverty a disgrace; and the colleges, beautiful islands of financial security where gross and celibate dons drank port, and few intellects were stirred by anything save a mild interest in the more obvious beauties of Latin verse.

The enormous change from the first to the second was not the immediate result of the revived interest in literature characteristic of Waynflete's day. Throughout the sixteenth century, although the old religious fetters had been loosened, the sincerity and zeal with which theology was studied, both by Catholics and by Protestants, was as great as it had ever been; but all over Europe an old era was ending; and in Oxford, more even than in the rest of England, the religious changes brought about by Henry VIII, Edward VI, Mary, and Elizabeth had an inevitably unsettling effect.

LEICESTER'S SETTLEMENT

Early in Elizabeth's reign the University's new Chancellor, Lord Leicester, attempted to give it a thorough overhauling. The world had been turned upside down by that combination of factors we call the Renaissance, and the time had come to take stock. The keynote of the new regulations was regimentation. Every one's name was to be entered in the Matriculation Book, every one was to be in a college or hall, and oaths and tests were designed to ensure that every student conformed to type—the type, of wide limits, that the new Church of England fostered. The settlement, which was amplified during the remainder of Leicester's chancellorship, was finally completed, perhaps in an even more disciplinary spirit, by Laud, who became Chancellor in 1630. Opposition came, not from the Roman Catholics, who had all men's hands against them, but from the Puritans, who had the defects of their qualities, intolerance among them. Intellectually, perhaps, they provided a needed stimulus to the University; and till their final brief triumph in the Civil War they are a presence that can never be forgotten behind the façade of Oxford conformity.

Party differences, however, were all apparently swept away in loyalty to the King, when he made Oxford his head-quarters in 1642. While the war lasted it does not appear that much academic work was done in Oxford; but on the victory of Parliament the University settled down in a praiseworthy way under its new masters. Once more, however, studies were upset in 1660, by the Restoration. It was not that unduly many were expelled from the colleges; but few of the new Fellows and scholars were academically minded, and the University, unsettled by nearly twenty years of war and revolution, was in no case to resist the disintegrating tendency of Restoration morality. The Oxford of the years that followed may pride itself on its loyalty to Church and King, but on little else; and the corruption, idleness, and self-indulgence that Gibbon castigated have their roots in the seventeenth century.[1]

ABANDONMENT OF THE FOUNDER'S AIMS

How did Magdalen School fare in these troubled times? Which of the turning-points in Oxford history robbed it of the unique character that was discussed in our first chapter? Even if nothing were known otherwise of Leicester's settlement, a study of the facts concerning the Magdalen Choristers and Demies would make it clear that the change happened in the early 1560's.

The choristerships become little more than extra demyships—singing, no doubt, was looked on without favour by the Puritan President, Humfrey. This can be deduced from the ages of the Choristers. Nowadays, when Choristers are chosen entirely for their singing, they are appointed at the age of nine or ten, and resign when their voices break at the age of about fifteen. Before 1564 in the comparatively few cases where information is available Choristers were appointed at the average age of $11\frac{2}{3}$, and resigned at the average age of $15\frac{3}{4}$. From 1564 to 1591 the average age of appointment is $15\frac{1}{2}$, that of resignation is 20. The conclusion is clear that, either by the Chancellor's command, or, more probably, by the wish of President Humfrey, who shared Leicester's Calvinism, from 1564 onwards the endowments of the Choristers were used, not to provide skilled musicians, but to open more gateways for scholars. About 1592, apparently, President Bond, who succeeded Humfrey in 1589, could stand the lack of boys' voices no longer, for the age of appointment

[1] For Oxford at this time see Mallet, vol. ii.

drops, and thereafter, with not infrequent exceptions, remains about 10 or 11. But the age of resignation remains far above that of the breaking of the voice; and it was not long before to get a choristership was to be settled for one's University life. After the Restoration it became the exception for a Chorister to resign before taking his degree, unless to become a Demy or a Clerk (singing man). What Waynflete would have thought of this use of his foundation one cannot say. The School was little affected by it.

But it was far otherwise with the Demies. As we have seen above (pp. 8, 19, 20), they were the unique feature of Magdalen College and School, on them depending two of Waynflete's aims— to give homogeneity to the training of his scholars by starting them in the College School; and to rear up an unending series of grammar teachers by making two or three of the Demies continue to study grammar long enough not only to profit themselves 'but to be able also to instruct and educate others'. Both these aims were now suddenly shelved. From 1534 to 1563 the average age of appointment of the Demies had been 15¼, from 1564 to 1703 it was 16½; and the change was not gradual: in the years 1561–3 of the twenty-seven appointed twenty were under 16; from 1564 to 1569 of thirty-six appointed only three were under 16 and eighteen were 17 or more.

From about 1576 another innovation appears, which further stultified Waynflete's intention of providing a complete Magdalen education from start to finish. Demies begin to be appointed who have already matriculated as members of other colleges and halls. At first these are mainly from Magdalen Hall, within whose precincts the Grammar School stood, and it may very well be that most of these Demies had, in fact, studied in the School; but the number of those from other colleges grows continually, and by the end of the seventeenth century most of the demyships were being filled from among resident undergraduates.[1]

The figures concerning the training of teachers are even more striking than those relating to the age of appointment. From 1482 to 1563 of 67 Demies whose subsequent careers are definitely known 16 became teachers; there are a large number of unknowns in these early years, but the figure—which amounts to about 24 per cent—is convincing proof that Waynflete's injunction was being carried out. After 1564 the percentage of teachers drops to 5, about the number that might be expected in any school. Here, too, the change is sudden; from 1543 to 1563 the number of teachers among the known careers is 7 out of 31; from 1564 to 1582 the number is 1 out of 37.[2]

There was no ill will behind this curtailment of the School's activities. Humfrey speaks of the School in the most enthusiastic terms;[3] but the changes in statutes that necessity had demanded, combined with the root and branch logicality of the Calvinism then in power, did not stimulate respect for tradition. Mallet records

---

[1] The figures are as follows:

				Percentage of the total of coming from *Magdalen Hall*	Demies appointed coming from *other colleges*
Before 1576	.	.	.	nil	nil
1576–1615	.	.	.	14	5
1616–43	.	.	.	17	17
1644–60	.	.	.	13	12
1661–1703	.	.	.	19	41

[2] All figures concerning Choristers and Demies are based on Bloxam's *Register*.

[3] 'Hoc consilio . . . fundator scholam Wainflettensem, Brackleiensem et vestram domi celeberrimam extrui et aperiri voluit ut diversis locis graecarum et humanarum literarum semina sparsa in fecundam segetem totius reipublicae excrescerent.' *Cornucopia Hadriani Junii*, Basil 1558, ap. Knight's *Life of Colet*, p. 107.

Leicester's charge, 'Yow are driven everie day to dispense with your statutes', to which 'the University had no adequate reply';[1] and in the case we are considering it is doubtful whether anything save strict adherence to the letter and spirit of the statutes could have saved the unique child of Waynflete's subtle genius. The Elizabethan organizers could not tolerate the unusual—both Choristers and Demies had to be approximated as far as possible to the ordinary undergraduates; and so it came about that the School had to be approximated to the ordinary grammar school.

But as an ordinary grammar school Magdalen School continued to flourish for many years. Though the Demies no longer played such an essential part in it as before, many young Demies were still appointed, and they and the Choristers and Servitors of the College still formed an important element in the School. This ensured the keen interest of the College in its efficiency, and there are many signs throughout this period that it was kept up. In the amplitude of the field from which it could draw its teachers and in its continued connexion with the University the School had advantages which the grammar school elsewhere lacked. But in 1703 a further change took place. The College passed a resolution that no Demy should count time spent in the Grammar School as residence for a degree,[2] and therewith the School's connexion with University education may be said to have ended.

[1] ii. 116.
[2] Resolution quoted in Bloxam, vi. 151. 'Decretum et ordinatum est a Dno. Praesidente, Vice-Praesidente, reliquis officiariis et sex simpliciter senioribus, in scaccario congregatis, quod in posterum nullus de minore numero scholarium, vulgo dictorum Demies, gradum Baccalaureatus ambiat priusquam sedecim terminos (relicta Schola grammaticali) sub Tutorum regimine in Universitate compleverit.' V.P. Reg.

H

The change was a result of changing circumstances. The type of student whom the Restoration brought to Oxford might justly be suspected of taking the line of least resistance in gaining the degree that would qualify him for a fellowship or a living, and in 1703 four years' residence was almost the only requisite for a degree. It thus became necessary to ensure that the four years were, at any rate in theory, spent in University studies. Probably the number of Demies in the School had been dwindling for some time, and was not immediately cut off by the regulation of 1703. It would be a mistake to suppose that from 1703 the School sank in a flash to the mere Choristers' school that it was by the end of the century; but it is nevertheless right to note 1703 as the day when the School ceased to be marked out among schools by that intimate link with the University.

THE PUPILS

For most of this period pupils continued to be drawn largely from the same sources as before, though of the Demies, as explained above, it is probable that only that comparatively small proportion who were appointed young attended the School. The Choristers would all attend until they started their University course, and the number of Servitors or poor scholars tended to grow.

These Servitors provide an interesting commentary on changed times. No mention is made in the original statutes of any servants in College except a manciple with an assistant, a cook with two assistants, two grooms, two porters who should also act as barbers, and a laundress (if no man can be found) 'of such age and condition that evil suspicion ought not to fall on her with verisimilitude'; personal servants are foreign to the scheme, but with the passing of medieval times arose the conception of 'menial' tasks; and by the end of the sixteenth century it appears that every adult member of the College found it necessary to have a personal attendant.

There were poor lads whose only chance of education was to become a Servitor. Many of them profited exceedingly by their opportunity, and the institution had obvious advantages; but there were also difficulties, the main one being that no one was really responsible for the boys, and there was an irrepressible tendency for the College to be surrounded by hangers-on, anxious to gain a meal by doing an odd job, but with no interest in education at all. The following records tell the story clearly enough.

In 1585 Cooper, as Visitor, decrees that the 'useless and too burdensome[1] number of so-called poor scholars' shall be rigorously cut down; the thirteen senior Fellows, Doctors, and the Reader in Theology may each have a servant but must pay for him; and they are urged to choose servants who show promise in scholarship. Ten years later the President and thirteen seniors make an order that all poor scholars must be formally admitted and go to the Grammar School or take the University course: no one except the thirteen seniors may have an attendant who is not one of these formally admitted poor scholars. Cooper's rule has clearly been interpreted with a generosity that would have surprised its framer, and it is not strange to find that in 1612 there are seventy-six poor scholars and Servitors. By 1636-7 the Visitor is again complaining of the 'idle and unschollerly' 'multitude of poor schollers and servitors'. All must

[1] There was clearly a tendency to reward the poor scholar with a free meal 'on the College'.

'goe to the grammar schoole, or if their abilitie be beyond that degree of learning, shall diligently frequent lectures etc.' There exists a list of this date containing sixty-six names with the member of the foundation responsible for most of them. In 1665 the Visitor allows any one to have a poor scholar as servant; he has given up the struggle against progress, and henceforth the only stipulation is that servants shall not be an expense to the College.[1]

Numbers of townsmen, as before, would send their children to the School. John Harmar, Usher 1617–26, wrote a little Latin phrase-book (*Praxis Grammatica*, 1623) 'in usum Schol. Magdal. Oxon.', parts of which show that among his pupils were boys living at home with their parents: 'My mother asked my schoolmaster to be a little gentler to me' is an example.

A more doubtful matter is the extent to which members of Magdalen Hall still attended the School. It will be remembered that the Hall had been built round the School to accommodate the undergraduates who wished to attend the early grammar lectures. By the eighteenth century it was no more intimately connected with the School, except architecturally, than any other hall; but this had probably not been so for very long. In the period before the Civil War Magdalen Hall was the most flourishing of all the colleges and halls; it numbered some three hundred members who excelled in literary productiveness as they did in number; and in view of the Hall's origin it is difficult not to suppose that its popularity had been due in the first place to its proximity to the School. Another significant fact is the number of Demies from 1576 onwards appointed after being matriculated as mem-

---

[1] The records are printed in Bloxam, iii. 133, 136, 137, 163, 164; Macray, iii. 42, 51, iv. 22.

bers of Magdalen Hall. Here cause and effect were intertwined. It is certain that boys went to the Hall to wait for a demyship, and probably the College tended to appoint Demies from the Hall because they had got some idea of their capabilities from the school-master, while boys wishing to get demyships would enter at Magdalen Hall in the hope of catching the schoolmaster's eye. We have some confirmation of this supposition in a letter from Lord Clarendon to the President in 1667, recommending for a demyship 'one I did some time since mention to you, then I think in your College School, called William Reekes, whom as I remember you seemed to look upon as a hopeful youth'. We cannot, however, say anything more definite than that the young or backward entrants to the Hall probably attended the School, at any rate until fairly late in our period.[1]

Connected with the gradual transformation of Magdalen Hall into a home for University students only is the rise of what may be called a boarders' house for the School. In early times Magdalen Hall had fulfilled this function, but from the Civil War onwards we find the schoolmaster drawing an income from boarders.[2] This suggests that till then such members of the School

[1] See also the case of Hurst in 1643–8 (p. 117).

[2] See Price's letter, quoted on p. 118. James Carkesse, Master 1663, also sought for boarders, as Wood tells us (Wood's MSS. Ashmol. 19 D 13, ap. Bloxam, ii. 165, 166): 'Mr Thomas Gilbert living near Magdalen Hall, and receiving the sons of fanatics to be his hosts, sending them to school at Magdalen to Mr Carcasse, and Mr Carcasse, minding to have them to be his own hosts, complained to Dr Fell that he did great injury hereby to youths, for that what he infused in them one way Mr Gilbert did undoe another, and the like. Upon the which Mr Fell told the Vice-Chancellor, Dr Blandford, and he the Chancellor, Whereupon for that reason, it is thought, and because Mr Carcasse had a mind to the boys himself, he was turned out of town; but Mr Carcasse was crossed in this his design, for the boys were taken away and sent elsewhere.'

as came from outside Oxford had lived at Magdalen Hall; but, of course, these boarders, from the later sixteenth century onwards, would be less numerous than in the days when Anwykyll and his successors were setting new standards in teaching.

SCHOOL LIFE

The curriculum throughout this period probably varied little in its principal aim; Latin was the main subject, and everything led up to the production in a boy's last years of themes (in English and Latin), verses, and orations. The main purpose of these was to fit the boy for disputations at the University, and even for ordinary conversation. At any rate, in 1590 President Bond could claim that in Magdalen the scholars 'dared not presume to speak any other language then Latine'. No doubt in good hands the system gave a boy a good general education.

The authors read included the old classics of Wolsey's curriculum, but John Harmar's phrasebook, referred to above, shows that the school was also reading Erasmus's *Colloquies*, Corderius's *Dialogues*, and Politian's *Letters*, all of them books which might help pupils to adapt classical Latin to the needs of modern conversation and correspondence. Greek, which had early entered the curriculum, was still taught, as, apparently, was French. Quantities of Greek and Latin verse and prose were produced by the School to celebrate Queen Elizabeth's visit to Oxford in 1566.[1]

Within these broad limits masters had their own idiosyncrasies, and a manuscript in the Bodleian[2] gives an interesting set of remarks, jotted down,

[1] For these see Nichols's *Progresses of Queen Elizabeth*.
[2] Rawl. MS.D 191.

apparently, by some anonymous student of teaching, about the methods of three Magdalen Masters: William White, Master 1632–48, James Carkesse, Usher 1655–6, Master 1663, and Richard Reeve(s), Usher 1668–70, Master 1670–3.

'Mr White framed Latine sentences in the belly of each other, as he phrased it.'

'Mr Fulman [the antiquarian: see below, p. 115] says he was better at Latine at school than now, for tho' he reads books he studyes them not. He was but a quarter of a yeare with Mr White and so is yet much to seek in Greek.'

'Mr Carkas used no printed phrase books but marked those in lectures commanding the boyes to shew them once a week. He would at the giving of a theme explain it fully —He used much translation into Greek and Latin—He read but one theme sc. the worst, which a whipping attended.'

'Mr Carkas would say the boyes had dictionaryes to English words in construeing so trouble not him—His scholars made themes one night and verses another—he went the ordinary way to work to teach them versifying—He gave a theme somewhat neer of sense to the lecture—made great use of Terence which will (sayde young Mr Davis) teach one to speak Latine.'

He made use of Ciceronis works epitomised.'

'Mr Carkes says making Latine too soon breeds an habit of ill Latine.'

'Mr Reeves, schoolmaster of Magdalen School gives the sense of an English theme first.'

'Mr Reeves at Magdalen College makes boyes read their Greek Grammar in the lower forms on Saturday because its out of their weekly course.'

'Mr Reeves the best grammarian in England (Davis jr.)'

'Reeves reads Ovid's metamorphoses mornings after syntaxis, and nothing else.'

For most of the period we are discussing the schoolboy's way of life did not differ greatly from that of earlier days, except that, like his elders', it was becoming more civilized and luxurious. The hours of work and the holidays remained about the same, except that when the Puritans were in power there was more church-going, more attention and note-taking demanded at sermon-time, and less account taken of Saints' Days. Harmar's phrase-book again gives one some ideas. The phrases, translated here from the original Latin, may be left to tell their own tale.

'Let all the boys be at school to-morrow at dawn.'

'I shall not be read out to-morrow in the absentees' list, because I was at school all this week.'

'If I were read out in the absentees' list as often as you and your brothers I should most certainly be beaten by the schoolmaster.'

'When our schoolmaster was teaching us yesterday in school your mother asked a holiday (ludendi veniam) of him.'

'If Peter, William, and George, and the schoolmaster's eldest son had been with me in the market I should have bought each of them several arrows.'

'If we are not careful the schoolmaster will catch us here playing draughts (tesseris).'

Besides the amusements Harmar mentions, in this, the age of Shakespeare, play-acting was common in Oxford. The Magdalen accounts from 1560 onwards contain many references to those acted in the College, and it is quite likely that members of the School acted in them: Latin plays were encouraged in schools as improving the boys' speaking of the language, and Samuel Barnard, Master 1617–25, wrote three plays which were acted in Magdalen in 1617, 1618, and 1619.[1] Francis White, Master 1614–17, was also a writer of plays.

But apart from the work and games which he shared

---

[1] Macray, iii. 45.

with boys elsewhere, the schoolboy at Oxford was in the centre of a more animated life and more stirring events than most: the life of the Magdalen schoolboy in particular, so closely linked to Magdalen College and Magdalen Hall, was diversified by many excitements which he enjoyed together with the University.

The six-day visits to Oxford of Queen Elizabeth in 1566 and 1592, the visit of James I, his Queen, and eldest son in 1605 must have been exciting enough, particularly as Prince Henry was entertained at Magdalen; but perhaps the boys at school in 1586 would remember still better the adventure of that year. Some Magdalen men had been deer-stealing on Shotover, and one of them had been arrested by Lord Norris, so that his fellows, by way of revenge, made a determined attack on Lord Norris when he next visited Oxford. They were restrained by the Vice-Chancellor and every one confined to his College to enable Lord Norris to leave Oxford in safety.

'But the Scholars of Magdalen College, being not able to pocket these affronts, went up privately to the top of their Tower and waiting till he should pass by towards Ricot sent down a shower of stones that they had picked up, upon him and his retinew, wounding some and endangering others of their lives. It is said that upon foresight of this storm, divers had got boards, others tables on their heads to keep them from it, and that if the Lord had not been in his coach or chariot he would certainly have been killed. But however it was, the result came to this pass, that some of the offenders were severely punished, others expelled, and the Lord with much ado pacified by the sages of the University.'[1]

Another red-letter day occurred in 1640, when the Puritans or 'precisians' of Magdalen Hall, boys

[1] *Annals*, 1586.

among them, no doubt, showed their strength.

'At the salute of Flora, two May-poles were set up in Halywell near Oxford, in despite of the Precisians. On the top of one was placed a Tub, and therein the picture of one Edw. Golledge or College, a Musitian and great Puritan . . . and because he had formerly stole wood (as 'twas reported) a little fagot was tied to his back. This mockery had not stood a day or two but exciting much the precise people, the Scholars of New Inne and some of Magdalen Hall came armed and pluckt it down, which giving offence to the Parishioners of Halywell, much harm would have followed, had not certain officers interposed themselves.'[1]

But greater disturbances than these were at hand. In August 1642 the schoolboys could watch a barricade being built across Magdalen Bridge against the Parliamentary army, and loads of stones being carried up into the Tower to be rained down as they had been on Lord Norris. The King entered Oxford after Edgehill, parking his artillery in Magdalen Grove; parts of his earthworks still exist in the school's grounds. The city then remained his head-quarters till 1646, when it at last surrendered to Parliament; Wood[2] gives a telling picture of the result of those four years: Oxford was 'empty as to scholars, but pretty well replenished with parliamentarian soldiers . . . as for the yong men of the city and university, he found many of them to have been debauch'd by bearing armes and doing the duties belonging to soldiers, as watching, warding, and sitting in tipling houses for whole nights together.'

The year 1648 brought a Parliamentary visitation which was more severe on Magdalen than on most colleges. Most of the Choristers and the Schoolmaster were expelled, though the School as a whole was little

---

[1] Ibid., 1640.   [2] Wood's *Life and Times*, i. 129.

altered: and the same may be said of the restoration in 1660. Thereafter, though the School cannot but have been affected by the dissolute life prevalent all around, the only major excitement was the affair of 1687, when Magdalen College became the storm-centre of anti-Roman Catholic feeling in England. James II's determination to appoint a President, and Magdalen's determination to resist, James's preliminary victory and ultimate defeat are part of English history; but the situation must have been doubly piquant for the boys of the School, owing to the equivocal part played by their Schoolmaster. Wood's diary for January 10th, 1688, notes, 'Mr Thos. Collins, schoolmaster of Magdalen College, returned from London after he had been there some time to gaine a fellowship of Magdalen College and not turn Roman Catholic. In his absence Mr [Richard] Wright, his usher, left his place and carried away most [of] his scholars to teach them privately. . . . 'Tis said Mr Collins hath lost his reputation among his friends.'[1] Collins was also Chaplain to Parker, the Bishop of Oxford whom James nominated as President, and we are told by an eyewitness how, as Parker was too ill to take possession of the new home on which he had been thrust, 'The very day the Lodgings were Broke open, the Bishop's Lady, led in by Tom Collins, went to view them.'[2] But when all was over and done, when William was King, and Hough, the College's choice, was President again, Collins seems not to have suffered for his excessive loyalty to James. Oxford was Jacobite when James was gone, and Collins lasted another thirty-five years as Schoolmaster.

[1] Wood's *Life and Times*, iii. 253.
[2] Letter of John Aldworth quoted by Bloxam, *Magdalen College and James II*, p. 178.

CHAPTER V

SOME MASTERS, USHERS, AND PUPILS
1564-1703

Balguay, Hooker, Forman—The Symonds Scandal—Featley, Nicholson—
Hobbes, Clarendon, Harmar, Chillingworth—Fulman, Pierce, Sherley—
Hopkins, Price, Coles—Thomas Smith—Reeve, Collins, Yalden

BALGUAY, HOOKER, FORMAN

To succeed so great a scholar as Cooper, who had retired at the height of his fame as a teacher, a man of learning was necessary, and Nicholas Balguay, who became Master in 1567, had earned his place. In his later years, to judge by the disclosures under his successor (p. 110), his efficiency was not great; but before his appointment he had won a good name as a scholar. He was one of the Magdalen men who, in 1566, had greeted Queen Elizabeth in both Latin and Greek, and before that, in 1563, he had been appointed Greek Lecturer in the College, receiving an additional £2 per annum from 1569 onwards for reading Greek to the School. He retired in 1583, becoming a Prebendary of Salisbury, and from 1591 till his death ten years later he was Master of the Temple.

Balguay's most famous pupil, other than Hooker, was that wayward genius, Simon Forman. Forman was born at a village in Wiltshire in 1552, and on the death of his father in 1563 was put by his 'ill-natured and clownish mother' to 'keep sheep, plow and pick up sticks'. Simon, however, by becoming apprentice to a druggist, acquired the rudiments of medicine, and educated himself a little by picking the brains of a boy who shared his bedchamber; later he betook himself to Oxford, where, as a Servitor, he 'improved himself much in learning' at Magdalen School. But the two benefactors that maintained him were wastrels—though one of them afterwards became a bishop—and spent all their time courting the two daughters of a certain doctor at Cowley, and 'thither did Simon go almost every day with bottle and bag, to the great loss of his time'. After two years Forman left Magdalen, and maintaining himself as a schoolmaster, studied astrology, magic, and medicine until in 1579 he found himself, according to his own claim, possessed of miraculous powers. Thereafter his life was one long battle with his more regularly qualified rivals, and it is to Forman's credit that the turning-point in his career came with his work among the poor during the plague of 1592, when most regular doctors were frightened away. Less reputable was his work among the upper classes, which consisted largely in fostering illicit intrigues with love-philtres; but to the powerful friends thus acquired he doubtless owed the licence to practise which Cambridge University gave him in 1603. His work for the plague-stricken poor in 1592 had resulted only in a summons by the College of Physicians for practising without a licence. Forman's death, it is said, took place for no visible reason in a boat on the Thames in 1611, a triumphant vindication of his methods, as he had prophesied that he would not outlive the day on which it occurred.[1]

THE SYMONDS SCANDAL

Balguay's successor, William Symonds, held office from 1583 to 1586, at which time a storm that had been gathering broke, and swept him deservedly away. Piecing together the very consistent complaints that were made and the action taken by the Visitor in

[1] See *Athenae*, ii. 371.

1585, one can deduce that corruption and inefficiency were rife. 'The School', said one Fellow, 'has been taught either by Vice-gerents or very bad Schoolmasters, about these ten years together, and by such a one now as hath two benefices, who only keeps the School until he can compass the twenty pounds in money which he gave for it.' 'A general complaint', says another, 'has been made of default therein for ten or twelve years, that whereas heretofore Masters of Arts have resorted thither to hear, now Scholars are necessarily taken away and privately taught. He that is now Schoolmaster had at his coming a Benefice in Lincolnshire, and now is said to have another.' It is suggestive of jobbery also that John Bedo, who was Usher from 1554 to 1571, became on his resignation Master of the School at Brackley, and Roger Webster, who succeeded Bedo as Usher, succeeded him also in 1576 at Brackley. Webster's successor as Usher was Henry Mercer, whose resignation in 1585 suggests that he shared Symond's guilt.

The Visitor, among other things—for there was much to find fault with in the College at the time—rebuked the President and Fellows for allowing the School to become an object of contempt (*derisui et despectui haberi*), and commanded them to appoint to it a man, honest, industrious, learned, and elegantly instructed in the humanities (*vir probus, industrius, eruditus et humanioribus disciplinis eleganter instructus*) and to see that he was treated with respect, and that all the boys and young men not yet fit for dialectic frequented the School, whether they were Demies or commoners.

FEATLEY, NICHOLSON

Paul Smith, the first Master appointed after the visitation, had at any rate two famous names among his pupils—John Milton, the father of the poet, and Daniel Featley or Fairclough. Featley was one of the most eminent theologians of the seventeenth century. From Magdalen School he went as scholar to Corpus Christi College, and later 'his admirable disputations, his excellent sermons, his grave, yet affable demeanour, and his other rare accomplishments, made him so renown'd, that Sir Thomas Edmunds being dispatched by king James to lie leiger-ambassador in France', chose Featley as his Chaplain. While he was in France 'he became the honour of the Protestant religion and the English nation; insomuch as his many conflicts with, and conquests of, the learned Sorbonists in defence of the protestants, and opposition to the papists, caused even those adversaries to give him this encomium, that he was "Featlaeus acutiss. & acerrimus" '.[1] In 1617 he became Chaplain to Abbott, the Archbishop of Canterbury, retiring in 1625 to 'the study and practice of piety and charity', but his retirement was rudely disturbed at the outbreak of the Civil War by a visit of some rebel soldiers, who 'after they had missed our author Featley, whom they took to be a papist, or at least that he had a pope in his belly, they drank and eat up his provision, burnt down a barn of his full of corn and two stables, the loss amounting to £211'. The Parliament, nevertheless, made an effort to enlist Featley's services in the assembly of divines, for 'he was esteemed by the generality to be one of the most resolute and victorious champions of the reformed protestant religion in his time, a most smart scourge of the church of Rome, a compendium of the learned tongues, and of all the liberal arts and sciences'; but Featley's Protestantism was neither extreme nor pliable enough, and he was

[1] This and the following quotations are from *Athenae*, iii. 157–60.

imprisoned for a short time, and released only to die soon after.

Edward Lapworth, who was Master from 1598 to 1610, had, like Cooper, leanings towards medicine; and after he resigned the School he became Doctor of Physic, and, in 1618, Linacre Physics Lecturer and a noted practitioner. His pupils at Magdalen School include some eminent and perhaps some very great names.

William Nicholson, Bishop of Gloucester from 1660 to 1672, entered the School as a Chorister in 1598, became Master of the Free School at Croydon, and during the Rebellion taught a private school in Wales.

'After the King's restoration he was by the endeavours of Edward Earl of Clarendon lord Chancellor of England designed bishop of Glocester by his majesty. . . . Which bishoprick he kept, without any translation to another see, to his dying day. . . . He was a right learned divine, well seen and read in the fathers and schoolmen, but above all most excellent he was in the critical part of grammar, in which faculty none in his time, or perhaps before, went beyond him.'[1]

Another eminent pupil was Accepted Frewen. Frewen was elected Demy in 1603 at the age of 14; he matriculated in January 1605 and took his B.A. in January 1609, so that it is fairly certain that the four years between his matriculation and his B.A. are those of his University course, the time between 1603 and 1605 being spent at the School. He later became President of the College (1626-46) and showed himself a keen supporter of Laud. In 1643 he became Bishop of Lichfield, and after the Restoration in 1660 Archbishop of York.

[1] *Athenae*, iii. 950.

HOBBES, CLARENDON, HARMAR, CHILLINGWORTH

It is possible that Thomas Hobbes, the famous philosopher and author of *Leviathan*, and Edward Hyde, Lord Clarendon, Chancellor and author of the *History of the Great Rebellion*, were also taught by Lapworth in the College School, though, as has been said, one cannot be certain about members of Magdalen Hall at this time. Certainly both came into residence at the very early age of thirteen, and it would be pleasant to think that, in endeavouring to get Nicholson made Bishop of Gloucester, Hyde was merely serving an old school-fellow; it must be mentioned, however, that Wood insinuates that the Chancellor's zeal was really due to a bribe of £1,000.[1]

Little of interest is known about the next few Masters and Ushers except that Lawrence Snelling (Master 1610 to 1614) was a Puritan whose evidence later contributed to Laud's condemnation; and his successors, Francis White (1614-17) and Samuel Bernard (1617-25), both wrote plays for performance in the College. The most interesting of their Ushers was John Harmar (1617-26), whose *Praxis Grammatica* has already been mentioned. Wood disliked him as a Puritan, but has to commend his learning.

'He was a most excellent philologist, and a tolerable Latin poet; was happy in rendring Greek into Latin, or Latin into English, or English into Greek or Latin, whether in prose or verse; which we now call transversing and transposing. But as in these he did excell, and therefore often made use of by scholars, so did he go beyond all that I knew of his condition, that affected popular applause, he being of so credulous a humour, as to take all that was said or done to him, to redound to his honour and credit. . . . Besides all

[1] *Athenae*, iv. 825.

J

this, he beeing also a meer scholar, and therefore mostly in a poor and shabbed condition, whether in his way of living or habit, he flatter'd all men and powers that were uppermost, whether lawful or usurping, and endeavoured to make himself known to all patrons of learning if it were only for a meal's meat, or to gain applause.'[1]

After leaving Magdalen he became successively Master of St Albans School, Under-master of Westminster, and Greek Professor at Oxford and Rector of Dewhurst; 'but losing those two places after the restoration of King Charles II he retired to Steventon in Hampshire, where he mostly lived on the joynture of his wife'. It was while Greek Professor that he gave an instance of the 'credulous humour' that Wood refers to. In October 1659 a 'mock-Patriarch' visited Oxford, and Harmar was sufficiently deluded to put on his robes and make him a solemn Greek oration.[2]

William Chillingworth, the theologian, may have been at the School under Snelling or White and Harmar. Wood[3] says that he was born in 1602 and 'educated under Edward Sylvester . . . or in the free school joyning Magdalen College or in both'. One of the greatest thinkers of his time, he earned the friendship and respect of such men as John Hales and Lord Falkland, not only by his ability, but also by the moderation, disinterestedness, and sincerity that led him to the Church of Rome and back again to the Church of England, and, for a long time after he had returned, barred him from all preferment through a scruple about signing the Articles. Wood aptly quotes Hobbes 'that he was a lusty fighting fellow that did drive his enemies before him, but would often give his own party smart back blows'. His greatest work

[1] Ibid. iii. 918.   [2] *D.N.B.*
[3] *Athenae*, iii. 87.

was *The Religion of Protestants a Safe Way to Salvation*, a book produced after his return to the Church of England in answer to the views of the Jesuits that had formerly appealed to him. 'Chillingworth's argumentative clearness was regarded by Locke as a model . . . he never strains a point against his adversary, but overwhelms him by the massiveness of his learning, and the loftiness of his intellectual attitude.'[1] Chillingworth took the Royal side during the Civil War, was captured, and died in honourable captivity.

FULMAN, PIERCE, SHERLEY

Of John Allibond, Master from 1625 to 1632, nothing need be said except that he bore a reputation as 'the witty man of Magd. Coll.'; his Usher after Harmar's departure was John Langton (1626-32), and his only eminent pupil was Henry Langley, who was Chorister from 1627 to 1632, and was Master of Pembroke from 1647 to the Restoration.

From 1632 to 1648 the Master was William White and the Usher John Hyde. White was ejected by the Parliamentary Visitors of 1648, Hyde having resigned just before. Fulman's implied compliment to White as a Greek teacher has already been quoted; but perhaps the number of his eminent pupils is an even better testimonial. Fulman himself was made a scholar of Corpus Christi in 1647, expelled in 1648, and returning in 1660 was 'a severe student in various sorts of learning' till his death in 1688.[2] The historian of Oxford University pays a hearty tribute to his zeal as an antiquarian.[3] Another pupil of White's was Thomas Pierce, Chorister 1633-8. Pierce was elected President of Magdalen in 1660 on the King's recommendation, but 'the true government of that house being much

---

[1] *D.N.B.*   [2] *Athenae*, iv. 240.   [3] Mallett, ii. 441-4.

interrupted and disturbed while he sat at the stern there (he being more fit for the pulpit than to be a governor)', he resigned in 1672 to become Dean of Salisbury.

'The quicker pregnancy of his parts, the ingenious keenness of his pen, and the compleat excellency of his learning, many of his greatest adversaries did often confess and acknowledge, but oftner found experiment in those most notorious overthrows and palpable foils which he gave them. He was a resolute maintainer of the antient establishment of the English church, and a stout assertor of her due rights, especially in such a time, when it was accounted matter of the deepest guilt to have so much courage, as either to own the one, or publicly to appear in defence of the other. He, Hammond and Heylin (all formerly of Magd. Coll.) were the chiefest champions among the old, regular and comfortable clergy, who victoriously engaged many of the most specious and plausible pamphleteers, whose scurrilous and violent libels, the rank liberty of the boundless press midwiv'd into the miserably torn and distracted nation.'[1]

Pepys also pays tribute to Pierce's ability as a preacher: 'he hath as much of natural eloquence as most men that I ever heard in my life, mixed with so much learning'.[2]

Thomas Sherley, a famous doctor and Physician in Ordinary to Charles II, was also White's pupil, having attended the School as a day-boy. Besides practising he wrote or translated various medical books ranging from *A philosophical essay, declaring the probable causes whence stones are produced in the greater world . . . being the Prodromus to a medicinal truth concerning the cause and cure of the stone in the kidneys and bladder of man* to *Cochlearia Curiosa, or the Curiosities of Scurvy-Grass.* He finally died of grief, arising 'upon a

[1] *Athenae*, iv. 301.   [2] *Pepys' Diary*, April 8th, 1663.

just suspicion that he should be totally defeated of an estate in Sussex, worth about £3000 per annum, descended to him from his great-grandfather . . .'[1]

Mention must also be made of Henry Hurst, one of the most notable Nonconformist preachers after the Restoration. His case is interesting, as Wood[2] records him as being a batteler of Magdalen Hall in 1648. Actually he was a Chorister of Magdalen from 1643 to 1647, a fact which further confirms the close connexion between the School and Magdalen Hall.

White, after his ejection, secured the Rectory of Pusey, and 'kept it during the interval by the favour of friends and the smallness of the profits'. After the Restoration his old pupil, Dr Pierce, gained him the Rectory of Appleton as well, 'both which livings he kept to his dying day'.[3]

HOPKINS, PRICE, COLES

Of the Masters and Ushers during the Protectorate Owen Price, Master (1657-60), and Ezekiel Hopkins, Usher (1655-6), call for some comment. Hopkins was a Chorister from 1648 to 1653, and after being Usher and Chaplain of Magdalen he preached for some time in London. 'Having retired to Exeter on account of the Plague, he became Minister of St Mary's Church there, was countenanced by Bishop Ward, and much admired for the comeliness of his person, and elegance of preaching. At length John, Lord Roberts (afterwards Earl of Truro) hearing him accidentally preach, was so pleased with him, that he gave him his daughter Araminta in marriage, and took him as his Chaplain to Ireland when he went as Lord Lieutenant in 1669.' There Hopkins became successively Dean and Bishop

---

[1] *Athenae*, ii. 495–6.   [2] Ibid. 841.
[3] *Athenae*, iii. 1167.

of Raphoe and Bishop of Londonderry; 'where con-
tinuing till the forces in Ireland under the Earl of
Tyrconnel stood up in defence of K. James II in 1688,
he retired to England', and soon died.[1]

Owen Price had been Master of a school in Wales,
'where he advanced his pupils much in Presbyterian
principles', but in 1655 he returned to Oxford and
entered Christ Church.

'Soon after he became Master of the free-school near
Magdalen College, where by his industry and good way of
teaching, he drew many youths of the city, whose parents
were fanatically given to be his scholars. But upon the king's
restoration being ejected for nonconformity, taught school
in which he much delighted, in several places, as in Devon-
shire, Besills-lee near Abingdon &c. and became useful
among the brethren, and a noted professor in the art of
pedagogy.'[2]

He was clearly an excellent teacher, for at one time
the Independents designed to put him into Busby's
place as Master of Westminster. Price's letter on that
occasion to the Secretary of Cromwell's Council is
worth quoting in full.

'Dear and honoured Sir, 1. I cannot but be troubled at
the slownes of the governors in putting a period to my
busines, which you were pleased when I took my leave of
you, to look upon as done. And, being the report of it is
spread in this countrey, that is, has disswaded several persons
from sending their children to me upon the ensuing quarter
of Misdummer (to say nothing of many other inconveniences)
I fear I shall suffer by it very much if it does not succeed.

'2. In the judgment of all those wise Christians, both here
and among you, whom I have advised with, there appears
very much of God in this unexpected providence of bringing
me to the place, but there appears more of the divell in
keeping me out of it, in that he is so arrowsed as to incense

_____
[1] Bloxam, i. 67, based on *Athenae*, iv. 287.   [2] *Athenae*, iii. 942.

all his agents, both here and at Westminster, to set all their witts on work to conspire against me.

'3. What the *Remora* is I would gladly know. For, if my parts and qualification for the place be called in question, let any scholars in Oxford be appointed to make tryall of my boyes here; or I will wayt upon the Governors to the School at Westminster, and they shall hear me teach.

'4. But whatever they have to object, I doubt not but that I shall satisfye them that I am *par negocio*, if they will be so uncivill as to call my abilitie in question, who can produce of my Scholars, during these eight years that I have bin Schoolmaster (through grace) more godly men and preachers (some whereof have passed the approvers) than some (that keepe greater noise than I doe) have with their twenty years labour.

'5. But the Lord that teaches to profitt, gives the increase. If he will so vindicate his own name and interest, as to put it into your hearts to make choice of me, I shall labour in his strength and fear to be faythfull. If not, I shall trouble you no more, but rest yours in the firmest bonds. Owen Price.'[1]

Price's pupils would mostly be 'fanatically given' and therefore at a disadvantage in their years of manhood. The only one known is Elisha Coles, who acquired moderate fame as a teacher and as writer of numerous books on the teaching of Latin, English, spelling, and shorthand. However 'upon some default not now to be named he left all and went into Ireland, where he ended his course. He was a curious and critical person in the English and Latin tongues, did much good in his calling and wrote several useful and necessary books for the instruction of beginners'.[2]

THOMAS SMITH

Of the first two Masters after the Restoration, Parker (1660-3) and Carkesse (1663), little is known except what has been already said about Carkesse's

---

[1] Quoted by Bloxam, iii. 180–1.   [2] *Athenae*, iii. 1275.

methods of teaching and of acquiring pupils (p. 103).
Thomas Smith, who succeeded Carkesse in 1663 or
1664 and ruled the School till 1666, was a much greater
man. From 1668 to 1671 he was Chaplain to the British
Ambassador at Constantinople, and used the opportunity to make himself an expert in Oriental languages
and the history of the Greek Church, topics on which
several of his numerous books were written. On his
return to England he was given the nickname of
'Rabbi' or 'Tograi' Smith (Tograi being the name
of an Arabian author he had edited); but owing to
his desire to compromise in the great conflict with
James II in 1687, the name was altered by his enemies
to 'Roguery' Smith. The injustice of this is shown by
the fact that he was expelled from his fellowship by
the Roman Catholic intruders under James, and when
restored under William was promptly expelled again
as a Non-juror. As Dr Routh put it, 'no one ought to
doubt the veracity of Smith, that signal martyr to
conscience, who was fated to be a loser, whatever side
was uppermost'. It is impossible to read without
emotion the last letter that he wrote to his friend
Hearne in 1710, when old, blind, and in pain, having
lived for the last eighteen years of his life as a depen-
dant of Sir John Cotton;[1] and it is doing him bare
justice to quote Hearne's tribute to him.

'As he was a man of very great learning, so he was withall
modest, humble, and wonderfull communicative, of indefatigable industry, and of more than ordinary curiosity in
discovering and preserving the writings of learned men,
especially those of our own country, which are much
indebted to him for the lives of divers of them, as well as
for several other usefull and good works. . . . He was a person
well vers'd in all sorts of learning, and one of the best scholars

---

[1] The letter is quoted by Bloxam, iii. 200, from *Oxoniana*, iii. 118.

that ever were bred in Magdalen College, and indeed in the University, for he had an extraordinary good collection of books in all faculties, which he took care to digest in the best order. These books he picked up in his Travells, and at other times when he had a good convenient opportunity. This knowledge of books was so exstensive, that men of the best reputation, such as have spent not only hundreds but thousands of pounds for furnishing libraries, apply'd themselves to him for his advice and direction, and were glad when they could receive a line or two from him to assist them in that affair.'[1]

Smith still lives as the author of the Latin hymn that is sung on Magdalen Tower on May morning.

REEVE, COLLINS, YALDEN

Richard Reeve, who was Usher from 1668 to 1670 and Master from then to 1673, is another noteworthy man. A compliment to him has already been quoted;[2] and that it was not undeserved is shown by the fact that Dr Fell employed him to translate Wood's *History and Antiquities of the University of Oxford* into Latin. But having been converted to Roman Catholicism in 1667 and becoming known as a proselytizer, he was in 1673 forced to leave his post at Magdalen School and go to Douai, where he became a monk. Recalled to England in 1688 by James II, his resumed teaching activities were cut short by James's flight, and he died five years later.

'He was accounted a perfect philologist, admirably well vers'd in all classical learning, a good Grecian, and has been so sedulous in his profession of pedagogy, that he hath educated 60 ministers of the church of England and about 40 Rom. priests, as I have often heard him say: and having been lame from the beginning, as I have before told you, so

---

[1] *Collections*, May 13th and June 19th, 1710.   [2] p. 103.

consequently taken off from the rambles of the world, he spent his time altogether in studies and devotion.'[1]

Thomas Collins, who succeeded Reeve as Master, held the position from 1673 to 1723. He had been a Chorister, but as he won his choristership at the age of nineteen, it is not likely that he was educated at the School. His long career as Master opened in a blaze of glory, for Wood's diary (Dec. 19th, 1673) notes that on his appointment 'Mr Alexander Pudsey, mad by reason of pride, caused a poor boy of the College to make a bonfire over against the school door'. Pudsey was a vigorous Protestant, and one of the most determined opponents of James II in 1687, at which time, as we have seen (p. 107), he had less cause for approving of Mr Collins; but Collins's fifty years as Master gave ample time for the gathering and burning of his wild oats, and the evidence of his epitaph, which was composed by the famous Dr Sacheverell, coupled with that of the frequent references made by Hearne in his diary to 'this old ingenious man', enable us to construct a picture of one whose wit and scholarship made him good company everywhere, and whose ambition in his later days aimed no higher than a comfortable living.

Collins's first three Ushers call for no comment, but John Smith (Usher 1689-1717), who had been his pupil as a Chorister, appears to have been a man after Collins's own heart. His epitaph, with the incisive delicacy that only Latin is capable of, makes it clear that he was a great wag,[2] but his sense of humour was apt to outrun discretion. In his days as a Clerk he

---

[1] *Athenae*, iv. 387.

[2] 'Vir ingenio, voce, ac gestu honeste comicus; abundans facetiarum sine veneno; ficti amans, salva integritate; innocuus laetitiae artifex; lepidus poeta; amicus plane simplex; comes jucundissimus.'

once had to be fined 2*s*. for 'a scandalous error in celebrating divine service when in place of the Venite Exultemus he struck up Cantate Domino, and sang a whole verse against the sense and efforts of the rest who were trying to sing the right hymn'.[1] Hearne's diary (May 7th, 1713) records, apropos of the publication of *Poems on sevral occasions, by Mr Smith,* 'he was always looked upon as a very ingenious man, but I am afraid he hath not acted advisedly in printing these poems'. Hearne was probably thinking of their occasional indecency, but to a modern taste they are all extremely dull.

Of Collins's pupils who come within this period the most eminent were Henry Holyoake, Chorister in 1672, who later becoming Headmaster of Rugby, was largely responsible for its rise to greatness, and Thomas Yalden. Yalden was born in Oxford in 1670, and entered Magdalen School as a Chorister in 1678; he later won sufficient literary fame to be included in Johnson's *Lives of the Poets,* though he did not escape at least one typically Johnsonian reproof. 'In the last stanza (sc. of his *Hymn to Light*), having mentioned the sudden eruption of new-created Light, he says, "Awhile the Almighty wondering stood." He ought to have remembered, that Infinite Knowledge can never wonder. All wonder is the effect of novelty upon ignorance.' Collins's later pupils take us into the period covered by the next chapter.

[1] MS. Clerke, Pres., ap. Bloxam, iii. 225.

CHAPTER VI

THE PERIOD OF ECLIPSE

1703–76: Oxford in the Eighteenth Century: Decay of Magdalen College and School—Some Old Boys: John Parsons. 1776–1840: Cox's Reminiscences: Gilchrist: Ellerton—Jenkins: Changes in the School's Buildings —Reminiscences of Knight and Millard—School Life: Battles: Barring-out —Literary Interests—Games

1703-1776

OXFORD IN THE EIGHTEENTH CENTURY: DECAY OF MAGDALEN COLLEGE AND SCHOOL

THE eighteenth century, at any rate until its closing years, is the most discreditable period in the long history of Oxford University, and has been for ever damned in most men's minds by Gibbon's description of the fourteen months he spent at Magdalen, which he calls 'the most idle and unprofitable of my whole life'. In the words of Magdalen's historian,[1]

'Gibbon's description . . . though not free from inaccuracies of detail, is probably, on the whole, a truthful account of the College as it was in his Oxford days; and it may be said that the same description would have applied, with equal truth, for a good many years both before and after the middle of the eighteenth century. It would have applied also, *mutatis mutandis*, to a good many other Colleges in the University. Indeed, Gibbon's quarrel was not so much with Magdalen as with Oxford. He describes his own College rather as an instance of the general state of things than as an exception. But at Magdalen some of the conditions which favoured the slothfulness of the time were even more powerful than in other societies.'

At Magdalen the Demies, instead of resigning, in accordance with the statutes, at the age of twenty-five,

---

[1] Wilson, p. 222.

retained their places until they succeeded to fellowships, as of right, the result being that most of the
Demies at any period were graduates, and many of
them quite old men; apart from a few Demies, the
only undergraduates were 'gentleman-commoners', a
class whose uselessness made them the first victims of
the spirit of reform in the nineteenth century. An
assured future, and the absence of any but formal
obstacles to a degree, encouraged idleness in these
undergraduates; and among their seniors little teaching
was done, for there were few to be taught, while
research, that might have been claimed as their
raison d'être, appears to have been almost entirely
neglected. The Fellows waited for College livings to
fall vacant, and meanwhile were frequently non-
resident, supplementing their share of the College
income with teachers' or curates' stipends elsewhere.
Many members of the College were worthy men, no
doubt, but Tory Oxford was suffering from a frustrated
loyalty that soon degenerated into grumbling impo-
tence, an atmosphere not conducive to energy or
natural growth.

Inevitably the School declined, too, both in numbers and efficiency, though some slight stimulus was
given to the Master and Usher by the fact that their
salaries were eked out by the fees of 'pay-boys', as the
members of the School not on the Foundation were
called. These pay-boys, however, were not many:
Oxford was a very small place, and in the eighteenth
century the grammar schools that stuck rigidly to a
classical curriculum were not popular with the
mercantile and working classes who had come to
demand more up-to-date methods of education. Nor
is this surprising when we find that under Robert
Bryne (Master 1752-76) a considerable part at any

rate of some of his pupils' time was spent in preparing long lists of all the words found in such works as the *Epistles* of Phalaris.[1] The ordinary work, presumably, was not quite so meaningless as this; but by Bryne's day the average number of pay-boys seems to have dropped to about a dozen, a total only occasionally exceeded thereafter until the reconstitution of the School.[2]

Certainly the Choristers were the main interest of the Schoolmaster[3] and of the College. Any Chorister of ordinary ability in the eighteenth century could look forward to a placid and unalarming career, supported throughout his University life by the College to which the interest of some Fellow had given him the *entrée* at the age of eight or nine, and thereafter standing a good chance of a comfortable living in which to end his days, as useful or as useless to his parishioners as he chose.[4]

Take Andrew Etty. He is appointed Chorister in 1728 at the age of nine. No sooner has he left his choristership than he becomes a Demy, and remains one till, ten years after he has become a Master of Arts, a fellowship falls to him; this he holds for some eight years, and then, in 1758, he is appointed to the

---

[1] Bodl. MSS. S.C. 27998, 9. The other works indexed in this painful way were *Gabriae sive Babriae Fabulae, Hannonis Periplus, Hieroclis liber de providentia et fato, Hieroclis fragmenta, Mithridatis et Bruti Epistolae, Secundi Philosophi Sententiae, Libellum περὶ τοῦ Ἐπισταλτικοῦ Χαρακτῆρος.*

[2] In 1775 and 1780 there were about thirty (according to witnesses in the lawsuit of 1845), but this must have been due to the fact that in 1771 Bryne gained nineteen boys as the result of the Master of New College School being appointed to Southampton (Bloxam, iii. 236, 5). The numbers soon fell again.

[3] Bryne's diary (quoted ibid., 231 ff.) alludes to various old pupils to whom he gave recommendations, &c. They are all ex-Choristers.

[4] From 1703 to 1791, of 219 Choristers appointed 135 matriculated, and of these 78 did not resign their choristerships until they had become Demy, Clerk, or Usher of the College.

Vicarage of Selborne. Here he remains for the last twenty-five years of his life, performing 'many useful repairs' to the vicarage, and 'wainscotting up to the bottom of the windows the whole of the Chancel; to the neatness and decency of which he always paid the most exact attention'.[1] In his character, according to his epitaph,

'the conjugal, the parental, and the sacerdotal virtues were so happily combined, as to deserve the imitation of mankind; and if in any particular he followed more invariably the steps of his blessed Master, it was in his humility.'

His career, if not his virtues, can be paralleled over and over again among the Magdalen Choristers of the first three-quarters of the eighteenth century.

SOME OLD BOYS: JOHN PARSONS

The list of eminent Old Boys between 1703 and 1776 is not a long one. Thomas Jenner, who was President of Magdalen between 1745 and 1768, had been educated at the School under Collins. His presidency is notable chiefly for the fact that it included Gibbon's period of residence. Thomas Winchester's claim to fame is similar. He was Chorister from 1722 to 1729, and during his fellowship he was the second tutor of Gibbon, who says of him,

'Dr Winchester well remembered that he had a salary to receive, and only forgot that he had a duty to perform. Instead of guiding the studies and watching over the behaviour of his disciple, I was never summoned to attend even the ceremony of a Lecture; and excepting one voluntary visit to his rooms, during the eight months of his titular office, the Tutor and Pupil lived in the same College as strangers to each other.'

[1] White's *Antiquities of Selborne*, p. 472.

It is only fair to give the other side of the picture:

'His talents', says Archdeacon Churton, summing up a biographical memoir, 'if not splendid, were sound and good; his attainments various and useful; and he was a true son of the Church of England.'[1]

Another eminent Fellow was Thomas West, who had been Chorister from 1720 to 1727, and filling most of the College offices before his death in 1781, was wont to declare, 'with affectionate gratitude and reverence to the memory of the pious Founder', that he had 'eaten the bread of William Patten for three-quarters of a century'. Many stories were told of his simplicity, among them the following:

'An attempt to go as far as London, defeated by getting into the same coach again at the half-way house, which coach according to the awkward arrangement of that time returned to Oxford, while a different coach conveyed the passengers to Town;—this attempt, though recorded of other worthies of similar life and conversation, was really made by Dr West, as well as the very natural remark on repassing the bridge that commands a view of the walks where Addison once mused,—"Well, if I did not know that I was going into London, I could almost swear that *that* was Magdalen Tower." '[2]

Of those who earned fame outside Oxford the best known is Sir Richard Aston, who was at the School before going on to Winchester in 1728.[3] He was an eminent lawyer in his day, and, after displaying considerable energy as Lord Chief Justice in the Court of Common Pleas in Ireland, and earning some odium for his share in the invalidation of the writ of outlawry against Wilkes in 1768, won his greatest honour when

[1] Quoted Bloxam, i. 154.　　　　　　　　[2] Bloxam, i. 147.
[3] See *Notes and Queries*, x. v, p. 364.

the office of Lord Chancellor was put in commission in 1770 and he was one of the three commissioners. Aston died in 1778.

Worthier Old Boys, perhaps, were Richard Wooddeson and Henry John Todd. Wooddeson was Chorister from 1712 to 1722, and later became Headmaster of the Free-School at Kingston-on-Thames, where Gibbon and several other writers, less famous but well known in their day, were among his pupils. Bloxam's quotations make it clear that he was an excellent schoolmaster,[1] and even Gibbon does not condemn him. Todd was Chorister from 1771 to 1779; after many preferments he became Archdeacon of Cleveland in 1832; but the principal achievements of his life were literary. Among many other writings he edited the works of Milton and of Spenser, and revised Johnson's *Dictionary*.

The greatest pupil of the School, however, during this period was John Parsons, Master of Balliol and Bishop of Peterborough. Born in 1761, the son of the butler of Corpus Christi, he was educated principally at Magdalen School and Wadham. He became Master of Balliol in 1798, and 'with the Mastership of Dr Parsons the real revival of Balliol, and it may be said of the University generally, began'.[2] Mallet[3] gives a full account of his great work in rendering the University examinations a reality and promoting the efficiency of the tutorial system. When Parsons became Bishop of Peterborough in 1813 he continued to work for education by helping in the establishment and encouragement of the 'National Society' for the education of the poor.

---

[1] Bloxam, i. 137–43.   [2] *D.N.B.*   [3] iii. 166 ff., 178 ff.

K

1776-1840

COX'S REMINISCENCES: GILCHRIST: ELLERTON

The schooldays of Parsons and Todd take us to a period when the reforming spirit, of which Parsons was so worthy an example, was in the air; and if it took some time to affect his old school, we can at any rate see the stages by which it crept in. At the celebrated lawsuit of 1845[1] evidence about the School of as early a date as possible was called, some of which goes back to the days of Bryne's successor, Thomas Robinson, Master from 1776 to 1795; and, more helpful still, among Robinson's latest pupils was George Valentine Cox, later Master of New College School, and author of *Recollections of Oxford*, whose well-stored memory Bloxam drew on for his accounts of Robinson and his successors.

When Robinson took over the School in 1776 the pay-boys, as we have seen, were still at the number of 30, to which Bryne had raised them; but by the time Cox entered the School in 1794 they had dwindled almost to none. Nor is this surprising; the wildness that we shall see to be prevalent in 1838-40 no doubt was as bad at this time, and, moreover, the Master had given up the habit of attending the School. 'Being what was then called "a martyr to the gout", he heard the senior boys their lessons (when he was well enough) at his house, not far off.'[2] His most distinguished pupil was one Octavius Gilchrist, who, after being a

---

[1] See below, pp. 151 ff.

[2] The Schoolmaster's house was then in High Street, next door to what was later Dr Millard's boarding-house (see p. 154); but by the time of Dr Ellerton, Master 1798–1810, the Master's rooms were those in the Magdalen Hall buildings with a large bay-window, overlooking the Gravel Walk, and, on the other side of the room, commanding the entrance to the Schoolroom.

Chorister from 1787 to 1791, had the originality to become a grocer in Stamford. While thus engaged he made himself an expert in the then little studied subject of Old English plays, and, but for the timidity of his publishers, would have produced a massive edition of them in fifteen volumes. He was also a Fellow of the Antiquarian Society and an esteemed correspondent of Sir Walter Scott and Dr Bliss, the editor of Wood's *Athenae Oxonienses*.

Perhaps the worst thing that could be said about Robinson is that Cox considered him worse than his successor, William Rust Cobbold, and yet gives the following account of the latter:

'Having during one or two of his last years been a pupil of Mr Cobbold, I am entitled to speak of the impressions left upon me by his teaching: they are these—that from a bilious constitution, betrayed by his yellow-tinted complexion, he was ill-qualified to bear kindly and patiently with little ignorant boys. "Alphezibeus, Sir," he would say, "don't you know *s* from *z*? Listen, Sir, Al-phe-*si*-be-us;" every syllable, especially the third, being impressed by a sharp cut with a cane, or a sharper twitch of an ear. Indeed this latter punishment, his favourite one, extended *several times* to the *partial tearing* the ear from the head of a dull boy.'

Cobbold died in 1841, having been knocked down by a cart in the street.

'Being a very corpulent man it was two days before it was discovered that his ribs were broken. A Coroner's jury returned a verdict of accidental death, accompanied by a censure on the surgeon, who had not paid the case sufficient attention.'

Cox was happier with his third Master, Dr Edward Ellerton, of whom he gives a charming character-sketch, too long to be quoted here in full. Ellerton had his faults—some said there was a want of system in his method of running the School, and 'he carried his jealousy of interference with his boys to great length'—but 'he really loved his boys', and they loved him, not only for his kindness and his efficiency and his modesty—'carried even to blushing in his answers to rough boys' rude questions'—but even for his punishments. The main one was locking up in School during breakfast time; but

'he connived at the motherly kindness of old Mrs Lister, (the wife of the porter of old Magdalen Hall) who would often pass bread and butter and even hot tea through the barred School windows, looking into the Hall quadrangle.'

The usual reward was an invitation to share his frugal breakfast in the Schoolmaster's room,

'one egg apiece being the only addition to the College allowance of bread and butter; I beg pardon, there was another addition, and as he himself called it of a *Classical character*; "The ancients", he told us, "had their ἀναγνώστης, or reader, at their meals"; and so he, or one of his guests, read out by turns some English book of his choosing.'

But an especial treat was an invitation to share the six-mile walk to Islip, where Ellerton had the usufruct of the rectory garden, with all its strawberries. A solid proof of his thoughtfulness is to be found in the somewhat ungrammatical entry in the College Order Book in Ellerton's first year of Office:

'Ordered, that a stove be erected in the Schoolroom, and a fire at the expense of the College for one month before the Christmas holidays, and two months after the return of the boys to School.'

One of Cox's stories is worth quoting:

'Knowing (for what do not boys know of their Masters?) that the Dr, from his large head, his "*vultus taurinus*" and "*omnia magna*" was called "Bull"—we were not a little amused one day at his expatiating on the emphatic mono-syllable with which Virgil (*Aen.* v. 481) makes the sound expressive of the sense:

' "*Sternitur, exanimisque tremens procumbit humi* bos." The word (bos), the knock-down blow, etc. were illustrated by his relation of a similar prostration inflicted in a row upon a person nick-named (as I well remember) *Bull* Allen. The class tittered, the Dr beginning to suspect our knowledge of his own *praenomen*, turned off our attention to the distinction between the *bos* and the *taurus*, following it up with that between the *equus castratus* and the *equus integer*; till, finding by the increased tittering, etc. that he was *going further than he need*, his blushing fit came on, and the lesson ended abruptly.'

Ellerton came to the School as Usher under Cobbold, succeeding him in 1798. In 1803 while still Master he was elected Fellow, and remained Fellow till his death in 1851. Both during his lifetime and by will he was a generous benefactor to the University, the College, and the School, whose Choristers still compete yearly for the Ellerton Exhibition. But perhaps his greatest service to the world at large was done in 1822. At that time the architectural passions which had simmered since the erection of the New Buildings in 1733 had recently boiled up again, and a proposal was on foot to remove the northern side of the Cloister Quadrangle in order to clear the view between the New Buildings and the Chapel and Hall. The advocates of destruc-tion, by rapid work in the absence of their opponents, had not only removed the northern side of the Cloisters but would have demolished the eastern side as well, save for the timely arrival of Dr Ellerton, to whom is due the present unspoiled restoration of Waynflete's original quadrangle.[1]

---

[1] Buckler, p. 127.

JENKINS

Ellerton's successor, Henry Jenkins, ruled the School conscientiously and well from 1810 to 1828, when he became a Fellow of the College. He took an interest in the games as well as the work of his pupils, and the Magdalen Cricket Ground on Cowley Marsh (from which the present 'Magdalen Road' and 'Magdalen Arms' take their names), for many years the centre of the University's cricket, was originally inaugurated by him for the boys of Magdalen School. The number of non-Choristers grew to about twenty, including some boarders, and the College showed its appreciation of Jenkins's work by a testimonial of £100, and by raising the Master's salary to £120, exclusive of 'Vest.' and 'Increment'.

Towards the end of Jenkins's mastership various changes in the School's accommodation took place. It will be remembered that for many years the School-room had formed the eastern side of the main quad-rangle of Magdalen Hall, separating it, as it were, from the College, the Schoolmaster's room being at one end of the quadrangle and the Lodgings of the Principal of the Hall at the other, the end farthest from High Street. From about 1812 the authorities of Magdalen College had seen in the approaching dis-solution of Hertford College an opportunity to rid themselves of Magdalen Hall; and it was arranged that the latter should migrate to the disused buildings of Hertford, which Magdalen College would put in repair. The change was accelerated by an accidental fire which destroyed most of Magdalen Hall in 1820, and by 1822 the Hall had gone, and its quadrangle had become a playground of Magdalen College School. A further change took place in 1828, when

THE QUADRANGLE OF MAGDALEN HALL

On the right is the western side of Waynflete's Schoolroom. In the centre is the Principal's Lodging which was used as a schoolroom in the early nineteenth century

From a water-colour by Buckler in Magdalen College

the old Grammar School, having become unsafe, was pulled down, except for the northern end with the bell-turret, which was left attached to the 1614 extension to stand as it now does under the name of Grammar-Hall. The late lodgings of the Principal of Magdalen Hall, which still stood, thereupon became the Schoolroom for the next seventeen years.[1]

REMINISCENCES OF KNIGHT AND MILLARD

Jenkins's successor, Richard Walker, was Master from 1828 to 1844. A remarkably vivid light is thrown on the School in his time by a manuscript now in the College Library, entitled 'Reminiscences of a Chorister'; it was written in 1840 by a boy then in the School, and its facts are amply vouched for, not only by the fact that the author was none other than Millard, the first Master of the revived School, who reaffirmed their truth when he was grown up, but also by some independently produced reminiscences by a Chorister named Knight, which were published in 1938 in the *Oxford Magazine*.[2]

Knight, in his reminiscences, said of Walker that he was not a very efficient master, and there was not much work done under him; but

'he was a man of some learning, something of a Hebrew scholar, and had published a book on botany; he belonged to a family in which gout was hereditary, and having experienced some twinges of the family complaint he was exceedingly careful in the matter of diet.

'He was rather given to studying French during school time, and would sit in front of the fire with his back to the boys with a French book in his hand reading half aloud,

[1] See Wilson, pp. 236 ff.
[2] January 27th, 1938. Most of Millard's reminiscences have been printed in the *Lily* from Dec. 1883 onwards.

while the boys were supposed to be preparing their lesson, very unconscious of what was passing behind him, unless an unusually loud titter or other noise caused him to turn.'

Grantham, who was Usher from 1801 till he fell out of his study window into the deer park and broke his neck in 1840, left a vivid impression behind him. He took the juniors in his room, and the curriculum is described thus:

'The three youngest boys had the following duties assigned to them: one had to light the fire, another to fetch water from the college pump in the cloisters, and the third to sweep the room. We called Mr G. as soon as the water boiled, and he came out with a pair of trousers drawn on over his nightgown, which was open in front, and proceeded to wash himself in a large basin which was set on a stool before the fire, during which time he heard lessons said. He was troubled with weak eyes which prevented him from reading, but he knew the grammars and elementary books by heart. For this weakness of the eyes he used to plunge his head into the aforesaid great basin, keeping his eyes wide open in the water. For cleaning his teeth he used to take a large spoonful of salt into his mouth and then brush his teeth: he used to say that salt was the best tooth powder. Having finished his ablutions he shaved before a small looking glass, in which on one occasion he caught a young boy making long noses at him behind his back; he happened, however, to be in a good humour, and only smiled before the glass, and the boy, observing this, was aware that he was found out. He was a passionate man and very severe when he lost his temper. . . . He had a fine black horse with a rat tail, which he used to call Dan O'Connell because of his bad tail—Dan O'Connell being the leader of the Irish party of those days, with rather a disreputable tail or following; . . . coming back from the College stables after a ride his delight was to flick any of us who came in his way with his whip, all in very good humour.'

Millard's reminiscences tell us of other masters;

Thomas Lancaster, who succeeded Grantham as Usher, was a milder man, famous for relying on good and bad marks rather than the cane. There was also an arithmetic master, paid by the boys themselves; this was one Lockey, who was succeeded by his son, Angel Lockey, and he by one Morton, who was extremely unpopular, being only eighteen, but conceited, and fancying himself at searching out 'what he conceives to be hard passages, or as he calls them "sweaters" in Virgil or " 'Orace", with the hope of puzzling the choristers,' but 'he has good nature, and is really clever'.[1]

[1] The characteristics of the staff are summed up in what Millard calls the School Song.

1 Rod of birch with iron rule
Keeps our boyant spirits under
Till with joy we quit the school
Bursting all restraint asunder.

2 O, who can express the pain
Which each idler feels or talker
Underneath the mighty cane
Wielded by the potent Walker.

3 Or who under his command
Dares stern Grantham to deride,
So the rod upraised in hand
Threats his aching back or side.*

4 Not less Lockey skilled in figure,
Learned in the scribbling art
Strikes with equal will and vigour
Each poor truant's hinder part.

5 Walker skilled in Botany,
To his appetite most cruel,
Lives in dull monotony
On brown-bread and water gruel.

6 His floggings, like to Angel's
visits
Are both few and far between,
But, when he doth exercise it,
Then his arm is strong, I ween.

7 Not so Grantham, his are many,
Sometimes mighty, sometimes
slight,
But his cane while he has any
Ne'er will be esteemed too light.

8 He, equipped with spur and boot
Each bright noontide without fail
Mounts his black four-footed brute
A courser whereby hangs no tail.†

9 Lockey too can boast much skill
In the *practice* of his cane;
Tho' there be no *fractions*, still
There is 'quantum suff.' of pain.

10 With *angelic* disposition
Angel in his father's station
Learned young arithmetician
Multiplies the castigation.

* Some MSS. omit the 'or'. *Millard's note.*
† Famous O'Connell had a rat-tail. *Millard's note.*

SCHOOL LIFE: BATTLES: BARRING-OUT

The Choristers at this time lived in lodging-houses in Holywell and Longwall. Knight spent a year in one in Holywell, where he slept with three other boys,

'two of them big fellows, and the other about a year older than myself. One of the occasional amusements of the two big boys was as follows: the house was an old-fashioned one and our room had a beam running across the ceiling, in which a large spike projected, and we were made in our turn to hang on by our hands to this spike to see who could hang on the longest, and the one who was beaten was slippered. . . .

'After about a year in this house, as I was not very happy there, I was transferred to No. 7 Longwall Street, where about four other boys were. This was kept by a college servant. It was more comfortable than the other, and we were very fairly fed: we had bread and milk for breakfast, meat at dinner, and bread and butter at tea. Our landlord used to set himself at times to teach us manners, which I daresay was needful occasionally, and used to say, "I must get you a book of Hetiquette". There was only one sitting room, which was used partly as a nursery in the day time, and we got to know a good deal about the washing and dressing of little children. They were kind-hearted people, however, and did not do badly by us according to their means.'

The wildness of the Choristers' life at this time is almost incredible. Fights with the 'blackguards', or town boys, were apt to occur, the big Choristers bullied the small ones out of money, some robbed the

---

11 *Stern* Vicary* with *treble* power
Our smarting *sterns* chastises too
Till our extremities are sore
And bruises rise both black and
blue.

12 This beating *base bars* out all *rest*;
With pain and fear we *shake* and
quaver,
And though they say 'tis for the
best
We think it no such mighty favour.

* Vicary was Organist of the College from 1797 to 1845.

GRAMMAR HALL AFTER THE DEMOLITION OF WAYNFLETE'S SCHOOLROOM

The building on the left is the Principal's Lodging of Magdalen Hall. Compare the picture facing page 135

From a print in the School Dining Hall

Usher of money and clothes, one shot a barking dog belonging to a Mr Brown with a pistol, another descended from the top of the Tower in a basket, another was expelled for threatening to horsewhip a Fellow, and another filled a pudding destined for the High Table with nails. Barrows and carts used to be seized and dragged into the quadrangle, sometimes remaining there for days while the owners inquired fruitlessly all over the town. The old custom was revived of hurling rotten eggs off the Tower on May Morning.[1] The 'Daily Express', a manuscript paper produced daily by the Choristers for some time, in its issue of May 1st, 1840, informs us that 'nearly a hundred rotten eggs descended on to the multitude of spectators below, bedaubing their garments with the fragrant contents'.

A pay-boy called Charles Barnett seems to have been a ringleader in most of these matters. He was

'of mean birth, bold, active and good-natured, but dissolute and attached to drinking . . . it is therefore no wonder that Barnett became a prime favourite among his companions. . . . At this time attacks from the town boys were constantly expected . . . and the army of the choristers was always kept in the most vigilant state of preparation. Of an evening or half-holiday, Barnett and his staff (chosen from the senior choristers) sat in state in the school with pipes, beer, etc.

[1] This custom apparently arose by way of retaliation against the town boys who attempted to drown the singing by blowing on trumpets and horns. It was forbidden by the authorities, 'who, however, did not at that time climb the Tower to enforce their orders. But what they failed to accomplish was quietly effected by the sagacious old Porter. Standing at the foot of the narrow staircase at the base of the Tower, as the boys ascended it in single file, with his heavy key he tapped the bulging pocket of the leader, and the rest, warned by the intolerable stench which followed, wisely retraced their steps and broke their eggs in the quad. below.' (Tuckwell, *Old Magdalen Days* p. 41.) From time to time the custom was, for short periods, renewed.

for drinking and smoking were then prevalent in the school to a very great extent, and scarcely a chorister, from the biggest to the least, could be found at any hour without a pipe of sixpenny china, home-made-wood, or halfpenny clay in his hand or mouth. It was here they hatched plans of attack or defence, excited each other by songs and verses written for the occasion, prepared their weapons and regulated the other transactions of warfare. The weapons were arranged on nails in the wall; sentinels, spies etc. were appointed, and Magdalen College School resembled more a camp or barrack than a seminary of learning. Strange to say, the town boys were not universally hostile; a few, principally inhabitants of Holywell Parish, declared themselves in favour of the choristers. On one occasion one of the latter, coming down the High Street by night, was startled by finding himself surrounded by bludgeon-armed citizens. He was, however, soon relieved from his fears by their stating that they were friends, and had assisted the New College choristers, who were also, if I may say, at war, in an engagement on the previous night. A number of boys and children were accustomed to collect in the Gravel Walk of an evening with the hopes of seeing the choristers combat with the "Blackguards", and perhaps intending to join the latter. Once indeed two choristers met a large armed party parading and had a hard run to escape. They (the enemy) sometimes ventured into the playground and stole sticks and other articles therefrom, a casualty which is now prevented by the door being constantly kept locked, each chorister having a key. Barnett often speedily drove them off with the *red-hot-tongs* which they construed into a pair of pokers. Pistols were also fired in the air to intimidate the enemy. . . . About 1837 or 8 a formal challenge was given by the Blackguards and accepted and a day and hour fixed for the battle. The School again presented all the appearance of a fortified castle. Sentinels constantly guarded the playground door and every chorister carried arms both in the precincts of the school and in the street or elsewhere. Vast heaps of large stones were brought from the kitchen-yard in gowns and cloaks and deposited in the playground. Wardens of the Magazine and other officers were appointed and every preparation made for the anxiously expected hour. On the evening before the appointed day, a verse in the first lesson struck the choristers as peculiarly appropriate.

"And as soon as the morning shall appear and the sun shall come forth upon the earth, take ye every man his weapon and go forth every valiant man."

'The choristers received it enthusiastically, as almost a special promise of success, and many a pencil was employed to take down in writing the inspiring words. We have one of these copies now before us.'

After all this, it is quite disappointing to learn that the town boys, daunted no doubt by the formidable preparations of the Choristers, funked the appointment. Barnett was ultimately dismissed by the Master for 'wild freaks', on the accusation of one Hodgson, who later became a Minor Canon of Winchester.

'Barring-out' was another practice, particularly at the expense of the unpopular Morton. The *Daily Express* records various instances, of which the first two may be quoted as typical. Morton summoned the boys in on a half-holiday:

'The Choristers were resolved not to bow to the haughty supremacy claimed by their new *puppy pedagogue* and soon after two o'clock P.M. preparations were made for fortifying the Junior schoolroom. All the forms were brought from the other room. The table was piled against the door and most efficient defences contrived. . . . Morton's arrival was hailed with cheers, yells, groans and hallos; he marched up the stairs and on finding the door fastened proceeded to threats and threatening interrogations. . . . Finding his verbal exhortations vain Mr M. took to bodily violence and shoved vehemently etc. All was however in vain and at length the baffled pedagogue "brushed off as hot as Vesuvius" and raised the siege.'

The issue of three days later records a second fray.

'A yet more daring exploit than the barring-*out* took place this afternoon. Morton was barred *in*! Some of the boys who were in the school perfumed the room with asafoetida while those without secured the door strongly with cords. Those within escaped by the window looking towards the playground (the other was nailed up for this occasion) leaving Morton to enjoy the fragrance of the asafoetida etc. . . . At four o'clock he was of necessity released as two of the boys . . . could not get down by the windows, the one on account of his terror, the other on account of his corpulence.'[1]

LITERARY INTERESTS

In the School at this time were not only Millard, but R. H. Hill, his successor as Master, Benjamin Blyth, who became Organist in 1845 and did much for the revival of Magdalen music, and two brothers, C. P. Macray, who died young, and W. D. Macray, who ultimately became Assistant Librarian at the Bodleian Library and completed Bloxam's *Register of Magdalen*. It is not surprising, therefore, to find that the wild life described above had another side to it;[2] and Millard records an improvement in his later days, though the revival of polite letters was not unaccompanied by outbreaks of the old Adam:

'But in a short time, the propensities to drink were eradicated and smoking *fumed off*. The choristers became, if not more moral, more refined in their tastes, and their minds, when no longer engaged in warfare, turned to literature for entertainment. Some years before, under the auspices

[1] Four o'clock was the hour of Evensong, and, whatever they might venture with Morton, the two Choristers had to attend that.

[2] Millard once went to the Master, and asked leave to stay away from school as he wanted to work. 'He was flogged for impertinence, but obtained the desired permission.' Hill (not Macray, as the *Lily* suggests) had the same experience.

of the Headmaster, a library was established in the school, consisting of many volumes of miscellaneous literature. These were increased by presents and purchases made by subscriptions of 1d., 3d., and 6d. per half year from each member of the school, and in a short time amounted to some hundred books. At the present time the library consists of between five and six hundred volumes.'

Millard, writing in the third person, with the modesty of a Caesar, records that when he was Librarian he did a great deal to restore order among the books, and made various rules limiting the number of boys who could use the library, and the times when it was open.

'When, therefore, one day he found two dayboys named McRay using and disarranging the books out of school hours, he thought proper to request they would go out of the library. This, however, not being acceded to, the Librarian and the Dayboys fell to blows, and a fierce combat ensued for some fifteen minutes, which had at least the effect of clearing the library of the obnoxious individuals. But as the Headmaster did not altogether second the views of the Librarian in enforcing attention to the regulations of the institution Millard resigned.'

Chaos, according to the writer, followed for some time, until at last Millard was induced to resume office.

Plays also engaged the School's attention. A regular theatre was constructed on a small scale, and plays written by boys were acted; unfortunately only the titles survive. Millard produced *The Shepherd's Choice*, *The Love Token*, *Fridolin*, *Wholesale Wedlock*, *Howqua Mowqua and Sowqua*, Knight *The Vow*, *The Miser's Slippers*, and T. S. Hill (no relation of the future Master) *The Robber*. The literary activities of this small group of some twenty boys are astonishing. The *Daily Express* has already been quoted, and there were many other periodicials. The *Weekly Gazette* included such items as an 'Essay on the characteristics of the British Poets' by Millard and an 'Elegy on a hedgehog' by W. D. Macray, but it did not exist for many weeks; nor did *The Spectator* or *The Pearl*. Far the most successful was the *Choristers' Monthly Magazine*, which lasted for over two years (1838–40). Two copies were written out and circulated among Demies and Fellows every school month for all that time and a high standard of literary work was produced. The attention of the boys' elders was naturally attracted, and in 1840 not only did the undergraduates of the College offer a poetry prize for competition by the School, but a selection of the best poems that had appeared in the Magazine was published with the title of *Poems by Members of Magdalen College School, Oxford*. The poems included show plentiful signs of imitation of Byron, Wordsworth, Coleridge, Scott, &c., as is only natural when, as the preface says, 'none of the authors are above sixteen years of age'; to be able to imitate shows at any rate praiseworthy familiarity with contemporary poetry; and many of the poems are pleasing in themselves as well as technically skilful.[1]

GAMES

Games as well as literature and crime occupied the attention of this remarkable school.

'In cricket', says Millard, 'their triumphs have been very great, testified by their matches with the New College and Christ Church Choristers. The latter indeed, from the age and size of their players, were generally successful over Magdalen, but not without a hard contest, and the good play of the choristers was always conspicuous. With the New College our success was probably various in former

---

[1] See note at end of chapter.

days, but in 1838 Magdalen beat New College (after recount) by one run, and again by ten wickets.'

Millard also gives what must be one of the earliest references to hockey, under that name:

'They also in the playground practise during the cold weather an excellent game resembling the ancient "Golf" and the Scottish "Shinty", but by the Oxonians called "Bung and Hockey", being played with a bung and a hooked stick called a hockey. The players are divided into two parties and the object of each is to strike the bung to the wall or boundary defended by the opposite party.'

In summer 1839 the Lily Boat Club was formed, R. H. Hill, Millard, T. Hill, and Smyth rowing several races, while,

'on the procession night when the College crews (the annual races being over) pull down the river with splendid flags etc., the Magdalen School boat followed with an elegant little flag, blue with white lilies, at the stern. . . . The dress of the crew consisted of blue striped jerseys, straw hats and blue ribbons.'

Millard's own review of the School at this time, written many years later, may close the account. Bloxam had been given the manuscript volume of reminiscences and inquired if Millard owned it. He replied:

'I recognise the artistic illustrations, the handwriting, and, alas! the ἦθος of the whole. None of these are very creditable, but the *facts* are strictly correct and the picture of School life at Magdalen as it then was is perfectly faithful. We were so entirely uncontrolled—so completely a law unto ourselves that the evil compelled a remedy from within. Like settlers in San Francisco we could only maintain even an approach to morality or discipline by organising "vigilance committees", and taking the (Lynch) law into our own hands. We used to form an oligarchy of "four seniors" (I hardly know

L

how chosen) who were very arbitrary and severe, and upon the whole exercised a tolerably wholesome influence. . . .

'It was a strange state of things, and certainly had the effect of bringing out a considerable amount of originality and eccentric talent. The theatre with its scenery, drapes and *plays*, all of native production was a remarkable instance. At one time we actually had a *daily* newspaper of our own —of course in ms. One thing which saved us from absolute degradation was the extreme kindness shown us not only by senior men like yourself and some other Fellows, but also by high-minded undergraduates or bachelors, such as Hy. Balston, Henderson and my own voluntary tutor Hoskyn.'

Note to page 144

The writers represented are the two Macrays, R. H. Hill, Millard, and Knight. One of the best poems is 'The Enchanted Rose' by Millard. It tells how a knight, overtaken by a storm, takes refuge in a mysterious cavern 'like palace built by faerye'. He picks a magic rose with four thorns growing on it; a fairy band trips into view whose leader gives him a golden cross, urging him not to let it go, if he be a true Christian knight. At the same time,

> 'The rose, by magic touch convey'd,
> Was sudden in his bosom laid,
> And the thorns gave such bitter smart,
> He felt their venom in his heart.'

The knight is then assailed by temptations; as he successfully resists those of gluttony, cowardice, and avarice, three of the thorns fall from his heart, but one is left.

> 'Now, Holy Mary, watch his lot,
> The worst temptation comes, I wot.
> Behold, a comely damosel
> Adorns the fairy's gloomy cell,
> And fixed her eyes, so soft, so blue,
> 'Twere ruin to a knight less true.
> Around his neck her arms she flung,
> And sweetly smiling o'er him hung;
> And certes he had given way,
> By wanton beauty led astray,
> Had he not knelt him down and pray'd
> For the blest Virgin's saving aid.

Then up he rose, with strengthen'd heart,
Nor from his well-watch'd cross would part;
When in the fairy dancers bound,
And gambol gaily all around,
While falls the last thorn to the ground.'

The fairy monarch commends him, and the troop vanishes.

'Lo! all is chang'd—'tis now daylight
And in the forest lay the Knight,
His helm, his lance, his trusty sword,
Were hung around their sleeping lord,
And, waken'd by the beams of day,
Up rose Sir Ralph, and went his way.'

Another creditable poem, though it lacks the imaginativeness of 'The Enchanted Rose', is C. P. Macray's 'Caius Marius sitting amongst the ruins of Carthage'. After a good deal of moralizing—

'How frail and fading are terrestrial things!
The peasant's hut, the palaces of kings;
Th' embattled wall, the "dim receding aisle",
And man himself, who formed the wondrous pile,
May sink to nothing—in how short a while!—

it takes us to Carthage, where the ruins,

'—struck with dread to see a Roman nigh—
Trembled, and thought of cruelties gone by;
The awe-struck Poet, with ecstatic sight
Hails the great Marius, great, tho' courting flight,
Who, feebly resting on a mossy stone,
Thus to the tott'ring structures "made his moan" . . .'

Marius regrets that he ever left his peasant farm, but admits that he found it 'sweet to hear the trump of Fame' and to triumph above his envious foes,

'Who bit their lips to see me borne on high
Through grateful Rome in pomp of victory;
Like those crush'd stones, that crumble on the path,
I fell at length beneath their fateful wrath,
And he, once called the father of his Rome,
Wanders from place to place, without a friend, or home.'

The vision vanishes, and the poet is left.

'This truth the Roman teaches us, tho' dead—
That transient joy to man on earth is given,
And lasting peace is found alone—in Heaven!'

The best of the lighter poems, a parody of Pope's 'Man of Ross', far from being reprinted, had to be deleted from the copy of the Magazine in which it saw the light, for obvious reasons. Robert Meadows White, whom it celebrates, was a Fellow of the College and Professor of Anglo-Saxon, the Moberly referred to being one of his competitors for the Chair. (In spite of the poem, White was a competent Anglo-Saxon scholar.)

> 'But all our praises why should fools invite?
> Rise, honest Muse, and sing the genial W . . . e!
> Pleas'd Maudlin echoes to the classic name
> And either Common Room resounds his fame.
> Who beat great Moberly, unbeat before?
> Who gained the prize for Anglo-Saxon lore?
> And knows of Anglo-Saxon just as much
> As Ching Lan Lauro does of Double Dutch!
> Who, proudly aiming at the highest Class,
> Read sixteen books and just obtained a pass?
> Who bores the Dons? Who persecutes Demies?
> "The genial W . . . e," each Maudlin man replies.
> Lo, in his rooms admiring pupils sit,
> The genial W . . . e unlocks his stores of wit,
> Makes vile false quantities in pompous tone,
> Cons up the notes and spouts them for his own.
> All on his head their imprecations cast,
> The Dons who yawn—the cross'd Demies who fast.'

CHAPTER VII

THE REVIVED SCHOOL

*The Lawsuit of 1845 and the Reconstitution of the School—J. E. Millard—
Growth of the School—R. H. Hill: The Scheme of 1875—H. C. Ogle—
E. R. Christie—School Life, 1846–87—Choristers' Festivals*

THE LAWSUIT OF 1845–7 AND THE
RECONSTITUTION OF THE SCHOOL

By 1840, as we have seen, there were many in the College who were taking an interest in the School very different from anything that the eighteenth century could show. To a certain extent this must have been due to the boys then in the School, whose qualities, to a thoughtful mind, emphasised by contrast the wretchedness of the conditions in which they were taught. But, apart from that, the time had come when a school such as has just been described was an anomaly and an anachronism. Arnold at Rugby had been revivifying Public School education for thirteen years, and in Oxford itself, though the forces of reaction were by no means spent, what may be called the intellectual impulse to reform, associated with the names of Parsons and Eveleigh, had been reinforced by the Oxford Movement, which came as a moral awakening to its opponents no less than to its supporters.

In Magdalen Dr Routh, who had become President in 1791 and remained in office till his death in 1854, was a staunch Conservative, and for the duration of his life held at bay any reform which might be held to threaten a vested interest; but the School 'was practically the only department of the College in which vested interests and privileges did not stand in the way';[1] and such men as Bloxam, the Dean of Divinity, were able to carry through a great scheme of reform.

The most obvious step to be taken was the appointment of good Masters. Henry Cadwallader Adams, a Fellow of the College, who succeeded Walker in 1844, and in later days produced a wide variety of books, including poems, books of religious research, Latin and Greek text-books and school stories, resigned after two months; but his successor, William George Henderson, was a schoolmaster with a genuine vocation. He had obtained a First in Greats and a Second in Mathematics, and while a Fellow of the College had unofficially tutored such promising boys in the School as Millard himself. After he resigned the mastership he became successively Tutor at Durham University, Principal of Victoria College, Jersey, Headmaster of the Grammar School at Leeds, and Dean of Carlisle.

The third Master in this period of transition, and the one who was to see the School firmly established on its new footing, was James Elwin Millard. We have already met him as a boy, and seen how he then won the friendship of Bloxam. The modest and impersonal account which Bloxam gives of these days disguises his own share in events, but it seems likely that Millard had long been destined to tackle the job of building up the new School which the reforming Fellows had in mind, and that Adams and Henderson were merely keeping the place warm for him while he was at the University. At any rate Millard took his B.A. in 1845, and in 1846 Henderson resigned and Millard was appointed Master.

But something in addition to good Masters was necessary if the School was to grow in numbers and extend its sphere of usefulness as was now intended.

[1] Wilson, p. 240.

OLD BUILDINGS adjoining MAGDALEN COLLEGE.

Taken down in 1845.

Sketched Etched by W. Mathews 14 Grove St.

THE SITE OF THE SCHOOLROOM OF 1851

The accommodation in the old Lodgings of the Principal of Magdalen Hall was hopelessly inadequate; Bloxam's extracts from College Orders enable us to follow the prolonged effort that finally led to the erection of a new and worthy school.

On November 15th, 1843, an order was passed,

'That a new School and House for the Master be erected on the site of the Greyhound Inn, and of the house now occupied by Stevens.'[1]

Plans had been submitted, accepted, altered, extended, and approved by the end of 1844, but in March 1845 everything was suspended by the lawsuit brought against the College. The case was not finally settled till March 1849; and the new School was not opened till May 1851—nearly eight years after its erection had been decided on. In the meantime the Schoolroom in old Magdalen Hall had been pulled down, and the School dragged on what must have been a painful and tantalising existence in rooms in the Chaplains' Quadrangle, between the Tower and the old *aula bassa* that had been used as a schoolroom for a short time in 1480.[2]

The lawsuit was brought by one Hester, the Town Clerk of Oxford, acting, one may suppose, for his fellow townsmen. Hester's claims, put as briefly as possible, were these:

1. That the School should be maintained as a public Grammar School, with free tuition for all and

---

[1] The site of the Greyhound was that at the corner of Longwall where the School was finally built. Stevens (or Stephens) was Manciple of Magdalen and his house, according to Tuckwell (*Reminiscences of Oxford*, p. 247), was next door to Magdalen Hall. In some ways it is to be regretted that this original scheme of having the Boarders' House next door to the School, instead of on the other side of Longwall, was not followed.

[2] See above, pp. 13-15.

not, as was in 1845 the practice, for the Choristers only.

2. That the College should appoint a Master and Usher, and provide them with commons equal to those of the Fellows and with rooms in College, and allow them to participate, like the Fellows, in the increased revenues of the College.

3. That the College should pay the Master a stipend equal to half the President's and the Usher half the Master's.

4. That the College should either restore the old buildings or provide others on the same site.

The claims amounted to an attempt to restore the School, *mutatis mutandis*, to the position it had held in the fifteenth century—when, it will be remembered, the Master and Usher were financially on exactly the same footing as the Fellows, except that they received a salary, £10 for the Master, £5 for the Usher (the President got £20), while the Fellows did not.

But the College put forward two objections:

1. The Fellows' practice of dividing the surplus revenues of the College among themselves, if not strictly in accordance with the statutes, which had never visualised such an income as the College now had, had been authorised by the Visitor and was not relevant to the present case. Increased expenditure on commons enabled the Fellows to hold their own with the change in the value of money. The salaries of the Master and Usher had been raised with the same object. Hester now claimed that the Master's and Usher's financial position should be adapted to modern times in the same way as that of the Fellows; to which the College, in fact, if not explicitly, put forward a dilemma. If he stuck to the statutes he could not claim for the Master and Usher more than

the original allowances, no matter how the value of money might have altered: if he relied on common sense to surmount this difficulty the College was the judge of what was reasonable in the payment of its officers.

2. The Court of Chancery had no jurisdiction over the matter at all, as the School was not a trust in the relevant meaning of the word.

The College, as we have seen, before the suit began, had resolved to do its duty by the School. Its real objection to Hester's scheme was not that it asked more, financially, than the College was prepared to give (though no doubt the payments it suggested amounted to more than were finally settled), but that it attempted to set up the School as an independent entity, taking from the College the power of the purse, forcing it to provide free education for the boys of Oxford, and leaving it only financial obligations and the right of appointing and dismissing the Master and Usher.

On June 11th, 1847, Lord Langdale gave judgment for the defendants, the College, on the ground that the Court of Chancery had no standing in the case, the Bishop of Winchester, as Visitor, being the proper person to deal with any such appeal; but his summing up showed that he realised both that a scandal existed and that the College was really proposing to remedy it:

'The College have, no doubt, a very important duty to perform with reference to the School, and the performance of that duty may be enforced by proper authority; but, unless it be a duty founded on a trust which this Court can execute, the performance of that duty is not to be enforced here. Upon the best consideration which I have been able to give to the subject, I am of opinion this Court has not jurisdiction to give the relief which is here asked. Though there is sufficient proof of the duty or obligation, there is not, in my opinion, evidence of a trust, as the word *"trust"* is understood in this Court; I must therefore dismiss this Information. But considering what has been done with the School, as appears by the evidence, and considering the erroneous view which the Defendants admit they have taken of it, and the colour of right under which the Information has been prosecuted, I think I shall not do wrong in dismissing this Information without costs. The Information may have been productive of great benefit; and I have read with satisfaction in the Answer, as well as heard it stated at the Bar, that the Defendants intend, even without any interposition of authority, to render the School much more efficient and useful than it has for a long time been.'[1]

The case was thereupon immediately laid before the Bishop of Winchester; Hester renewed his appeal, and after pondering the matter for nearly two years the Bishop, influenced no doubt by the fact that the College had already decided on the reform of the School, decided against him.

Without delay, the way now being clear, the College proceeded to action, and on May 3rd, 1849, passed a College order:

'That Mr Buckler be applied to for a plan of the School, to be exactly of the same dimensions as the former one, and on the site of the Greyhound. . . . That a house in the neighbourhood of the College be either purchased or taken on lease for the reception of the Head Master, sixteen Choristers, and other boarders. . . .'

The second injunction was the first to be carried out; a large house was bought for the boarders, Number 58 High Street; the building has now been completely remodelled.

The Schoolroom built, now in use as the College

[1] Bloxam, iii. 284–5. The complete judgment of Lord Langdale, with its résumé of the facts and arguments, is quoted on pp. 278–85.

THE NEW SCHOOL OF 1851

From a lithograph in the School Dining Hall

Library, stands at the corner of Longwall and High Street. It is one of the most successful Victorian Gothic buildings in Oxford, or indeed in England, for Buckler, as his book on Magdalen's architecture shows, had a genuine reverence for, and a profound knowledge of, medieval building. The outside is still as Buckler left it, but the loftiness of the interior has been lessened, since the College took it over as a Library, by the insertion of an upper floor. The foundation stone was laid by Dr Routh on his ninety-fifth birthday, September 19th, 1849, and the building was opened on May 1st, 1851.[1]

J. E. MILLARD (1846-64)

The School, thus splendidly reconstituted, had the right man at its head. Millard, who had been waiting as Master for this moment for nearly five years, remained for another fourteen, and in that time completely altered the nature of the School. His obituary notice, in the *Lily* of November 1894, written by W. E. Sherwood, who had been a boy at school under him and later became Master, gives a clear picture of his character and methods:

'In School he was strict and regular in all his dealings, an excellent disciplinarian. Old boys will remember the sudden calm which settled upon the pandemonium of "Evening School", when the "cave Jim" was passed round the room, and the doctor stalked in grave and stately, to write his letters in the Usher's seat; or the hush which would come

[1] The day was marked by the performance of a concert in the new building under the direction of Benjamin Blyth, the College Organist, which Tuckwell records as the first good concert in Oxford: 'At the opening of the new Magdalen School in 1850 [*sic*], an amateur choir, conducted by Blyth, who had followed old Vickery [*sic*] at Magdalen, performed without instruments a series of pieces which would have done credit to the Berlin Choir. Oxford had become musical' (*Reminiscences of Oxford*, pp. 75-6).

over the School at other times if he but tapped his pencil on the desk. He ruled us well and wisely, dealing out equal measure to all, perhaps with too impartial a hand, as in its exceeding fairness it took too little thought of the different temperaments of the boys, which made rewards and punishments so unequal in their incidence. We all feared him, but we all respected and loved him.

'In work we should have called him a very successful Head Master, had he not been overshadowed by the extraordinary successes of Dr Hill. Still he laid the foundation on which those achievements were built, and without which they would, at any rate in the earlier period, have been impossible. It was he who brought Thomas Clayton to the School as master, and he too who built the Laboratory; the two things which enabled Dr Hill to turn out the constant series of Scholars which the School then produced. The tide of Scholarships was flowing steadily in Dr Millard's days, though it was in the days of his successor that it was in full flood. Among his pupils were John Richard Green, Canon E. L. Hicks, and the present Bishop of Thetford [Lloyd].

'But it was perhaps in other directions that his real greatness lay. The soul of honour himself, he looked for it in all his boys, and made the appeal to it his strongest lever in dealing with us, and, as a rule, he did not appeal in vain.[1]

[1] The reasonableness of Millard's treatment of boys may be illustrated by the 'Order Book' of the 50's, from which three extracts are here quoted:

'Oct. 14th. 1854. The boys are requested as a matter of good taste and propriety to salute in passing the chief officers of the College and all matriculated masters of the School.'

'March 12th. 1856. As the trees in the Playground which are not at present a great ornament and advantage to it have been very much injured and broken of late, The Head Master wishes boys to abstain from climbing into them.'

'Nov. 4th. 1858. (After stating that Public Houses in Oxford are out of bounds). When on the river or engaged in any long excursion, they (boys) will be allowed to take refreshment at inns, so long as no abuse of the liberty renders it necessary to withdraw it, but the Head Master begs that they will not frequent inns more often or longer than is necessary.'

Out of School he laid aside all his sternness, without losing a particle of his dignity, and became one of us, a thing very rare amongst masters of those days. In the Gymnasium he took one of the classes, whilst after Evening School the Schoolroom itself became a Gymnasium, where he took command and "set the exercises". He bathed at "Cox's" (Parson's Pleasure) all the year round, and was an enthusiastic oar, whilst he joined with us also in our paperchases and hockey. It was only some six years ago that, being in the playground when a hockey game was in progress, he was sorely tempted to join in, and finally refused only because he had no change of clothes.

'It was however the religious side of his character that had the most enduring effect on his boys. He was, for those days, an advanced High Churchman, in a period when that type was far more uncommon than it is now, and his reverence, his earnestness, and his great goodness of character had a very strong effect on all who came in contact with him. With him the Chapel and the Chapel services became the centre of the School life, and we were fortunate in having one who put this stamp upon the School in its early days, which, in all after changes, it has never entirely lost.'

Millard's High Churchmanship and his sternness provoked criticism at times,[1] but the picture given by Sherwood is amply borne out by other Old Boys who were at school under him.[2]

GROWTH OF THE SCHOOL

During Millard's mastership various buildings were added to the School. First of all Millard himself bought 'Fifty-Seven', as the house next door to the Boarders' House was called; then in 1856–7 a chapel was built, largely from the contributions of Old Boys

Millard, of course, replaced the 'Vigilance Committees' of his own schooldays with a proper system of prefects.
[1] Oscar, p. 13.
[2] See *Old Magdalen Days*, pp. 19, 20.

and parents, in which the service was daily performed, the boys providing both a choir and an organist, as they have continued to do ever since.[1] In 1863 a dining-hall and kitchen were added to the house, and in 1863 a laboratory.

The numbers both of boarders and day-boys grew steadily under Millard's rule from eighteen to more than eighty. From the first parents of all classes in Oxford sent their sons as day-boys, and though the College had anticipated a growth in the number of boarders, the increase exceeded expectation. In the year after Millard's retirement the School was inspected on behalf of the Schools' Enquiry Commission, and the report tells us that there were 63 boarders, including the Choristers, and 28 day-boys.[2]

---

[1] The *Oxford Herald* gives the following account of the Chapel (Jan. 10th, 1857): 'It will be, when completed, rather a singular building. The material employed is red brick, with dressings of stone and coloured brick; but the walls are much too slender, and will, we fear, be soon thrown down by the roof, unless it be of a wonderful construction indeed. There is a pretty door at the west end; it is trefoil-headed, and the relieving arch is built of different coloured stones. Above it is a tolerably original string-course: between a double row of black bricks are placed red bricks turned round, so as to present the appearance of a zig-zag ornament. The idea is an ingenious one; but it would have been far more satisfactory if the points of the bricks had been made to project beyond the plane of the wall. As it is the string course consists of a series of holes in the wall and suggests weakness. However the notion is a good one and conceived in the right spirit: the great drawback is the thinness of the walls; we feel confident they will be found of insufficient strength. The east window is of two lights widely separated, with a large circle in the head. The west window is of five lights, characteristically arranged.'

[2] The report notes the parentage of boys as follows:
Day-boys: The ten highest in the school: 1. Solicitor; 2. Shoemaker; 3. Land agent; 4. Head of St John's College; 5. Solicitor; 6. Captain R.N.; 7. Resident M.A.; 8. College butler; 9. Widow; 10. Alderman of Oxford.

The ten lowest: 1. College servant; 2. University professor; 3. Widow; 4. Tradesman; 5. Clergyman; 6. Clergyman; 7. Veteri-

Such was the School that Millard handed over to Hill in 1864.[1]

R. H. HILL (1864-76): THE SCHEME OF 1875

For this period some fresh sources are available, the *School Magazine*, and, in manuscript, a booklet of reminiscences written by R. P. Colomb, who was in the School under Hill and for most of Ogle's reign, and writes both of Headmasters and assistants.

Of Hill Colomb says that he would have made his mark anywhere:

'He was a very handsome man, with the heavy, reddish whiskers of the period, and very marked, well-cut features; a strict disciplinarian with a kind heart, understood boys, very just, and, I should say, honourable in all ways of life. The tone of the School was high and for that Dr Hill was mainly responsible. Little that went on among the boys was unknown to him, and his way of dealing with matters that were undesirable was rather by discussion and advice than by the use of corporal punishment, and he was generally successful. He was not sparing of corporal punishment when, in his judgment, he considered it necessary, but I do not think he liked administering it. . . . Sorry I was when he left. . . . I do not think he was a great scholar, but he was better—he was a moulder of boys.'

H. E. F. Garnsey, the Usher from 1861 to 1876 (with a short interval), made less impression: 'He was by way

---

nary surgeon; 8. Tradesman; 9. Alderman of Oxford; 10. I.C.S.
Boarders: Of the twenty parents given, ten are clergymen, and there are two widows, two merchants, one gentleman, one banker, one solicitor, two doctors, and one D.C.L.

[1] It was in Millard's time that the School Song, 'Sicut Lilium', was written by G. Booth, a Fellow of the College. It was set to music originally by Blyth; but the fine tune to which it is now sung is the work of Dr H. C. Stewart, also a Chorister once himself, and till lately Organist of Magdalen.

of teaching Latin and Greek, but he was right off with me, for I learnt nothing.'

Clayton was probably the ablest man on Hill's staff:

' "Tommy" Clayton was a marvel, bearded, of course, a great getter of scholarships. He was a Classical master, and I never shone in Classics, so I never reached "Tommy's" able hands. He was also a wit, and his latest witticism ran early through the School. He translated the Aeneid into English verse, and we boys at once dubbed "Tommy's" production infinitely better than Conington's. The way he got scholarships was almost uncanny.'

The French was under the charge of the Chevalier Jules Bué, the University teacher. The Inspector of 1866 expresses some doubt whether 'a teacher who may be perfectly suited to young men is equally well suited to the instruction of boys, and especially those in the junior classes'. However, Colomb says of him, 'Bué we all just loved; he was gentle, affectionate and kind, and an all-round dear.'

Under Hill the School continued to grow slightly in numbers, coming near the hundred mark for a short time; and various improvements were made in its accommodation. In 1871 a classroom was added to the Big School at its eastern end, running out north at right angles to it, and the fives court which had to be pulled down to make room for this was rebuilt farther up the playground. The science accommodation was also improved about this time, calling forth an article in the Magazine:

'We have now got for our students a spacious and well ventilated laboratory, provided with all the chemicals needed for practical work; and we have also got a class-room for Physics which has lately, owing to the energy of our excellent, though perhaps rather extravagant, Physics professor, been extensively fitted up with mechanical apparatus.'

The writer, who appears to have been a Classical student, criticises the science teaching with a freedom only possible in a Magazine run entirely by boys. The boys, he says, are not supervised, and are therefore idle; but his strictures are disproved to some extent by the fact that in the following three years the School won four Science scholarships. The Science Masters were C. A. Buckmaster and A. E. Donkin.

The gaining of scholarships was certainly the most remarkable feature of Hill's mastership. Competition was less keen then than now, but even so, for a school of less than a hundred boys in twelve years to win fifty open scholarships and exhibitions was a notable achievement. To a certain extent this was the direct outcome of the Master's policy. He designed to carry yet farther the development that had taken place under Millard, and to approximate the School even more closely to the Public School type that was beginning to be established through the country. This led to the encouragement of boarders who increased so far that it became necessary for some of the assistant masters to receive the younger boys in their houses. The day-boys had to conform to the boarders' standard in such matters as compulsory games and hours of work, and complaints began to be heard in the town that Magdalen School was unduly difficult to get into.

But what enabled Hill to carry out his policy so successfully, at any rate as regards the winning of scholarships, was the School's situation in the University, which he exploited to the full. Not only were University teachers employed as part-time masters, but access to the University lectures was obtained for the boys, and, in some mysterious way that no one living seems now able to explain, the Master contrived that boys, while still at school, could matriculate on

M

the books of colleges. Thus he could claim, in his prospectus, among the advantages which the School offered:

'The opportunity, often used, of proceeding while at school to the successive examinations of the University at a cost little beyond the ordinary school fees. Thus a fairly taught boy can leave school at nineteen, for civil or military employment, with an Oxford B.A. degree.'[1]

But in spite of Hill's success, 1875, nearly the end of his reign, saw something of a crisis. Why the College at this time decided to review the whole future of the School we cannot now be certain, but various reasons may be suggested. Hill, as is shown by the record in the Magazine of his speech at the dinner held in 1880 to celebrate the 400th anniversary of the School's foundation, took it as, to some extent, a reflection on his administration. Certainly some members of the College may have felt that the day-boys were not being sufficiently considered: to others the recently founded school of St Edward's may have seemed either a formidable competitor or an absolution from their own duties to secondary education. But probably the main cause of the crisis was that the College felt it necessary to put the School's position on a more regular footing before facing a second University Commission. It will be remembered that what the College had fought against in 1845–7 was the establishment of a School

[1] School lists show boys in the Sixth Form who have passed Responsions and Moderations, the best example surviving being that of July 1873, in which feature Stephen Hill (passed Moderations), Joseph Elliott (passed Moderations), Ludovic Gilbertson (passed Moderations), and C. H. Murphy (passed Moderations). Hill matriculated in Feb. 1872, Elliott and Murphy in May 1872, and Gilbertson in Feb. 1873, all four at Queen's. The *Lily* records that Elliott and Murphy went into residence in October 1873, i.e. nearly a year and a half after they had matriculated as members of Queen's, and Gilbertson left in Dec. 1873, presumably to go into residence in the following January.

with a definite constitution and endowment; and under the shelter of the studiously vague benevolence that had been substituted for this the School had developed and was developing like Frankenstein's monster. Clearly, Commission or no Commission, its position needed to be regularised. Hill's approaching retirement, which had been decided on in 1874, gave a favourable opportunity, and Regulations for the conduct of the School were drawn up. They were published in the Magazine of November 1875: and though not as favourable to the future development of the School as its friends had hoped, were at any rate not so bad as they had feared.[1]

Among numerous regulations that are largely formal and concern such matters as fees, salaries, appointments of masters, &c., it was ordered:

That all applications for admission should be submitted to the School Committee, and that all boys, except Choristers, should be formally admitted by the Committee after examination by the Master;

That the total number in the School should not exceed that easily accommodated in the existing buildings;

[1] The notice which Hill had inserted in the Magazine of Oct. 1875 shows clearly that rumour at any rate had talked of the abolition of the School or of its reduction to a Choir School:

'The future status of this School having been under the consideration of the President and Fellows of the College, it was resolved at their meeting of July 22, 1875, "That the College approve generally of the principle embodied in the School Committee's Report that the School shall be retained as a First-Grade Classical School." The general principle being thus affirmed, the College may be expected to deal with matters of detail at an early meeting. Meanwhile parents and those interested in the School may feel assured, and are hereby assured, that the School will for the future have opportunity and receive encouragement from the College to compete, as it has hitherto done for the great educational prizes open to Schools.

Richard H. Hill, D.C.L. Head Master.'

That the number of boarders, except for Choristers and ex-Choristers, received by the Master should not exceed forty;

That no boy matriculated in the University of Oxford should remain in the School beyond the term in which he matriculated;

That the Master should have a lease of all the School buildings at a nominal rent, and, lastly;

That the College should have the right of resuming the School buildings for College purposes after giving three years notice to the Master.

It should be said at once that the alarming effect of this last regulation, which the Magazine in a critical editorial compared to the sword of Damocles, was largely mitigated by the statute put forward in 1880 by the second University Commission, which laid down that the School 'shall always be maintained'.

Hill's resignation took effect the year after the Regulations were published; and his successor, Harman Chaloner Ogle, undertook the task of working the new scheme.

H. C. OGLE (1876–86)

Some idea of the new Master may be gathered from the obituary notice, too long to quote in full, which appeared in the *Lily* of May 1888:

'That Mr Ogle gained the most coveted honours the University had to bestow, it is hardly necessary to say. A voracious reader, he possessed the power of rapidly grasping and assimilating the contents of a book, a process in which he was aided by a memory truly prodigious. Page after page could he repeat of books which he had read years before, and without any attempt to learn them by heart; apt quotations flew to his lips, and he rarely failed in instantaneously tracing to their sources lines which baffled the keenness of others. . . . He was fond of saying that a Master should be a fountain of knowledge to his boys; truly few have succeeded so well in the endeavour as he. But vast and varied as his learning was, it sat lightly on its owner. No man was ever less of a pedant. . . .

'But if his friends admired Mr Ogle for his talents and his learning, it was for his heart and his character that they loved and revered him. . . . To say that he thought of self last would be a very inadequate statement of the case. He never thought of self at all. . . .

'Throughout Mr Ogle's tenure of office the School was foremost in his thoughts. . . . He was happiest among boys, especially the younger, for whose welfare he was always scheming. He entered into their feelings, sympathised with their joys, their sorrows, and, it must be added, with their pranks.[1] For Mr Ogle was gifted with a keen sense of humour, so needful for the schoolmaster, qualified by the equally needful shrewdness. . . . First-rate at telling a good story and drawing upon a fund of anecdote well-nigh inexhaustible, a generously appreciative listener, he was a most agreeable companion. Eccentric he was, but beneath the layer of oddity there ran veins of purest gold. . . . The effect of Mr Ogle's character on the boys who were with him some time can hardly be over-estimated. . . . The man who in this 19th century could inflict on himself bodily punishment because 'he who has to give pain ought to know how

[1] An old boy tells an illustrative anecdote. Some boys had adopted a stray dog, but, unable to feed it and unwilling to say good-bye for ever, they conceived the plan of stuffing it. The dog was drowned and skinned, and the body, with youthful insouciance, thrown over the wall. Unfortunately, the owner of the garden next door informed the police that the body of a murdered child had been put in his garden! The police saw it was a dog, and made inquiries of Ogle, who had meanwhile learned part of the truth. 'Being the soul of honour he was in a bad fix—but somehow managed, without saying what is not, to put the police off the scent. That very day he had some occasion to go into the study of the dog-fanciers, and found them, with singular failure to appreciate the situation, happily engaged in stuffing the skin. The skin went into the great school furnace, and the boys into the Headmaster's study.'

it feels", has something in him to kindle enthusiasm and to win disciples. . . .

'Another secret of Mr Ogle's influence was the transparent genuineness of his religion. . . . (he was) a man who, in a thorough-going, matter of fact sort of way, set about converting into practice that Gospel which so many are content with admiring as a theory.'

Such was the man who had to try to continue the successful administration of Hill under circumstances far more difficult than Hill had had to face. The School certainly was not in so strong a position when he left as it had been when he became Master. The record of scholarships, though excellent,[1] did not equal the remarkable achievements of the School in Hill's day; the numbers showed a tendency to decline, and for most of Ogle's time they were below rather than above eighty; but, though Ogle seems, without doubt, to have been too easy-going as a disciplinarian, it is doubtful how justly this retrogression can be laid to his charge.

The Regulation referred to above, preventing boys from staying in the School after matriculating, robbed the School of one great attraction that it had had under Hill; and in any case the number of boarders had to be reduced. Ogle's efforts were largely directed to making the School more suitable for day-boys. The local paper, on his appointment, expressed the hope 'that the freer introduction of a good industrious stamp of day-boys will benefit not only the boarders (for boarders are still to be a marked feature in the School) but also the citizens and residents of Oxford'. And a letter by Ogle to the paper in 1877, replying to charges of 'exclusiveness', claims that the new scheme was designed for the benefit of residents, and that admission was no longer

---

[1] In eleven years twenty scholarships and exhibitons were won.

hampered by 'exclusiveness' or any sort of social factor.

The abolition of compulsory games and chapel for day-boys, and the alteration of the School hours to suit them certainly sent their numbers up considerably in Ogle's first few years; but by 1884 they were back to their old level. This was due partly to the widespread depression that occurred in these years, partly to the birth of private schools in Oxford, partly to the impression of the School's exclusiveness that still existed in Oxford because of the cumbrous mode of admission laid down by the Regulations.[1]

Faced with this situation, the College appears to have changed its policy; there was a movement in favour of appointing a Master who could raise the number of boarders, whether by his personal connexions or by some other means. A delay, however, took place owing to divided counsels, and to a curious misunderstanding with Ogle about his resignation. Ogle had resigned in February 1883, with the idea of becoming either Master of Dulwich College or Proctor; disappointed in both, he had assumed from the fact that no steps were taken to appoint a successor that his resignation was held to have lapsed. However, in February 1884, he was officially reappointed, but only for two years, Ogle taking it that the appointment would be renewed if the School was in a healthy condition at the end of 1885; but, before the two years had elapsed, the College resolved to appoint a successor. Ogle, feeling that to accept his dismissal would be to admit—what he strongly denied—that the School was in an unhealthy condition, and unwilling

[1] These reasons are given by Ogle in a letter to the College. The private school he was particularly thinking of was probably Summerfields. The School was not being affected by the foundation of what is now the City of Oxford School in 1878, for Ogle says it was only in the junior department that boys were few.

to bring to an end the schooling of various boys for whom he had made himself financially responsible, resisted; and an arrangement was finally reached that Ogle should resign at the end of 1886. Immediately after his resignation Ogle prepared to set out as a missionary to the Assyrians, but he died suddenly before leaving England.

E. R. CHRISTIE (1887–8)

The successor appointed, E. R. Christie, had the merit of bringing with him some twenty boys from his old school at Brockley—West Kent Grammar School; and he added to the staff two illustrious names: Owen Seaman, who came from Rossall and ultimately became Editor of *Punch*, and A. W. Verity, whose editions of Shakespeare's plays have been familiar to examination candidates for many years. Both stayed on after Christie left, Seaman for one term, and Verity till 1890, and did the School valuable service in its period of reconstruction. Christie himself appears to have been in many ways an inspiring teacher and preacher. Ogle, it seems, had been unable to believe anything wrong in any boy, and this had led to a certain amount of bullying and abuse of authority by the older boys. Christie met this problem by degrading the old prefects and appointing new ones from among the boys he had brought to the School with him; any chance of success that this sweeping measure might have had was lost by the unyielding severity and brutal discipline of its author. It is not too much to say that Christie was feared and hated by most of his pupils.

Among the boys bitter hostility existed between the old and the new elements. The changes introduced by Christie were enthusiastically received by the 'Brockley boys', whose views on the matter are the only ones that survive, owing to the fact that the Magazine was remodelled and the Brockley boys put in charge. The views of the old members of the School can be deduced from the general tone of veiled hostility displayed by later references in the *Lily* to the Christie regime and, in particular, from a remark made by Sherwood at the first prize-giving after he had taken Christie's place: 'I have had the natural conservatism of the School entirely on my side in all the changes I have made, instead of against me.'

Some of Christie's severity may have been salutary, but the rumours about his moral character which began to circulate in Oxford effectually stilled any debate about the rights and wrongs of his measures. After a year the College took sudden action and Christie disappeared for ever. The School his successor inherited had been reduced to thirty-six boys.

SCHOOL LIFE, 1846–87

The School hours for most of this period were from 8 to 10, Chapel being at 10, then from 11 to 1, when dinner was taken; in the afternoon there was school from 3.0 to 4.0, and from 6.30 to 8.0, tea being before evening school and supper after it. Ogle appears to have adopted something more like the modern arrangement, filling up the afternoons and substituting for evening school Preparation for boarders only. Saturday under Millard was a half-holiday and all red-letter Saints' Days whole holidays, but before long Saints' Days came to be neglected and a regular three half-holidays a week substituted. There was a holiday of five weeks at Christmas, of six in the summer, and of one at Easter. The whole school was examined twice a year, once by the Master and once by University

Examiners appointed by the President, a generous allowance of prizes being given.

The curriculum consisted very largely of Latin and Greek, but English, Geography, History, and Scripture were represented, the last named being done by all the School on Sundays; Mathematics was done throughout the School, being ranked nearly as high as the Classics; and, as has been mentioned, before his retirement Millard had the Laboratory built and Science introduced for the benefit of the older boys. French, to begin with, was not encouraged, being taught in the evenings only and being an 'extra', as far as fees were concerned; but by the Regulations of 1875 both French and German became part of the regular curriculum.

The recollections of different types of boy combine to give us a good picture of school life. J. R. Green, the historian, was a boy under Millard. His letters show the effect on a sensitive boy of the School's environment.

'The College was a poem in itself; its dim cloisters, its noble chapel, its smooth lawns, its park with the deer browsing beneath venerable elms, its "walks" with Addison's Walk in the midst of them, but where we boys thought less of Addison than of wasps' nests and craw-fishing. Of all Oxford colleges it was the loveliest and the most secluded from the outer world, and though I can laugh now at the indolence and uselessness of the collegiate life of my boy-days, my boyish imagination was overpowered by the solemn services, the white-robed choir, the long train of divines and fellows, and the president—moving like some mysterious dream of the past among the punier creatures of the present. . . . May morning too was a burst of poetry every year of my boyhood. . . . At first we used to spring out of bed, and gather in the gray of dawn on the top of the College Tower, where choristers and singing men were already grouped in their surplices. Beneath us, all wrapped in the dim mists of the Spring morning lay the city, the silent reaches of the Cherwell, the great commons of Cowley Marsh and Bullingdon, now covered with houses, but then a desolate waste. There was a long hush of waiting just before five, and then the first bright point of sunlight gleamed out over the horizon; below at the base of the tower a mist of discordant noises from the tin horns of the town boys greeted its appearance, and above, in the stillness, rose the soft pathetic air of the hymn "Te Deum Patrem Colimus". As it closed the sun was fully up, surplices were thrown off, and with a burst of gay laughter the choristers rushed down the little tower stair and flung themselves on the bell-ropes, "jangling" the bells in rough medieval fashion till the tower shook from side to side. And then, as they were tired came the ringers; and the "jangle" died into one of those "peals", change after change, which used to cast such a spell over my boyhood.'[1]

Another of Millard's pupils tells us something of the lighter side:[2]

'There is no need to describe the games and pleasures of a public school (read "Tom Brown"), for we were "run" on Rugby lines, and, in addition, throw in the joys of boating and swimming. Magdalen became a boating College during my residence, and often have I screamed myself hoarse and squeezed over the two little bridges to see a bump in the Gut. As none of us were allowed on the river until we could swim fifty yards, every boy in the School could swim. I learned in one lesson. Every boy could also row. . . .

'We were well fed and were given beer twice a day, at dinner and supper, for "teetotalism" had not yet arrived. There was no stint, but we were not supposed to leave anything on our plate, and it was amusing to hear a fellow, when passing his plate for a second help, say: "Small piece, please, well done, no fat. . . ."

[1] Letter quoted in *Studies in Oxford History*, Green and Roberson, O.H.S.

[2] *School and Sea Days*, Alan Oscar (W. B. Whall).

'A certain amount of "bullying" went on, such as "roast-ing" a fellow before the fire; but a petty persecution and perhaps the worse, was "cobbing", done with a hard chest-nut on the end of a piece of string, the victim being first made to "touch his toes". . . .'

The games, football, cricket, hockey, rowing, swim-ming, running, went on under Hill and Ogle as before, and Old Boys played a worthy part in University athletics. To these official amusements were added in 1870 a Debating Society, which has flourished ever since, and a School Magazine, and in 1871 a Rifle Corps. In Millard's time a purely literary journal, called the *Magdalen College School Monthly Magazine*, had been founded but it had not lasted long. The *Magdalen College School Journal*, founded in 1870, was a school magazine of the modern type, mainly a chronicle of events. It is probably one of the oldest school magazines in existence, having lasted without a break, though with various changes of name, to the present day.[1]

Colomb gives a note about the Corps:

'A Rifle Corps we also had, a Cadet Company, attached to the 1st Oxford (University) R.V.C., a gallant band of some fifty boys, mostly small, who were ready to go any-where and do anything. . . . We wore a uniform of very dark blue, laced across the chest with black mohair braid, a busby of imitation astrakhan, with a blue and black plume, carbines, and the long sword-bayonets in black belts and frogs, and we fancied ourselves in this uniform quite a lot, though, looking back on things, it was a ridiculous dress and particularly ugly.'

The Magazine bears witness to the enthusiasm of the

---

[1] It became *The Lily* in 1880, *The Magdalen Magazine* under the Brockley boys in 1887, and has been *The Lily* ever since 1888.

Volunteers, at first, at any rate, and gives some illuminating advice after the first public parade:

'We must ask all members of the Corps to observe absolute silence in the ranks, as, otherwise, they cannot give their whole attention, which is a *sine qua non* in learning drill. They must also listen for the word of command, and, when they have received it, act upon it without delay, as by so doing they will render it much easier for the Officers in command to rectify any mistakes they may have committed: and we must also ask those of the School, who do not belong to the Corps, but who are led by their patriotic feelings to accompany it in its parades, to preserve a respectful distance, and on no account to attract the attention of those in the ranks.'

The Corps appears to have been allowed to drop about 1880.

Music flourished, particularly under Ogle. Not only did a Madrigal Society give quite elaborate concerts, but the prize-givings of his time became the occasion of musical performances by members of the School.

Another interesting event that took place under Ogle's mastership was the production of a Greek play: two performances of the *Cyclops* of Euripides were given in 1882. Special music was composed by Mr Franklin Harvey, who also trained the chorus. Walter Parratt, then Organist of the College, provided the piano accompaniment and A. Sidgwick, then Fellow of Corpus, helped the players with advice. All the actors were boys, and there seems no doubt that the performances were a great success, in spite of a technical hitch on the first night, when the omission of a 'not very edifying' conversation between Odysseus and the Chorus left insufficient time for Silenus, off stage, to struggle with 'the mechanical difficulties of the sheep and cheeses', Odysseus being left 'in a rather embarrassing position by no fault at all of his own'. The Choristers were unable to take part in the play owing to their musical duties.

Colomb is informative, too, about unofficial amusements. Every Saturday (when pocket money was given out) each study would pool its resources for a feast:

'Sausages and fried potatoes were usually our feast, with bread and butter, washed down with milkless cocoa. Oxford in those days produced a cheap form of sausage called "Dogs", a short, skinless gentleman, but oh! how good he was. One boy would volunteer as cook, "cut" evening chapel, and we found our meal ready by the time we returned.'

On summer Saturdays, when the nesting season was on,

'numbers of the boys in canoes found their way up the Cherwell to the upper reaches where the moor-hens' nests were, soon detected by young eyes, and we brought the eggs back in dozens. A complacent staff in the kitchen cooked them for us and we ate them at tea.'

A more questionable amusement took place for some time on Shrove Tuesdays. Pancakes were eaten of course at dinner, and the squeezed lemon-skins were carefully collected and hurled at selected passers-by on their way down Longwall.

'Usually there were rows, sometimes fights, and very naturally so. . . . Mind you, it was not only the wild spirits, boys who like myself were always in trouble, always in mischief, who took part in the pelting; it was all of us, the steady ones and the high-spirited ones.'

On one point Colomb pays the School under Hill and Ogle a remarkable tribute:

'We never smoked, we never drank, and we never swore. Had we done so I could not have failed to remember it.

I do remember one boy saying "damn", and I wondered why the heavens did not immediately drop and pulverise him.'

CHORISTERS' FESTIVALS

But the Choristers especially enjoyed memorable duties and privileges, both musical and traditional. To be in the Choir under John Stainer (1860–72) and Walter Parratt (1873–82) must have been a wonderful education, as a Chorister's life still is, though the Chorister, hurrying from class to practice and back again to class, may have doubted his good fortune.

But certain days were pure joy. May Morning has already been referred to: Gaudy Day, July 22nd, was another great event. After morning service came the School Prize-giving, and at the conclusion of his ceremony the Choristers went to the bursary to receive their Gaudy Money, the four seniors also receiving a bottle of College port apiece.[1] At 5.30 came the dinner.

'We boys went into Hall to take part in the singing of the Latin Grace. We did not dine, but according to ancient custom waited at the tables. It was usual for the Senior Chorister to wait upon the President, or in his absence on the Vice-President, and the rest stationed themselves here and there, ready to do anything required of them, being especially active in the opening of soda-water bottles, which offered us opportunities for startling guests at other tables with the falling corks, but I fear we were more of a hindrance than a help to the regular waiters engaged. *All* of

---

[1] L. S. Tuckwell (*Old Magdalen Days*, p. 13) adds the following story: 'I found a ready purchaser for mine in Dr Corfe, the Organist of the Cathedral, who knew what good wine was. He promised to pay me four and sixpence on condition I brought it to his house as soon as I received it. I did so but had he only seen how I shook up the precious wine in my struggle to save it from the clutches of two disappointed juniors, who pursued me to his very door, he would have refused to fulfil his part of the bargain.'

us were happy, but one especially had reason to be quite jubilant, and that was the one selected to sing the solo parts of the Grace, for he was entitled, according to an old tradition, to receive half-a-crown from each of the Senior Members present, a sum which was seldom refused. The boy thus privileged had the good taste not to ask for the present himself, but appointed one of his school chums as his deputy. My chum was sufficiently wide awake to defer his application for this gratuity until he had reason to believe that his victims were in a comfortable condition and inclined to be liberal, and in consequence met with such success that he brought me the handsome sum of three pounds fifteen shillings, of which I gave him ten shillings for his trouble, and thanked him for his sagacity.'[1]

Colomb tells how on one of these occasions he was told off to wait on Wilberforce, then Bishop of Winchester and Visitor, and,

'When all were seated I found that his opposite number was Dr Hill (who had previously told all the Choristers that on no account were they to drink any wine, no matter who offered it to them). During dinner the Bishop turned to me and called me to him. Putting his arm round my waist, he asked me my name, and I told him. Then he said, "Do you like hock?" I said I did. Then, pushing a glassful under my nose, he said, "Drink that!" I refused, he asked me why, and I told him. He said, "Oh, bother Dr Hill: never mind what he said! I say you are to drink it." I did drink it, and Dr Hill's face was a picture in his endeavour to pretend he did not mind.'[2]

The waiting, the port, and the collection have all been

[1] *Old Magdalen Days*, p. 14.
[2] Colomb tells another story of Wilberforce's exasperating sense of humour. At one of Stainer's concerts he managed to get hold of one of the little gadgets provided for guests to spray themselves with eau-de-Cologne, and he completely ruined a performance of 'Sweet, honeysucking bees' by puffing scent in the faces of the Choristers from his front-row seat.

abolished, though the Choir still sings at the Gaudy Dinner; but another old custom still goes on, the most popular of all, at any rate with the Choristers—the Christmas Eve party. It was started by Bloxam, as an entertainment for the Choristers in his rooms; but it soon grew so far that it had to move to the Hall. Oscar's description of 1860, with very slight alteration, would serve for any Christmas Eve to the present day:

'As night came on we mustered in the College hall, already filled with fellows and visitors. The side tables are laden with barrels of oysters and other matters. We group ourselves round the piano, and the overture to the Messiah begins. Then the opening solo, "Comfort ye my people!" rings out. We proceed on through solo and chorus to the Pastoral Symphony. Then, out of a silence rises a pure boy's treble, which brings tears to more than one rugged face:

' "There were shepherds, abiding in the field, keeping watch over their flocks by night."

And so we go on till the first part of the Oratorio is finished.

'Then we are conducted to the High Table, where the junior chorister takes the President's chair, and the others range themselves along the sides. And here the president himself and the senior fellows come and wait upon us. . . . A standing dish is "frumenty", being wheat, raisins and other things boiled in milk; but there is a goodly spread besides.'

After supper comes the lighting up of the Christmas tree, surely the most enormous there ever was, and the distribution to the Choristers of presents, bought previously by the Vice-President, not without the advice of the senior Chorister; then follow the carols:

'Presently, at the conclusion of a carol there is a pause, a hush falls over the company, several are looking at their watches. For some minutes there is listening silence.

Then from the tower, rings through the frosty air that plaintive prelude, sounding weird and distant.

N

The conductor raises his baton, and we burst into Pergolesi's Gloria in Excelsis; as the first duet is reached we hear the great booming strokes of "Twelve!"

Et in terra pax

The ten-bell peal rings down the scale in accompaniment.

Pax in terra
Pax hominibus bonae voluntatis
Pax
Pax

'For a moment, at the conclusion, we all stand silent, listening to the clashing of the bells. Then hand clasps hand, the loving-cup goes round.

' "A merry Christmas to you!'

' "And you!"

'And again tears stand in many eyes: they stand in mine as I write. Many a time since, when rocking in my hammock under the beams, have I recalled those moments, and, in my mind, sung myself to sleep with some of the sacred songs I learned at Maudelyn.'

JAMES ELWIN MILLARD

From the portrait by W. J. Burdett (?) in Big School

CHAPTER VIII

SHERWOOD AND BROWNRIGG

W. E. Sherwood: His Assistants—The New House—C. E. Brownrigg—The First World War—The Board of Education—New Class-rooms

W. E. SHERWOOD (1888–1900): HIS ASSISTANTS

THE School at the time of Sherwood's appointment seemed in danger of complete collapse. No better man could have been found to restore it to the position won by Millard:

'Though I have been away from Oxford for some years', he said at his first Prize-giving, 'I have come back again full of my old love for and belief in the School, and full of its old traditions, and to work, so far as I can, on the old lines, which were laid down so wisely by Dr Millard, and in the main preserved by Dr Hill and by Mr Ogle.'

Sherwood had been a boy at the School under Millard, and a Master under Ogle. At Christ Church he had won First Class Honours in Mathematics, and had both rowed and run for Oxford against Cambridge. But no enumeration of qualities can do justice to the new Master's character. The evidence of Old Boys and of the *Lilies* published during his mastership gives an impression, hard to convey in a condensed form, of a man working and thinking behind all that the School did, undaunted by difficulties, unsatisfied by anything short of the best or short of the ideal that he had set himself, whether in work or games, in boys, masters, or in himself; an active Christian.

The School immediately began to recover from its disastrous year under Christie. By November 1888 the numbers had risen from 36 to 46, by 1890 to 72, and by 1897 the 100 had been reached. The standard

of work improved commensurately, as was shown both
by the results of Certificate examinations, and by the
scholarships and exhibitions won by the School.[1]

One obvious cause for Sherwood's success was the
whole-hearted support he had from the College. In
1888 at his first Prize-giving every effort was made to
make the day memorable, the Bishop of Winchester,
as Visitor, taking the Chair, and the Bishop of
Chichester giving the prizes away; and this support
was extended throughout his mastership. With this
added to the School's natural advantages of location
and tradition it was likely that a quick recovery would
be made from what was merely a fortuituous period of
eclipse. But besides this Sherwood was supported by
a band of assistant masters such as few schools of the
same size can ever have possessed. Owen Seaman and
A. W. Verity, as has been said above, Sherwood took
over with the School; among his own appointments
during the twelve years that he was Master the best
known and loved by many generations of Magdalen
boys were Mr C. E. Brownrigg, Usher or Master from
1888 to 1930, and Mr P. D. Pullan, 1897 to 1935,
who for so long combined to continue Sherwood's
good work for the School; but more famous in the
world outside, and no less respected by those they
taught, were A. E. Cowley, later Bodley's Librarian,
A. W. T. Perowne, later Bishop of Worcester, P. S.
Allen, later President of Corpus Christi College, and
A. L. Dixon, later Waynflete Professor of Pure Mathematics. Another distinguished assistant master, though
the credit for his appointment must go to Mr Brownrigg rather than to Sherwood, is the present Regius
Professor of Ecclesiastical History and Canon of

[1] Twenty-two scholarships and exhibitions were won during the
twelve years of Sherwood's mastership.

Christ Church, Dr Claude Jenkins, who was a master from 1902 to 1903.

Besides the improvement in scholarship that Sherwood and his assistants brought about, games also were played with greater keenness and efficiency. The Master himself was directly responsible for the revival of rowing and gymnastics, and in cricket, football, and hockey old *Lilies* show how much the School owed to Mr Brownrigg, then Usher. The corporate life of the School was stimulated in other directions. Societies of all sorts, debating, chess, natural history, literary, and scientific, were formed or revived; and many old boys will also remember the concerts on Saturday evenings and Breaking-up days, in which Mrs Sherwood played such a large part. Old programmes record songs and recitations at these, not only by Messrs Cowley, Allen, Perowne, Dixon, Brownrigg, and Pullan, but also by Cosmo Lang, later Archbishop of Canterbury, and then Dean of Divinity at Magdalen. In all these activities the day-boys, who formed about half the School, were encouraged to join: the President, speaking at the Prize-giving of 1887, made it clear that the College planned the School to serve Oxford primarily, but by the retention of the boarders to give the day-boys a chance such as he himself had had at Clifton of profiting by the especial qualities of a Public School.

THE NEW HOUSE

Sherwood having done so much for the School, it is fitting that a permanent memorial of his mastership should exist in the shape of the present Boarders' House. It is symbolic of the justifiable confidence of the College in the School's future under its new Master. The old house at the corner of Longwall and High

Street had seen its best days, and in 1891 an outbreak of scarlet fever revealed deficiencies in the drainage which, added to the general dilapidation of the house, made the College decide on a completely new boarding-house. While the old drains were temporarily repaired the boarders were accommodated in one or two large houses elsewhere, mostly in 'Turrell's', a somewhat ramshackle building standing on the site of the present house. The new boarding-house was soon started, and in September 1894 the School moved in. The Chapel that Millard had attached to the old house was replaced by a stone Chapel on the north side of the playground, the interior decorations and furnishings of the old Chapel being moved to the new, which was opened on May 23rd, 1895. The service on this occasion was conducted by the Dean of Divinity, later Archbishop of Canterbury.

In 1893 the School obtained from Christ Church a lease of the present playing field. Much levelling and remaking was necessary before it could be used, and much of the ground was not levelled until Mr Brownrigg became Master; but in the winter of 1894–5 the first game of football was played on it, the players, before the bridges were made, being punted across; and, though its low position has always rendered it liable to occasional flooding, the School has since that date found it as useful as it is beautiful. The broad expanse of level turf, ringed with chestnuts, poplars, and willows, and encircled by the Cherwell, the graceful 'willow-pattern' bridges that connect it with the House, and the Tower of Magdalen overlooking all, make it perhaps the most beautiful of all grounds in Oxford or elsewhere.

In 1900 Sherwood, owing to the delicate health of his wife, found it necessary to retire from the mastership. This short account gives the main facts of his reign: the vivid words of Dr John Johnson, printed elsewhere in this book,[1] make superfluous any further impression of the School that Sherwood did so much to revitalize. He lived in Oxford for another twenty-seven years, giving bountifully of his ability and energy to his parish of Sandford, to the City of which he became Mayor—the first University man to do so—and to the University Boat Club, of which he was the Treasurer and the historian. Needless to say, he continued to take the keenest interest in the School—as late as 1913 he was still sometimes coaching the School's rowing—and he became, inevitably, the first President of the Old Boys' Club that was started in 1902.

C. E. BROWNRIGG (1900–30)

Mr Brownrigg's appointment as Master after his twelve years as Usher must have been welcomed by the boys that knew him. He remained Master for some thirty years, and was fortunate to have as his principal helper throughout that time Mr P. D. Pullan. Mr Pullan came to the School in 1897, was Housemaster from 1900 till his marriage in 1903, and Usher from 1901 to 1935. From many generations of boys these two won affectionate respect, and it is hard to estimate the gain they brought the School in steadiness and continuity through a period of such difficulties, including, as it did, the First World War, the entry on the Board of Education Scheme, and the change to new buildings.

Brownrigg instituted the Commemoration Service, which has ever since been one of the most important

---

[1] See appendix I.

events of the School's year, in 1906, the *Lily* giving the following account:

'Mr Brownrigg has taken a good deal of trouble this year to institute what we hope will become an Annual Com-memoration. On June 23rd, the second day of the School Sports, a service was held in Magdalen College Chapel in the morning, an address being delivered by Dr Field, the Warden of Radley. The many Old Boys who came up were given lunch in Magdalen, and in the afternoon a large number of parents and Old Boys were present at the sports, which were held on the Cricket Ground instead of the Iffley Running Ground, which has generally been used. Every-thing went well, and the first occasion was at any rate a success.'

A similar procedure, with some modifications described in the next chapter, is still followed, but since 1932 the Prize-giving has been moved to Com-memoration Day.

Old *Lilies* reveal Mr Brownrigg's untiring services to the School's games, and his utterances as Master, modestly though they read, cannot conceal his ready sense of humour. But the boys he taught knew Mr Brownrigg to be more than an athlete and a wit. One who was at the School after the First War writes:

'With a few exceptions, who passed quickly on, I believe we all had faith in our teaching. The higher one went the more certainly was this true: Pullan and Brigger[1] we regarded as without peer in teaching and accepted all they said as gospel. Exam results and the general standard of education show that we were justified in this. . . . Teaching in class is only a section of education. As important is the guidance that a boy can get from the master on the viewpoint which ought to be taken up in facing certain problems—the foundation of a philosophy of life, and the general apprecia-tion of the way mature minds work which follows from an

[1] Brownrigg and Brigger are synonymous.

easy, yet dignified, relationship between masters and boys. As one rose through the school one found more and more of this *desideratum*. In Pullan, especially, and Brigger one was able to realise the humanity behind the pedagogy, and many who knew their influence, must find, I am sure, that these great teachers helped to lay the foundations of their own philosophy.'

It appears that one of the features of the School at this time was the large share of responsibility enjoyed by the prefects. The Old Boy quoted above writes:

'Even in spheres of activity controlled by authority such as the O.T.C. boys always were allowed to wield great influence. Games-captains made their own fixture lists without necessarily any consultation of authority: managed the discipline of games themselves: picked the teams, and were responsible for all arrangements for away matches. No master ever went away with a team to keep order; it was unnecessary. Prefects called Roll in the morning, took a large share of Prep, saw the boys to bed at night, had wide punitive powers—very rarely abused—and wielded an autocratic but generally just authority. In general this was a good thing: it developed character early, made away with all fear of responsibility and built up powers of decision and independent thought. I myself have never ceased to be grateful for this early chance to wield authority.'

To a certain extent the benefit to the character of the average boy from this prefectorial influence had become generally recognised in Public Schools at the beginning of the century; but at Magdalen, perhaps more than elsewhere, partly owing to the smallness of the School, the individual's energy and corporate loyalty were brought out by this appeal to his sense of responsibility. Perhaps the system was more suited to boarders than to day-boys. At any rate, until after the Great War there was a tendency for the proportion of boarders to day-boys to increase.

Some small extensions to the School premises were made. In 1901 the march of progress was recognised by the provision of a bicycle-shed in the playground. In 1905 two new class-rooms, of a temporary character, were built. In 1907 the remainder of the playing-field was levelled, and in 1913, thanks very largely to Mr Brownrigg's generosity as well as to his energy, the present pavilion was erected.

THE FIRST WORLD WAR

When war came the School underwent the same experience as all schools. The *Lily* through those four years tells the sad tale of lives full of promise courageously laid down, the sadness illuminated by the honours that came plentifully and by pride in those that lived no less than in those that died. Only two of the many can be mentioned here—Noel Chavasse, who won the Victoria Cross with bar, and died of wounds in 1917, and John Fox Russell, who was also killed in 1917, and was posthumously awarded the Victoria Cross.

The ordinary work and ordinary games continued; but behind all the School's activities thoughts of war were never very far distant. Many of the staff left to join the Army, and two of the Fellows of the College, Mr P. V. M. Benecke and Mr A. L. Pedder, helped with the school work; speaking at the first Prize-giving after the War Mr Brownrigg recorded: 'We also made some trial of learned ladies, though for the last two years we have returned to the sex of more dingy-hued socks.' A Cadet Corps was quickly formed, and the Master became its Commanding Officer. Drill and manoeuvres absorbed the boys' spare time and War Loan their spare money. Day-boys dining at school brought their ration coupons with them. In the *Lily* of March 1917 one reads, not without amusement, among the records of ordinary school life, 'We are indebted to the Master for the purchase of a number of bombs, by the help of which we hope soon to have a bombing class in full swing.'

THE BOARD OF EDUCATION

When peace at last returned it brought with it some rather unexpected developments. The most important was that the School came partially under the control of the Board of Education. This meant that the School received a grant from the Board, based on its total numbers and the numbers of its Sixth Form, and in return admitted a number of scholars from the Oxford elementary schools, the Masters' salaries and pensions being adjusted to the Burnham Scale.[1] It may be that nothing but the prospect of a financial grant would have induced those responsible to make the change—for some time the School's numbers had been appreciably below the level to which Sherwood had raised them, though they were soon to soar, even without the scholarship-boys, far above the previous highest level—but it cannot be questioned that the change has proved of benefit to both the old and the new elements in the School, and to Oxford as a whole.

In a changing world, paradoxical as it may sound, Magdalen School had to change if it was to remain the same—if it was to remain, in fact, a first-rate school giving to boarders the advantage of an education in Oxford and to Oxford boys those advantages of the Public School system of which President Warren had

[1] The School admits each September twenty-five per cent of the previous year's total entry, so that about one quarter of the school at any given time are likely to have come as scholarship winners from state schools.

spoken in 1887. More money was necessary in order
to keep up to date, and, at the same time, the claims
of the University left the College less able than before
to increase its expenditure on the School. The need
might easily have been met by an increase of fees,
for which the School's situation and its record of
scholarship and athletics would, as it were, have given
good value; but the financial was not the only side to
the question. To allow the School to develop into
another rich man's Public School would have been to
betray a heritage and a tradition. Magdalen School
had never been a school of rich men's sons, and genuine
democracy had flourished in it, not only through the
conscious efforts of such Masters as Millard, Ogle,
and Sherwood, but also through the peculiar nature
of Oxford. The City till recently was populated almost
entirely by academic persons and tradesmen, and a
mixed day- and boarding-school in such circumstances
was likely to prove a meeting-place of classes. The
population was now vastly increased, and if Magdalen
School was to continue its old role of bridge between
University and City its relations with the City
demanded more rather than less attention. The effect
of the changes of 1920 has been to preserve for every
able boy in Oxford a road into a Public School linked
to the University like no other in the country.

NEW CLASS-ROOMS[1]

An equally important, and in some ways less
welcome, change took place in 1928, when the School

[1] As long ago as 1851, the very year in which Buckler's schoolroom was
completed, a number of Fellows had drawn up a scheme for providing
accommodation for Commoners in the area adjoining Long Wall, the
Schoolroom to be their Hall, and another schoolroom to be provided
elsewhere. Fortunately or unfortunately, President Routh's opposition
sufficed to suppress the scheme. See T. S. R. Boase, *Journal of the Warburg
and Courtauld Institutes XVIII, iii-iv, p.*181.

moved from its old quarters in and around the School-room of 1851 to the new class-rooms on the west of Iffley Road. The old premises were the result of gradual accumulation rather than planning. Big School bounded one end of the playground; at the opposite end, dividing it from the Deer Park, stood the Chapel and the bicycle-shed. On the Longwall side there was only one wooden edifice that moved with the School and, filling various purposes, survived until 1956. On the opposite side of the playground, separating the School from the main College buildings, was a row of class-rooms, broken by a fives court, and, at the Deer Park end, the Laboratory.

In 1928 it became necessary for the College to increase its living and library accommodation, and it was decided to take over the Schoolroom as a library and build a court round what had been the playground. New class-rooms were to be built for the School on the western side of Iffley Road, near the Boarders' House. Plans for the new buildings had been drawn by Sir Giles Gilbert Scott, and sad though the parting from the old Big School was, the change to properly designed class-rooms would in other ways have been of great benefit. But before the plans could be put into execution it was decided that the expense would be too great, and buildings of similar design but of far cheaper, temporary construction were put up. As far as practical use went there was no fault to be found with the new buildings, but the fact of their 'temporary' nature caused some apprehension among the friends of the School, which grew when it was realised that at a revising of the College statutes in 1926 the statute referring to the School had been altered. Where before it had ordained that the College should always maintain the School, it now ran, 'So long as the grammar school of the College in Oxford is maintained . . . .' Nothing permanent could be done at the moment, but the School's future remained uneasily a problem at the back of the minds of its friends and Governors, till it emerged again, as will be shown below.

The new buildings at first consisted of the symmetrical block with Big School in the middle. The Chapel was added in 1929, the Old Boys contributing the shrine. Both in the Chapel and in Big School every effort was made to preserve as far as possible the internal appearance of the old buildings. Stained-glass windows and furniture were transferred from the old Chapel, and from the old School came the shields bearing the names of winners of scholarships and other honours and the fine collection of portraits of former Masters, Ushers, and Old Boys.

Two other changes that took place in Mr Brownrigg's mastership must be mentioned. In 1926 the efficiency of the Cadet Corps was recognised by the War Office, and it became a contingent of the O.T.C. Since that time the School has regularly sent a team to Bisley and has met with very creditable success in the Ashburton Competition.

In the years following the War, when boarding-schools generally enjoyed a boom, the School's boarders increased so much that it became necessary to open a supplementary boarding-house. Lanercost was therefore opened by Major Shepherd, he having previously received a few boys elsewhere. The total of boarders rose as high as 90 in 1925 but the 'boom' was, as elsewhere, only temporary; and Lanercost was closed in 1933, the number of boarders thereafter remaining about 60. The total numbers of the school reached about 170 in 1925, and continued about that figure

WILLIAM EDWARD SHERWOOD

From the portrait by T. F. M. Sheard in Big School

until the expansion described in the next chapter.

Having seen the new buildings in, Mr Brownrigg retired in 1930, but only as far as Iffley, where he lived until his death in 1942. He continued to take a keen interest in school affairs and in particular to 'fire the gun' at the school sports, which he did for fifty years. His portrait, painted by Hayward and presented by the Old Boys, hangs in Big School among those of his predecessors. A memorial window designed by Lawrence Lee in the School Chapel was dedicated in 1955.

CHAPTER XI

RECENT TIMES

The School in 1935—Commemoration and Prizegiving—Building Problems—The Second World War—Growth in size—New Buildings—Other Developments

THE SCHOOL IN 1935

WHEN a school history reaches or comes near the present-day, the writer's point of view necessarily changes, particularly if he is closely connected with what he is describing, and I hope therefore that I may be forgiven a free use of the first person singular in this concluding chapter.

Mr Brownrigg was succeeded by Mr Kennard Davis as Master in 1930, Mr Pullan by me as Usher in 1935, so that I have vivid recollections of those two great schoolmasters who had done so much for Magdalen School in the first thirty years of the century; and I also remember very well not only what the school was like when Kennard Davis left it, but also what it was like very soon after his arrival.

It was of course very much smaller than it is now. The number of boarders ranged between 50 and 60, there were 100, or a very few more dayboys. Mr Kennard Davis was form-master of the Sixth (about 30 strong), I of the Fifth, C. H. B. Shepherd (the Major) of IVa, H. S. Johns of IVb, E. S. Riley of the Third and P. B. Halewood, the Chaplain, of the miscellaneous mites who were lumped together under the name of II and I. E. W. Stoneham taught all the French, while J. C. Simmons, E. S. Riley and H. J. Cox respectively (but with some overlapping of function) supplied the Chemistry, Physics and Mathematics.

The classrooms consisted of the recently built 'semi-permanent' block which still, though re-modelled internally, runs along the southern side of Cowley Place. The block then contained three classrooms on one side of Big School and, on the other, two class-rooms, a Chemistry laboratory, a lecture-room, a small changing room with lavatories and, at the Plain End, a Physics laboratory which had been added to the main block shortly after Kennard Davis's arrival. The only other accommodation (apart from the Chapel and the Boarding House) was a wooden hut which had been brought over from the Longwall site and which later generations knew as the library and prefects' study or as the junior Physics laboratory. In 1935 it was divided in two, one half being used as a classroom and, spasmodically, as a library, the other being the masters' common room.

The playground was bounded by a wooden fence running at right angles to the Iffley Road past the end of the Chapel and returning at an angle to Cowley Place. Beyond this fence lay 'Milham Ford', which then meant not only a stretch of grass, but Milham Ford School. Milham Ford School, rehoused in 1938 beside the Marston Road, then consisted of the brick building now used by the Oxford School of Architec-ture and, by way of overflow, four wooden huts of varying size disposed about the area of grass. To the best of my belief the two schools interfered with one another surprisingly little.

One of the main differences between the school then and the school now was the small size of the Sixth form. Classics, Chemistry, Physics, Mathematics French and History were taught with considerable efficiency, but there was a tendency for French and History to require 'fitting in'; English and Biology

o

were only exceptionally taken for Certificate purposes.

In the lower school the working arrangements were on the whole similar to those of the present day, except that there was no art-room or gymnasium. Mr A. E. Rost used to come in intermittently to teach art in classrooms, forms used to march up the town to do gymnastics in the Alfred St gymnasium under Mr Morley; and the whole school, under Capt. Simmons's eye, did P.T. in the playground during the morning break. The junior forms then, and until Mr Burton's retirement in 1956, did their singing in the School House dining hall.

Games, then as now, were rugger in the Christmas term, hockey in the Easter term and cricket in the summer, but rowing took place only in the Easter term and only in fours, which were housed under Magdalen Bridge. Games took place on the playing field on Wednesday and Saturday afternoons; during the winter terms afternoon school did not start until three. Games were also played (mainly team practices) between dinner and school time. All day-boys went home to dinner except the very few who could be fitted into the boarders' dining hall, and it was customary for them to change at home for games. They did not in my opinion suffer appreciably from this as the number coming from far away was then very small.

In the summer lawn-tennis was played quite seriously, though the small numbers of the school caused the cricket authorities to keep a vigilant eye on such counter-attractions. Athletic sports took place on the Thursday and Saturday of Commemoration week. The Callender (Cross Country) race also took place in the summer and terminated with a plunge into the river at the end of the Broad Walk and a scramble

THE SCHOOL AND PLAYGROUND ABOUT 1890

From a photograph given to the author by Dr. W. F. Audland

out and on to the playing field. This was discontinued when in the very hot summer of 1936, the favourite was overcome by the heat and was found singing hymns and running round in circles near the Christ Church Memorial Garden.

Of what are now called 'out of school' activities there were, apart from games, comparatively few. Until Miss Mary Wiblin's lamented death in 1937, the Choral Society used to meet on Saturday evenings in the Christmas term in the Dining Hall. Their annual concert was given in the Town Hall and reached a high standard. Professional soloists were often engaged, some distinguished volunteers, such as Dr Armstrong of Christ Church and Dr Watson of New College, used to sing with the choir; and there was a volunteer orchestra in which only two or three boys were usually good enough to play.

On the Friday evening before Commemoration Major Shepherd, with some assistance from Old Boys and also such friends of the school as the Magdalen men who coached school boats, used to organise a light-hearted entertainment, consisting mainly of Gilbert and Sullivan numbers, in Big School. As the years passed this concert tended to become more elaborate.

A lively Debating Society met on Sunday evenings in the School House, and the boarders performed fairly frequent 'end of term' plays produced by Capt. Simmons, who was then housemaster. In 1938 a very successful performance of 'The Tempest' was given on the school field by both boarders and day-boys. For the time being this was an isolated effort, but it pointed the way to later developments.

On Friday afternoons most of the seniors paraded in the O.T.C. and the paramilitary pursuits of shooting and playing in the band occupied numbers of them at other times. Mr Kennard Davis had also in 1931 started a Scout Troup, mainly for the younger boys.

COMMEMORATION AND PRIZE-GIVING

The biggest event of the school year was the Commemoration and Prize-giving, which had been held on the same day, near the end of the University's summer term, since 1932. The prize-giving goes back to the earliest days of the reconstituted School. It will be remembered that the President appointed examiners to examine the School yearly, and prizes were awarded on the results of the examination. It was customary for a meeting to be held in the School-room at the end of the Summer term, to hear the Examiners' report and to receive the prizes from the hand of the President or Vice-President. For a few years in Ogle's time and from 1888 to 1931 the Prize-giving was held in the Michaelmas term, and a custom arose of inviting some distinguished man, often an Old Boy or former master of the School, to give the prizes away. Until the Second World War the day began with the Commemoration Service in the College Chapel, the service itself beginning with '*The Lilies of the Field*'. The writing of the words of this beautiful hymn was one of Mr Kennard Davis' first services to the school. The music was composed by Dr H. C. Stewart, who had been at the school under Ogle and was Organist of the College, with a brief interval, from 1915 to 1942. The Lesson—'Let us now praise famous men'—was read by the Master; the sermon was commonly preached by an Old Boy; the Bidding Prayer was introduced in 1939.

After the Service every one proceeded for the Prize-giving to Big School, then just large enough to contain the boys and their parents. When all had been squeezed in, the Prize-giver, the President and Governors and the Master advanced to the platform which had been specially erected for the occasion and decorated with flowers—there was then no stage in Big School. The rest of us then sang the old hymn '*Miles Christi*' in the translation by D. L. L. Clarke, an Old boy and now a master; the music, like that of *The Lilies of the Field*, was composed by H. C. Stewart. In the afternoon came the Sports, and in the evening the Old Boys Dinner.

BUILDING PROBLEMS

Such was the school when I first came to know it after five years of Mr Kennard Davis' rule; a small community with a strong and lively corporate sense; an ethos which immediately and favourably impressed those who came in contact with it; an excellent record of scholarship, sweetened with music and leavened by contact with the academic atmosphere of the University and with the cultural opportunities offered by a civilized city; proud of but slightly overawed by its connection with the great college of St Mary Magdalen, and rather vaguely aware of its own past greatnesses. It was a happy school, but it lived under a perpetual challenge and threat. Like many small Public Schools in the inter-war years it needed money, and money in those days of depression was hard to come by. The semi-permanent buildings put up in 1928 could not be expected to last for ever, and their replacement was a problem that would soon need to be faced realistically. The Old Boys, as a Club, learned in August 1937 that the College was discussing it, and, as when the old buildings were vacated, some alarm was felt about the future of the School. When

approached, the College, which was already sub-
sidising the School to the extent of some £1,500 a
year, intimated that it was unable to find the money
for new buildings. This was owing to its statutory
financial obligations to the University, because of
which no additional money could be spent on such a
College matter as the School without the University's
approval and at the wish of a two-thirds majority of
the College itself. Some hope existed of financial
assistance from the City, which was being relieved by
the School of the expense of educating about a hundred
boys but was paying fees for only a small fraction of
them. An approach was made by the College to the
Higher Education Sub-Committee, but, with the
greatest goodwill, the Sub-Committee could not hold
out hope of practical help.

It was in this atmosphere of frustration and almost
of despair that the School assembled for the Prize-
giving in June 1938. Dr John Johnson then gave his
electrifying address with its constructive proposal for
the raising of a building-fund. Those who had ears to
hear felt, even before Dr Johnson came to his own
generous offer, that the hour of difficulty had brought
forth the man. Such readers as did not hear the address
should turn to it and read it now. Before the meeting
broke up two others had each offered a thousand
pounds; at the Old Boys' dinner that night the total
promised was raised to £4,244, which by the end of
July had become £6,800 and by the following December was raised to over £8,000.

But there were difficulties. As Dr Johnson had said
in his address, the Old Boys of a small and never rich
school could not hope to raise £20,000 from their
own numbers. The wider public that he had appealed
to must be publicly approached, and before this could

be done it was necessary for the College, which had been impressed and gratified by the work of the Old Boys, to make a convincing gesture of confidence in the School's permanence. A majority of the College favoured the proposal to give this gesture by increasing the yearly grant to the School by £300; but there were many who felt that it would be premature to make this alteration in the statutes until some detailed scheme had been contrived for the School's working and government, and for the trusteeship of the fund that was to be raised. The majority in favour of the proposal, therefore, was not a two-thirds majority. A great deal of devoted thought was then given to the problem, but in the spring of 1939 the College came to the conclusion that, in view of the political situation, the launching of an appeal would be ill-timed, and the whole question was therefore postponed. Some urgent needs of the School were met by extending the changing accommodation of the Boarders' House, and by taking over some of the temporary buildings adjoining the School that had been recently vacated by Milham Ford School. But, for the moment, nothing further could be done.

THE SECOND WORLD WAR

Mr Kennard Davis, as Master, was thus faced with a daunting and almost desperate situation as the war grew visibly nearer, and it was largely through his tenacity and courage that the school came through it larger and perhaps more flourishing than ever before, and through his cheerful and imperturbable good humour that it did so without any damage to its ethos and spirit and without any serious loss of efficiency. Nor should one forget the tireless labours of Mrs Davis who coped successfully with the enormous difficulties of running the Boarding House under wartime conditions.

Oxford was fortunately spared the horrors of air-raid damage, but the war brought her, in common with the rest of the country, many tasks to be done and shortages and inconveniences which, however trivial when compared with those of the fighting line and of the blitzed cities, might be held in their sum to amount to hardship.

Blacking out all the windows in the Boarding House every night was a considerable operation; the basement library was shored up with immense balks of timber to serve as an air-raid shelter, brick shelters were built at the edges of the playground, and all the windows of the classroms were painted with a substance which was intended to prevent them from splintering and which certainly shut out a good deal of the light and all the visibility. The Junior Training Corps—as the present C.C.F. was then called—played its part in the defence of Oxford against possible enemy parachutists and fifth-columnists, guarding the river banks at night with fixed bayonets! Fire-watching arrangements were concerted with St Hilda's; and sporadic outbursts of digging for victory turned the grass alongside Cowley Place and a large number of miscellaneous rectangles at the edge of the playing field into allotments. The ground could be the more easily spared because shortage of petrol made it impossible to keep the whole field mown; the grass at the far end was allowed to grow and a haystack made a picturesque but regrettable appearance in the autumn.

GROWTH IN SIZE

An unexpected result of the war was the growth in the school's size. This was partly due to Oxford's being a 'safe' area, to which people from threatened towns were evacuated. Even in September 1939 the school's numbers had risen to 192, and a decision was soon taken to duplicate the bottom forms, thus starting the process of becoming a 'two-stream' school. Thereafter, as the double stream rose higher, the total continued to increase by an average of more than twenty per year until the 400 mark was reached in 1949, since when it has remained fairly constant.

Fortune enabled the school to cope with the problem of accommodating these extra numbers, if not comfortably, at any rate adequately. Just before the war Milham Ford School had moved to their new buildings in the Marston Road, leaving their hut classrooms empty. The large wooden building adjoining Iffley Road was taken over by the ambulance department of the A.R.P. and later by the First Aid and Rescue Service. The latter also took over the wooden hut adjoining the Chapel (and, incidentally, gave it the name, which stuck so long, of 'The Nest'). The Hut adjoining the Christ Church ground was taken over by St Clement Dane's School, which had been evacuated to Oxford from London. Very soon, however, the bulk of St Clement Dane's returned to London, and the Rescue Squad, having mercifully little rescue-work to do, proceeded to build for themselves the more durable quarters, which now form the L-shaped part of the school's 'concrete block'. Things thus worked out in such a way that as the school's numbers mounted there was always a fresh wooden hut available to serve as a classroom.

It is needless to say that these wooden huts, though they lasted until 1957, were far from solving the school's building problem. When the war ended, the question of the school's future, which had been, so to

speak, in cold storage since 1939, had to be met afresh
and solved in circumstances very considerably altered.
If the school was to be continued—and the enthusiastic support given to John Johnson's appeal in 1938
had made it almost unthinkable that it should not—
there were three broad possibilities open to the
Governors; and each of these possibilities was very
closely considered. The first was to give up the Direct
Grant and become Independent; this would have
involved reducing the school probably to its old size
of about 170 and confining it to those whose parents
could afford to pay the fees economically necessary.
The second possibility was to hand over the control of
the school to the Local Authority, as had been done
with the College School at Brackley; this would have
involved not only a horrifying breach of tradition but
also the abandonment of the boarding element in the
school and in particular of the choristers, who have
been for so many years not only a link with the College
and a symbol of the school's past but also a fertilising
element in the school's cultural life. The third possibility was that the College should continue the school
as a Direct Grant School under the slightly altered
conditions of the Education Act of 1944.

When Mr Kennard Davis retired, in July 1944, the
question had not been finally decided, but there can
be no doubt that the increase of the school's numbers
under his régime, the maintenance of its standards
and traditions in spite of war-time difficulties, and
the fresh developments which his interest in literature
and the arts had fostered were all potent argument
against revolutionary change. The President, Sir
Henry Tizard, took the keenest possible interest in
the school's well-being. At one time he came danger-
ously near to the second alternative, of handing the

School over to the City; but the arguments against this course were gradually seen by both College and City to be of prevailing force, and in 1945 the College decided to apply for the School to be retained on the Direct Grant list. The School could feel with some satisfaction that this decision had been reached not on sentimental grounds, but on the basis of evidence scientifically weighed. It could feel satisfaction and pleasure in a token of confidence extended by the College to the Old Boys; in 1944 Basil Blackwell and John Johnson were invited to serve on the School Committee of the Governing Body as representatives of the Old Boys. John Johnson continued to serve the School he had done so much for until his death in 1956; Sir Basil Blackwell remains an invaluable member of the Committee.

The decision taken by the College in 1945 was not exactly a matter of maintaining the status quo, for the Education Act of 1944 had introduced a new principle into the Direct Grant system. Henceforth no boy was to be debarred from admission through inability to pay the fees, and to that end parents of day boys whose income was below a certain level were to be assisted by remission of all or part of the tuition fee. These remissions are repaid to the School by the Ministry, which therefore controls the amount of the fee. The Ministry allows Direct Grant Schools to borrow for building purposes and to fix a fee at a level which will allow repayment of building loans over a period of years. It thus became possible for the College to advance money for School buildings without facing a permanent impoverishment. Problems of building licences and materials continued to be acute for some years after the war, but the general situation was hopeful instead of almost hopeless. We could feel not only that the School *must* go on, but also that the road ahead was tolerably clear.

NEW BUILDINGS

The first steps in the provision of new buildings were modest. At the end of the war the concrete block built by the Rescue Squad was taken over and in 1951 the classrooms and laboratories to the north of Big School were remodelled in such a way as to provide a Senior and a Junior Chemistry laboratory and a Senior Physics laboratory; the old wooden hut adjoining them became a Junior Physics laboratory; and another concrete block containing five rooms was built to replace and extend the accommodation lost elsewhere.

A far bigger stride was taken with the building begun in 1955 and completed in 1956, after the Visitor, the Bishop of Winchester, had conducted a dedicatory ceremony at Commemoration that year. This block contains three storeys extending almost from the Iffley Road to the Chapel with a changing room running out at right angles. It includes eleven classrooms, a large art room, a craft room, and cloak-rooms. Its completion released the School from the squalor of the wooden huts in which it had been for so long constrained to dwell; and even before this the prospect of another advance had become clear.

In 1955 a number of firms started the Industrial Fund for the Advancement of Science in Schools, whose intention was to give grants to Independent and Direct Grant Schools for laboratory building, the fund commonly paying for about two-thirds of the cost, the school for the remainder. The Fund listened sympathetically to the School's application, and approved the planning of two chemistry laboratories, two physics laboratories and a lecture room together with workshop, preparation rooms, dark room, balance room and science library. All this was completed by December 1957 and the block formally opened on January 30th, 1958, by Sir Robert Robinson, O.M., Honorary Fellow of Magdalen and Past President of the Royal Society. Thus in little over two years almost the whole of the School's shaky and superannuated classroom and laboratory accommodation was replaced by permanent, solidly constructed and seemly modern buildings. The architect for all this was Mr David Booth, the builders Hinkins and Frewin.

OTHER DEVELOPMENTS

Since 1938 the growth of the School has led to various changes in the House system. The original six were named in memory of Prefects killed in the First War; the boarders being divided among Callender, Chavasse and Leicester, the day-boys among Blagden, Wilkinson and Maltby. In 1938 the houses were divided into pairs; Maltby-Callender, Wilkinson-Blagden, Chavasse-Leicester. In 1945 two more were added, named after Bruce Dunn and Geoffrey Walker who died in the Second War. In 1955 Maltby and Callender became two separate houses, making five in all and the present tutorial system was started. By this each Housemaster is assisted by two tutors, and each house is divided into three 'rooms' with 25 to 30 boys in each, grouped according to age and position in the school, under a tutor assisted usually by two or three prefects. House-Prefects were instituted in 1945.

With growing numbers the activities pursued out of school have also been greatly increased. Music, Debating and Drama continue to flourish and a host of other activities, mostly in the form of societies, are carried on; a recent circular for the information of parents listed over twenty. The entertainment of the evening before Commemoration has developed into an annual concert or opera; since 1944 a service with carols sung by the Choral Society and lessons read by members of the School has been held every Christmas. The Musical Society has given an annual concert since 1946. The end of term plays produced by the boarders gradually developed into a Dramatic Society for the whole school. The first two stages in its progress were '*Journey's End*' in 1943 and '*St Joan*' in 1944. '*Hamlet*' was produced in 1945, and since then a Shakespearian play has been produced each year.[1]

Many other developments have become either possible or necessary since the school reached its present numbers. The most important is that much greater variety and choice of VI-form work is possible. There has been a great extension of science; biology is a regular subject and those doing physics and chemistry have become so numerous that they have had to be divided into two sets.

With some 400 boys and 800 parents, neither Big School nor the College Chapel is big enough for the Commemoration Service and Prize-giving; and since 1945 they have been held in St Mary's Church and the Town Hall or Sheldonian Theatre. In 1945 great improvements were made in the School Library under the direction of Mr Oates, then Usher. It was possible at this stage to set aside a large room for library purposes; and it was handsomely furnished with a presentation bookcase given by parents as a tribute to Mr Kennard Davis and other bookcases given as a

---

[1] Subsequent plays have been: '46, *Henry IV* 2; '47, *Macbeth*; '48, *Twelfth Night*; '49, *Julius Caesar*; '50, *Othello*; '51, *Romeo and Juliet*; '52, *Winter's Tale*; '53, *Merchant of Venice*; '54, *Hamlet*; '55 (Hilary) *Tempest*; '55 (Michaelmas), *Henry IV* 2; '56, *As You Like It*; '57, *Midsummer Night's Dream*.

MAGDALEN COLLEGE AND SCHOOL IN 1958

The chapel, classrooms, and laboratories can be seen in the foreground

War Memorial by the Old Waynfletes. Further developments have become possible through the extra space made available by the new laboratories in 1958.

A Parents Association, founded in 1955, has already proved its value. The parents have been able to enter more into the life of the school, competing against it in such activities as cricket and debating; and giving it invaluable help in many ways; they have taken over the running of an annual Christmas Fair, which had taken place intermittently since 1947, and have raised large sums for school clubs and societies; and they have organised teas on the playing field for cricket and tennis matches and—an even bigger task—for the vast crowds at Commemoration.

The School has been served in the last twenty years by a distinguished staff of assistant masters, in addition to those already mentioned. Four have moved on to Headmasterships elsewhere; R. C. A. Oates (Crewkerne); W. E. Northover (Sandown); L. L. S. Lowe (Royal Commercial Travellers' School, Bushey); P. C. Manwaring (Saltburn). The present members of staff are: I. W. Thomson (Usher); A. S. T. Fisher (Chaplain); E. W. Stoneham, J. C. Simmons, H. Elam, T. P. Swann, F. A. Garside, G. C. Howden, D. L. L. Clarke, F. H. Porter, H. E. T. Summers, L. H. Fenn, J. S. Millward, D. Marsh, H. P. Arnold-Craft, B. A. Field, C. S. Bishop, R. H. Holmes, H. K. Maitland, R. C. Olby, A. E. Best, D. L. Curtis, R. Avery, J. D. North.

CHAPTER X

RECENT OLD BOYS

IN an account of the Old Boys for this period first place must be given to the seven who have become Bishops.

A. T. Lloyd was at school under Millard, went up in 1863, and became Bishop of Thetford in 1894; from 1903 until his death in 1907 he was Bishop of New-castle. 'To the Tractarian theology', said the *Oxford Magazine* on his death, 'Bishop Lloyd united the moral beauty which marked the Tractarian leaders. . . . Though a south countryman he completely won the hearts of the people of Newcastle. . . . Probably few Bishops were personally so popular as he.'

Edward Lee Hicks was another Bishop who carried to his work the High Church principles he had imbibed under Millard; he was also a great classical scholar and archaeologist. He was Bishop of Lincoln from 1910 to 1919. To some he is better known as a scholar. At Oxford he won a double first, the Craven Scholarship, and the Chancellor's Prize for Latin Essay; but his greatest achievement was his *Manual of Greek Historical Inscriptions*. Inscriptions constitute perhaps the most vital field of Greek historical study today, and Hicks was one of the first Englishmen to realise their importance.

J. P. A. Bowers, who was at School under Hill and became Canon of Gloucester in 1885, was Bishop of Thetford from 1903 till his death in 1926. H. J. Embling was Bishop of Korea from 1926 to 1930. W. V. Lucas was Bishop of Masasi until his retirement in 1944. A. G. Parham, who was at school from 1895 to 1902, was Bishop of Reading until his retirement in

1944. He has in recent years preached the Commemoration Sermon, taken a Confirmation Service in the School Chapel and given the prizes away at the Prize-giving.

C. M. Chavasse, a former President of the Old Boys Club, is still Bishop of Rochester. At school from 1896 to 1900, he was distinguished at the University both in scholarship and athletics. He ran with his twin-brother for Oxford against Cambridge, and he has presented his and his brother's athletic medals to the school. In the First World War he won the Military Cross and the Croix de Guerre. As Master of St Peter's Hall he was largely responsible for the high position that the Hall has won for itself among Oxford foundations. He became Bishop of Rochester in 1939.

Many Old Boys eminent in scholarship have been produced at all periods. From Millard's day Hicks has already been mentioned, as has his fellow-historian J. R. Green. Also under Millard were Sir Edgeworth David and E. B. Elliott. David was Professor at Sydney University from 1891 to 1924, and during that period took part in the Shackleton Antarctic Expedition, being leader of the party of three which reached the South Magnetic Pole for the first time. He was a Fellow of the Royal Society, an Honorary Doctor of the Universities of Oxford, Cambridge, St Andrews and Wales, and won the D.S.O. during the First War by his applied science. E. B. Elliott became a Fellow of the Royal Society in 1891, and from 1892 to 1921 was Waynflete Professor of Pure Mathematics in the University of Oxford. He was a Fellow of Magdalen, and until his death in 1927 took the keenest interest in the School.

Among Hill's pupils were C. Plummer and

P

G. T. Prior. Plummer, after a double first in classics, became a Fellow of Corpus and a Lecturer in Modern History, but his real study was Anglo-Saxon and Celtic History and Literature. He edited numerous books in this field, including two of the Saxon Chronicles, and Bede's *History* and *Lives of the Irish Saints*. 'Charles Plummer', said Professor R. W. Chambers, 'seemed the reincarnation of Bede, if ever one man seemed the reincarnation of another—in his vast learning, his humility, his piety, his care for the young.' (*Man's Unconquerable Mind*, p. 51.) Prior, who went up to Magdalen in 1881, won a first in Natural Science and in Physics, and from 1909 to 1928 was Keeper of the Department of Mineralogy at the British Museum.

Under Sherwood were E. O. Winstedt, discoverer in the Bodleian of a missing portion of Juvenal's Sixth Satire, and a papyrologist of repute; and John Johnson, who, after winning fame by the discovery in Egypt of the oldest known manuscript of Theocritus, became Printer to the University. His heroic work for the School in recent years appears elsewhere in this book.

Under Brownrigg were Austin Lane Poole, who retired from the Presidency of St John's College, Oxford, in 1957, D. H. Hey, Fellow of the Royal Society and Daniell Professor of Chemistry at London, A. A. Miller, Professor of Geography at Reading and President of the Geography section of the British Association in 1955, W. N. Sage, Professor of History at the University of British Columbia, J. E. V. Crofts, Professor of English at Bristol, and W. S. Vines, Professor of English at Hull. Of a still later generation is J. B. Segal, who, after obtaining at Cambridge a first in Oriental Languages, the Mason Prize and a

Senior Hebrew Scholarship, and at Oxford a Doctorate of Philosophy, has recently become Lecturer in Aramaic and Syriac at London. Such younger men as Brian Shefton (Scheftelowitz) of Newcastle, K. W. H. Stevens of Nottingham and Harvard, and J. V. M. Sturdy, winner of Oxford University's Senior Septuagint Prize, show that the flow of eminent scholars has not dried up.

Of Headmasters too the School has borne a rich crop. H. A. P. Sawyer was at school under Ogle; he was Headmaster of St Bees from 1903 to 1916, and then of Shrewsbury till 1932. W. H. Ferguson, before becoming a Canon of Salisbury, was Warden of St Edward's, Oxford and Warden of Radley. A well-known Oxford figure for many years was A. W. Cave, Headmaster of the High School (now the City of Oxford School), whose great work earned him the Freedom of the City on his retirement in 1925. Besides these there were P. K. Tollit (Derby), A. F. Titherington (Brighton), F. B. Welch (Oswestry), E. C. Sherwood (Ipswich and Ramsgate), A. H. Coombes (Hurstpierpoint), H. Woolsey (Denstone), H. B. Jacks (Bedales), L. S. Powell (Chard), B. J. Rushby-Smith (Southwell Minster), and, greatest man of them all perhaps, the autochthonous Master of Magdalen, W. E. Sherwood.

Among eminent musicians are H. C. Stewart, for many years Organist of Magdalen and Choragus of the University; Sumner Austin, of operatic fame; Hylton Stewart, Organist of the cathedrals of Rochester and Chester and of St George's, Windsor; Norman C. Cocker, Organist of Manchester Cathedral; Cyril Taylor, Principal of the Royal School of Church Music; and J. H. Alden, formerly Organist of St Martin-in-the-Fields. The stage is represented by

F. E. Aylmer-Jones, better known as Felix Aylmer, President of Equity, A. A. Bushell and John Chapman. Ivor Novello combined musical with dramatic fame to an unusual degree.

Among physicians mention must be made of George Ernest Beaumont, and, among surgeons, of Ronald Ogier Ward, who served with the British Red Cross during the Balkan War, and in the First World War won the D.S.O. and M.C. He served again in France in the Second World War.

Other eminent Old Waynfletes are Sir Raymond Unwin, President of the Royal Institute of British Architects, Sir George Bonner, King's Remembrancer and Chief Master of the High Court, A. M. Walker, Chief Accountant of the Bank of England, T. F. M. Sheard, the painter, Sir Richard Winstedt, the orientalist, A. R. Cooper, Chief Engineer to the London Passenger Transport Board, who also helped to build the Moscow Underground, Major General T. B. L. Churchill, c.b.e., c.b., and Stefan Schimanski, whose promising career as a writer was tragically cut short when he was shot down over Korea in 1950 while acting as a War Correspondent. Most widely known of all perhaps, and the greatest and most constant server of the School among her Old Boys is Sir Basil Blackwell, whose publishing and selling of books have made him honoured throughout the world by book-lovers.

Old Boys of athletic distinction are recorded in the next chapter.

CHAPTER XI

GAMES

MILLARD's reminiscences, quoted from above, give some idea of the games played in 1840—cricket, rowing, hockey. The hockey was played in the playground, and the cricket on the old Magdalen ground (see p. 134). This continued to be used till the acquisition of the present ground in 1894, and football, when introduced in Millard's Mastership was played on various grounds, sometimes those of Colleges, sometimes borrowed fields. Those who know the present ground may be comforted to know that before its acquisition flooding was a worse trouble than it is now. In all games masters used to take part, and until the time of the First War it was common for them to play in matches other than those against schools. I have met men who were up at Oxford between 1890 and 1910, and who still associate Magdalen School with recollections of 'leather-hunting' while Mr Brownrigg hit their bowling all over the field.

CRICKET

At cricket the School's earliest opponents—apart from the Colleges—were Bradfield, Bedford, St Paul's at Stony Stratford, and Reading, but all these fixtures have now been dropped, and the School's oldest opponents are Bloxham and Abingdon. More recently fixtures have been arranged with Oratory; Leighton Park; the King's School, Worcester; the City of Oxford School; Berkhamsted; the Nautical College, Pangbourne; and Newbury. In recent years occasional matches against touring sides from Manchester Grammar School and Bradford Grammar School have been played. Among famous cricketers that the School has produced may be mentioned E. R. Bartleet, who played for Sussex while still at school in the 1860s; T. A. Belcher, a cricket blue of 1870; C. J. M. Godfrey, who played for Sussex and Oxford in the 80's; and O. G. Radcliffe of Gloucestershire (1891). H. C. Stewart played for the Gentlemen in 1897 and for Kent in the 90's; and while at school he and A. J. Willson in a match against Reading put on 249 in an unfinished ninth-wicket stand, Stewart scoring 148 and Willson 100. During the present century F. B. Roberts, who proceeded from the School to Cambridge via Rossall, won his blue in 1903; and more recent worthies are S. Pether and J. E. Bush, Oxford blues of 1939 and 1952 respectively, and G. W. G. Walker, who played for the Public Schools against the Army in 1938. Many Old Boys have played for minor counties, especially Oxfordshire and Lincolnshire; since the Second World War, J. E. Bush (as captain), A. H. Birchall, J. W. Carter, D. Laitt, T. A. Gibson, R. A. Winstone and J. S. Baxter have played for Oxfordshire. An Old Waynflete Cricket Week was started in 1949 and has been held every year since then.

FOOTBALL

The School's football history is variegated. When first started the game was rugger, but of a less stereotyped nature than is now fashionable. The School actually played a 'soccer' match with the College in 1871, though rugger was then theoretically the school game. In 1870 the customary arrangement of the side was two halves, two or three backs, and nine or ten forwards. In 1872 two of the forwards became three-quarters, but for the rest of the seventies the normal arrangement seems to have been nine forwards and six outsides—two halves, two quarters and two backs. The schools played in those days were Stony Stratford, Bedford, Reading, Worcester and St Edwards; but the St Edward's match was dropped after a serio-comic incident in 1880-1. Magdalen committed the *gaffe* of 'heeling the ball out of the scrummage', thereby winning the game by one goal and two touchdowns to nil. St Edward's claimed that heeling-out was illegal, and wrote to the Secretary of the Rugby Union, who, however, replied that he was 'sorry to say' that it was allowable. The variance about Rugby ethics was exacerbated by the fact that, in spite of the two captains having agreed not to publish the result of the game while the question was still *sub judice*, an enthusiastic Magdalenensian had sent the result on his own to the *Field*.

In 1885 the School, finding that owing to lack of weight they could not cope with the College sides against whom most of their matches were played, changed over to Association football, and played regular matches with Reading, which apparently changed at the same time, Bloxham, Abingdon, and, later, Oxford High School, Brackley and Leighton Park.

After the First War there was a general tendency among Public Schools to change from soccer to rugger and in 1928-9 rugger was adopted at Magdalen. The schools now played are Abingdon; Oratory; Leighton Park; City of Oxford; Southfield; King's School, Worcester; Newbury; Nautical College, Pangbourne; Douai; Reading; and Berkhamsted. Coached by Mr H. S. Johns from 1928 until his retirement in 1957, the standard of teams has often been very high; and

J. E. Bush's team in 1945 and G. B. Skates's in 1954 enjoyed unbeaten seasons.

The most distinguished players produced by the School in the last century were W. A. Douglas, who played rugger for Oxford in 1878-9; J. Eyre and B. M. H. Rogers, who played soccer for Oxford in 1880; R. D. G. Williams, who played soccer and rugger for Wales; H. C. Stewart, who played soccer for Oxford and rugger for Sussex; H. A. P. Sawyer, who played rugger for Sussex in the nineties; and G. S. A. Jones, who won his rugger blue in 1896. In the present century blues have been won at Oxford by H. S. H. Read (soccer, 1920) and S. Pether (rugger, 1938); and both in 1954 and 1956 two Old Waynfletes played for Oxford at the same time, S. C. Coles at scrum-half and W. S. Lawrence on the wing; Coles also played in 1957, when he was Honorary Secretary, and in 1956 he received an England Trial.

Since the Second World War E. T. Walters, P. H. Avery, A. V. W. Day, J. E. Bush, W. S. Lawrence, J. M. Kennah, E. E. Church, J. M. Walters, S. C. Coles, S. E. Oswin and P. C. Sibley have played for Oxfordshire in the County Championship, and six of them were in the team which reached the quarter-final in 1956-7.

HOCKEY

Hockey at the School has a long and distinguished history. It is likely that the reference to it in Millard's reminiscences is the oldest record of hockey at any school; the game was played at Magdalen from his time onwards and probably earlier. For a long time it was one of those games, whose disappearance is so much to be regretted, conditioned by the School's playground and therefore unique. One goal was the space between two buttresses of Big School, the other a similar portion of the wall at the other end of the playground. The principal difference from the ordinary game of hockey was that one could circumvent an opponent by bouncing the ball past him off a sidewall or buttress and at the same time running outside the man to meet the ball again behind him; also, either side of the 'hockey', which was made symmetrical, could be used. When properly played it was a game of great skill, and opponents who were more or less even on their own ground found themselves hopelessly outclassed on the School playground. At times, owing to the rival attractions of rowing or to the lack of suitable opponents, the game languished. In a powerful (and successful) plea for its revival in the *Lily* of 1898 Mr Brownrigg, then Usher, remarked that it had become 'a combination of an Irish row with shillelaghs and a series of golf drives from one end of the ground to the other'. At its best however the School could take on not only Colleges but the University itself on level terms. From time to time various modifications in the rules have been made, the effect of which has been to bring the game nearer ordinary hockey, until, on the School's leaving its old playground in 1928, all peculiarities disappeared except the characteristic hockey stick and ball.

From 1880 onwards ordinary hockey has been played with great success, due partly to the practice in the playground; moreover there were until recently comparatively few hockey-playing schools to dispute the supremacy of Magdalen. The School has produced three hockey internationals (H. R. Searby, England, M. D. A. Evans, Wales and J. R. Tindall, Scotland); ten blues at Oxford (G. V. M. Hickey, 1892-5; W. D. Coddington, 1892-5; A. E. Rambaut, 1905-8; E. M.

Venables, 1907; H. S. F. Smith, 1920-2; H. B. Jacks, 1925; E. S. Brown, 1933; D. F. G. Walker, 1939; J. H. Austin, 1947; and P. M. Gayton, 1954-5) and one at Cambridge (F. B. Roberts, 1903). Over forty Old Boys have played for counties, among whom J. E. Searby played over 100 consecutive times for Lincolnshire; since the Second War J. E. Bush, J. H. Austin, G. J. Wilsdon, R. S. Craig, A. H. Birchall, C. Blackwell, P. M. Gayton, D. H. J. Werrell, D. J. Parry, T. A. Gibson, H. T. Parry, S. G. Salway and R. J. Hubble have played for Oxfordshire. G. K. Archbold played for the Army in 1912-3, and P. M. Gayton in 1951. P. J. Haines played for the Royal Air Force in 1956-7. Since 1952 a Public School Hockey Festival, in which Magdalen has taken an active part, has been held every year in Oxford. No account of the School's hockey would be complete without referring to the debt owed over many years to the enthusiastic coaching of Major C. H. B. Shepherd.

ROWING

Rowing, as we have seen, started in Millard's days, and it has continued with slight intermissions ever since. Some reminiscences in the *Lily* of March, 1896, describe the rowing in the sixties. Practice meant a race to the boats after evening school had ended at eight, and a race for lock-up and chapel at nine. As the boats were kept on the bank of Christ Church Meadows, which were locked by the time the rowing ended, the boys had to scale the Merton or Rose Lane gates every night. In spite of these difficulties Fours were sent at times to regattas at Bedford, Worcester, or Henley, and in 1882 the Public Schools Cup at Henley was won, the four being A. F. Titherington,

A. F. S. Kent, T. N. Arkell, W. Kirkby (cox, P. Watson).[1] In spite of this success rowing seems to have lapsed for some little time after this, until it was vigorously revived by Sherwood, a blue himself, in 1889. Races were arranged with Bath College and, later, Worcester and Abingdon. T. H. T. Hopkins, for many years Bursar of Magdalen and a great friend of the School, used to coach the Four in the sixties and seventies. Thereafter Old Boys and Masters, conspicuously Sherwood, have frequently lent their help as coaches, and undergraduates of the College have also often coached boats. Old Boys and parents, too, have been generous in help with the heavy expenses of boats.

Blues among Old Boys are H. Schneider, 1865; F. H. Hall, 1871-3; W. E. Sherwood, 1873-4; J. H. T. Wharton, 1879-81; A. H. Higgins, who after getting a trial as a cox in 1881 stroked the boat to victory in 1882; W. S. Unwin, 1885, who also won the Diamonds and the Wingfield Sculls; A. F. Titherington, 1887; E. C. Sherwood, 1896; J. F. Clapperton, 1919; G. D. Clapperton, 1923-4, who has regularly commented on the Boat Race for the B.B.C.; and D. Glynne-Jones, 1952.

Fours, tubs and small boats have for many years been kept in the boathouse under Magdalen Bridge. Since D. L. L. Clarke returned to the School as a master and took charge of the rowing the club has taken to eights (1948), and since 1952 has rowed in the summer as well as in the Hilary Term. Regattas at which the School Eights compete include Marlow, Oxford Royal, Reading and Bedford, while a Four

[1] W. S. Unwin, who was in the School IV in 1880, tells how Bedford beat Magdalen that year by putting twelve-inch seats in their boat and buttering their shorts, so as to manufacture a kind of sliding seat!

has more than once been successful at the Serpentine Regatta. In 1957 for the first time the Eight entered for the Princess Elizabeth Cup at Henley.

ATHLETICS

The first Athletics meeting was held in a field, now part of the Parks, in 1861, when most people ran in socks and white flannels; W. Philpott, who was afterwards second in the Varsity hurdles, ran in bare feet and won both jumps, the hurdles and the hundred yards. Thereafter the Sports were transferred to Cowley Marsh, then to the Iffley Road track, and later to the new playing-field. Cross-country races against Bloxham and the Oxford High School used to be run at one time, and paper-chases were common. Old Boys include a number of Oxford blues: A. H. Hannam, mile 1864; W. G. Edwards, long jump 1867; F. O. Philpott, hurdles, high jump, long jump, hundred 1868-70; E. A. Bergman, mile 1869, high jump, long jump 1870; W. E. Sherwood, three miles 1872; E. L. Treffry, hurdles 1876; T. E. Wells, mile 1880-3; (also winner of the half-mile in the Amateur Championship); H. S. Alnutt, long jump 1883; S. E. V. Harcourt, cross-country 1904; C. M. Chavasse and N. G. Chavasse, who were up from 1905 to 1907 and won blues for the quarter-mile and hundred and ran in the Olympic Games in 1908; L. S. Powell, cross-country 1933; W. D. Paul, cross-country 1935; D. E. Fathers, mile 1949.

OTHER GAMES

Lawn tennis has been played at the School for some years, the best performers so far produced being A. C. Dobbs, who reached the final of the Public Schools Championship in 1937, and D. E. Mitchell, who won

the Oxford Mail and Times Championship while still
at school in 1956 and 1957. Matches are now played
against Abingdon, Berkhamsted, Nautical College
Pangbourne, Leighton Park, Reading and R.G.S.
High Wycombe.

The School regularly sends an Eight to Bisley, its
best performance so far being to come fifth in the
Ashburton Shield Competition in 1952, the year in
which I. A. Torrens-Burton achieved the almost
unprecedented feat of scoring a 'possible' at both
200 and 500 yards. Recent additions to the games
played are badminton, basket-ball and fencing.
H. L. O. Rees won a boxing blue in 1927; and S.
Pether, before winning his blues for cricket and rugger,
won one for golf.

Few boys in the School are unable to swim. The
non-swimmers are caught and taught early in the
City's baths, and thereafter admitted to the delights
of the School's own bathing place on the bank of the
Cherwell beside the Pavilion. Large numbers enter
every year for the Royal Humane Society's examinations and gain life-saving medals.

APPENDIXES

I

AN APPEAL MADE ON COMMEMORATION DAY
JUNE MCMXXXVIII BY JOHN JOHNSON, PRINTER
TO THE UNIVERSITY OF OXFORD

WHEN the Master, at the suggestion of the President of the College, first asked me to give away the prizes this year my first thought was of a shy boy who year by year used to go up and down the central alley-way of the old schoolroom to get his modest prizes. The boy was still father to the man. Then came a voice within me saying that here perhaps was the opportunity for doing something for the School which had done everything for me. And so I came to write down these words, taking care to write them because I was afraid lest one spoken word or another might be misconstrued.

IF you stand on the south-eastern edge of the Lincolnshire wolds, on the fringe of which I was born and spent my boyhood, the land falls away steeply. To the east of you, stretching between the hills and the sea is the rather grim and hungry country known as the marshes, to the south and adjoining the marshes are the bountiful fens. And there, on those flat lands adjoining the sea, where marsh joins fen, lies Wainfleet, looking across the plain to where Boston raises its lantern like a veritable torch of faith.

Here was born William of Wainfleet, Headmaster of Winchester, first Headmaster and Provost of Eton, successor to Cardinal Beaufort as Bishop of Winchester, and Lord Chancellor of England under Henry the Sixth. He was the founder of Magdalen College and this School.

But let there be no arrogance on the part of the School. The School was the servant of the College, an intramural convenience founded on Wainfleet's belief that the young students of his College must be taught Grammar because, as he said: 'A weak foundation betrays the superstructure and Grammar (i.e. language) is acknowledged to be the mother and basis of all Science.'

The history of the School for these centuries is an incident only in the life of the College, albeit a creditable incident, seeing that the early Grammarians of Magdalen College School must always form a separate chapter in any history of English education or scholarship. Was not one of them Wolsey himself?

I WANT you now to skip 370 years. For it is with the re-formed, or rather remodelled, Magdalen School of 1849 with which we are concerned today. You are all of you familiar with the manifold outbreaks of educational effort in the second and third quarters of the nineteenth century. Most of them were voluntary. Some of them came out of a pure spontaneity, others out of class-condescension or sectarian propaganda, yet others out of a stark reaction from the fear of revolution which haunted the whole country in the twenties and thirties. Almost all were devices of one kind or another for the spreading of education from the more well-to-do to the less well-to-do.

Thus in 1843, among public schools, Marlborough, of which school my own father is the oldest living member, was founded for the poorer professional classes. In 1849, whether from the personal effort of Dr Bloxam, or from a more impersonal movement of the tractarian conscience, the turn of this School came. I quote from a prospectus, issued in the mid-century with the cognizance of the College:

'At first Academic in its objects, and supplying purely Classical instruction to Members of the College and other matriculated persons, Magdalen School gradually changed its character, till in 1849 it was remodelled on the plan of the great Public Schools.'

Except in words the School ceased at this date to be an obligation imposed by the founder. Old obedience had given place to a new vision and the new had a greater obligation than the old. The School was the emancipated

Q

daughter of a free parent and as such we must consider her.

AND what of this School? What mark has the College set on this mid-nineteenth century School of its creating, and what mark has the School set on itself?

I have tried myself to recover the past. I remember a School of 45 years ago (we were then housed in the High Street) in which there was no cant and no humbug, and still less pocket-money. It was a School of almost naked equality, in which class-consciousness was not allowed to exist, in which masters and boys were alike disciplined before the law, yet in which disciplined equality and freedom from class-consciousness begat independence of the spirit. Culture, other than classical culture, was regarded shyly, although it was there all the same. And over all hung the friendly shadow of the humanities of the University. To me, in the life which the University has allotted to me, that freedom from class-consciousness has proved the most valuable gift of all.

Only the other day I had a letter from a friend I had not seen for more than 40 years who wrote similarly from his own heart:

'I do not know', he wrote, 'what H. G. Wells would have made of the Magdalen College School curriculum, but I feel it was a very sound education. Sherwood, with his robustness of character. Cowley and Pullan with their classical sense. Brownrigg with his culture. P. S. Allen with his almost medieval piety. The large measure of self-government exercised through the prefects. The cultural influence of the background of Oxford and the connexion with the College. The solid if unimaginative insistence upon Scripture. The Puritan simplicity of the studies and other rooms. The beauty of the Cherwell-encircled island. Sherwood's brief, incalculable explosions of tempestuous wrath. It was all very wholesome and helpful in its influence upon character. I at any rate look back on it all with gratitude.

'As a choirboy I had two other influences upon my character, Varley Roberts, that determined Yorkshireman, and Cosmo Gordon Lang, wise Lowlander and, at times, Highlander with second sight. Lang certainly made the Christian religion real to me, as Oxford introduced me to English culture. I went on to Cambridge, but Oxford was and is my first love.'

How continuous tradition has been! See how exactly what he wrote fits into something which the living Headmaster himself writes in this year of our Lord 1938:

'If I may be allowed to speak', he says, 'of my own experience, I can say that of the many schools with which I have been closely connected, I know of none in which this sense of individual character and organic life is so strong as in Magdalen College School. This impression is strengthened by all that I am told by my old boys. Many factors, I think contribute to it: the association with the College and the University; the strongly marked individuality of former Masters who have moulded the School's traditions; the comparative smallness of the School, which encourages intimacy among its members and favours personal development; the blending of varied elements in its composition; the beauty of its playing field and of its general setting, and even the sense of rather heroic striving to compete with larger and wealthier schools.

'All these, upon a background of long history, combine to produce a very distinctive character, to which all but the dullest boys are in a greater or less degree susceptible. I have never known a school with a more loveable atmosphere.'

Always there is the same iteration, reiteration, of the School as a link for youth between the humanities of the University and the outer world, a link often for those who can never have the opportunity of the full advantages of the University. That was one of the advantages laid down in the stilted phraseology of the early prospectus of the 1849 Re-foundation:

'So much contact (and no more) with, and influence from, the University, as to elevate the taste and raise the aspirations of boys.'

In whatever way you look on it, the School has fulfilled, even more than fulfilled, the purpose which the College laid down for it. Do you want me, as an employer of labour, to testify to this School? Yes, gladly I testify. Of the Schools in Oxford which offer me their older boys I regard this as the School which maintains the best balance between the humanities and the material, the man and the machine.

AND what of the present and the future? I need not myself recount the educational changes, in the country at large or particularly in this School, of the last 90 years since 1849—changes greater in content than all the changes of the 370 years which preceded—the growing absorption of private or institutional enterprise in Government hands, the construction of the educational ladder, the welcome coming of the scholarship boys from the elementary schools, and a hundred other changes. Yet it is true to say that the more the changes, the more thoroughly has Magdalen School fulfilled the purpose laid down for it in these enlarged opportunities.

'Our scholarship winners', writes a noted Headmaster of one of our elementary schools, 'come back to us at intervals from Magdalen School unspoiled by success, improved in speech and address, and obviously moving fast and far on the road on which we had tried to set them.'

There exists no better judge of value than the British working man whose wits are sharpened by his own narrow margin of living. His sure sense prefers for his son a 'free place' in this school where he must pay the cost of the books, to a scholarship with everything found elsewhere. The statistics of choice are inscribed on the rolls of education of this city and cannot be gainsaid.

If ever there was a school which could be called the school of the spiritual bridge, it is this School, a bridge between man and machine, spiritual and material, academic and civic, academic and the outer world.

BUT development has had its penalties. For this School must rely on the support of either its mother the College, or the city of its domicile, or the world at large.

The College gives it its support as far as it is able; gives it nobly. But nowadays its ability is confined.

The colleges of this University, if any of them were ever

wealthy corporations, are so no longer. More and more they are becoming integral parts of the University and face the huge (undefined and indefinable) obligations of the University unflinchingly, binding themselves by statute to hand over surplus revenues to the University. These duties of the colleges to the University are primary and inalienable.

Furthermore, it is only too true that each great benefaction which is given to the world, however carefully guarded it may be in its terms, creates in the long run administrative problems of its own. Expenditure begets expenditure. Wherefore great benefactions are like great reforms in the effect they may have on smaller beneficent institutions of the past like this School which lie outside their immediate sphere. The smaller institution is bound to suffer where the greater gains.

Already Magdalen College gives the equivalent of a salary of a first-class Professor to the maintenance of this invaluable School. It gives more in ground and buildings, and I guess will not be ungenerous in giving the ground of future buildings.

Buildings are the problem. Capital expenditure on classrooms, the provision of permanent brick for temporary wood, are needed to corroborate this great heritage of ours. New brick buildings to replace the wood and to give essential accommodation for the requisites of modern education would cost not less than £20,000. Veritably it would be crying for the moon to suppose that, in these later days of enlarged obligations in other and more primary fields, the College could dream of capital expenditure of this kind. Its revised statutes of fealty to the University forbid it.

Therefore to me these wooden sheds in which we sit today are no confession of bankruptcy by a College. They are a statesmanlike question addressed by a College to the world.

And what of this great city of ours? In the city there is old educational default to repair, which is eagerly being repaired. In the next few years Oxford city will have to face spending a quarter of a million, nay, perhaps half a million, on its educational problems. Would it not equally be crying for the moon to suppose that the city could at this very moment undertake obligations which were not conceived by itself? Co-operation and condominium in this School may very well develop in the future, but that condominium must be born in a School free of any complication of the past.

Meanwhile, in no present default of anyone, the urgent problem remains, daily, monthly, yearly, growing more and more urgent: bricks for wood, bricks for wood, bricks for wood.

It is clear that had the School not served its purpose of being this spiritual bridge, it would not have had these difficulties. Had it been wholly of the city, there could have been no doubt. Had it retained its old intramural responsibility to the College, equally there could have been no doubt.

It is just because the School has filled that place in the intervening world which the College itself planned for it in 1849, a place which is filled in the same intimate sense by no other School that I know in the British Isles, that its difficulties are those, not immediate but impending, which are summed up in my refrain: bricks for wood, bricks for wood, bricks for wood. How well the School has filled that place is attested by that same elementary school: 'All of us here', it says, 'would prefer to see Magdalen School continue in its wooden huts rather than send our best to the most sumptuous school which may be built but which may have a different tradition.' What better testimony can you have?

THERE remains the solution, and the only solution that I can see. Those who in a figure occupy the two bridge-ends can do no more. There remain those who use the bridge, or who have the opportunities of using the bridge, both in Oxford and in the great world outside.

I always like to think that the young William of Wainfleet was inspired by that great tower of Boston rearing up its

288 feet, the tallest tower in our British Isles, and that it was Wainfleet's inspiration which made Wolsey build the tallest tower in our Oxford midst. As Boston stump was both beacon to medieval shipping and signal of faith to William, so Magdalen Tower may be to us. I never pass it myself without wishing that I could do something to help the problems of that School-by-the-bridge which has always, both in its old restricted days, and in its less restricted days of the last 90 years, been the happy meeting-place for youth of University, city, and the world.

Twenty thousand pounds are needed if we are to replace wood by bricks. Twenty thousand pounds must be raised independently of City or of College. If, within the next six months, nineteen others can be found who will each contribute their twentieth share of this sum, then I myself shall be only too happy to substantiate my own overwhelming conviction in the great past and the great future of this School by adding the missing twentieth part. If more than nineteen contribute their quota then still my contribution will be there.

I am not appealing necessarily to the old boys who year by year have been doing everything in their power by persuasion or contribution to build a future scholarship fund. I am appealing to all men whose imagination can be caught by this pious foundation of a College and by the practical and spiritual purpose which it has served.

I see in my vision a brick building, plain and without any frills, as plain as the city will allow it to be. But that building will have one principal doorway, and over that doorway will be inscribed the names of men who are dead and who have done much or most to create or perpetuate the humane tradition of this School, virile in its body and in its spirit enlightened by the humanities of College and University. Those are WILLIAM EDWARD SHERWOOD, ARTHUR ERNEST COWLEY, PERCY STAFFORD ALLEN. There would be other names. But those are the men, no longer living, who made me what I am. Of the living I may not speak.

And there would be conditions, but only such conditions of shared responsibility as the College itself would welcome and accept.

Of all the thousands who study the financial columns of the papers in the morning in the hope of adding a little to their income by some clever prescience of their own, cannot nineteen be found who will make this investment in the spiritual future of our race?

Of all the thousands who are accustomed, over their morning newspaper, to throw breakfast-table stones at totalitarian governments, will not a bare nineteen be found who will show this substantial faith in the independence of man's character, and in the spiritual contacts of human life?

Of all the thousands who bow to the dictates of mass-psychology and to the mass-disseminated appeals through the air, will not a bare nineteen be found who will see this primary need, corroborated by their own experience, which is visible at their very doors?

Of the many others who live their own steadfast lives un-influenced by these things, may there not be found nineteen who will pay their tribute to such steadfastness of scholastic faith?

. Assuredly they will be found; does not our own faith tell us that opportunity vouchsafed will be seized? And on that day of fulfilment each one of those self-appointed twenty men or women will be able to repeat with humble satisfaction that motto which William of Wainfleet borrowed from the Magnificat:

'HE THAT IS MIGHTY HATH MAGNIFIED ME.'

II
LIST OF MASTERS AND USHERS

MASTERS	USHERS
1481 (?) JOHN ANWYKYLL	1485 (?) JOHN STANBRIDGE
1488 JOHN STANBRIDGE	1488 (?) ASHE
	1494 (?) JOHN HOLT
1494 ANDREW SCARBOTT	1495 JOHN HOWELL
	1496 *Two unknown men*
1498 THOMAS WOLSEY	1497 TURNER, ANDREWS, CLAY-DON
1498 WILLIAM BOTHEWOOD	1498 JOHN STOKESLEY
1498 RICHARD JACKSON	1498 EDWARD MARTYN, JOHN GOLDYFFE
	1499 HAMPTON
1502 THOMAS BRYNKNELL	1502 BURWAY *or* BORROW
	1504 JOHN GOLDYFFE**
	1504 MOORE
	1505 HALYE
	1507 FIELD
1509 BORROW*	1509 FULLER
1509 MOORE*	1510 MORGAN
1512 LEWYS *or* LUYT	1512 MAURICE BYRCHENSHAW
1513 HALYE*	(*as well as Morgan*)
1514 MOORE**	1516 STOKYS
1515 HALYE**	1516 BEDELL
1517 THOMAS STANBRIDGE	1518 SEND
	1518 FRYER
1523 THOMAS BYSSHOPPE	1523 WILLIAM HYNDE *or* HEYNE
1526 THOMAS ROBERTSON	1525 WILLIAM SARESON
	1529 PEARCE
1534 RICHARD SHERRY *or* SHIRREY	1534 ARMYLL
	1535 RALPH SMALLPAGE
	1537 JOHN (?) HERON
	1539 ROBERT DIGHTON
	1540 RICHARD HEWYS *or* HEWES *or* HUYS
1541 GODALL	1546 JOHN SLADE
1542 JOHN HARLEY	1548 JOHN BOLDERN
1548 JOHN SLADE*	1550 ROBERT LYLLIE
1549 THOMAS COOPER	1553 THOMAS GODDALL

| * *Previously Usher* | ** *Reappointed* |

MASTERS	USHERS
1557 PETER BACHYLER *or* BARSELER	1554 JOHN BEDO
1558 JOHN BOLDERN*	
1559 THOMAS COOPER**	
1567 NICHOLAS BALGUAY	1571 ROGER WEBSTER
1583 WILLIAM SYMONDS *or* SIMONS	1577 HENRY MERCER
1585 PAUL SMITH	1585 RICHARD NEWTON
1594 JOHN PELLING*	1589 JOHN PELLING
1598 EDWARD LAPWORTH	1606 NATHANIEL TOMKINS
1610 LAWRENCE SNELLING	1610 MERCADINE HUNNIS
1614 FRANCIS WHITE	1612 SAMUEL BERNARD *or* BARNARD
1617 SAMUEL BERNARD*	1617 JOHN HARMAR
1625 JOHN ALLIBOND	1626 JOHN LANGTON
1648 WILLIAM WHITE	1632 JOHN HYDE
1649 WILLIAM WROTH	1649 PHILIP ORMSTON
	1651 JOHN HOOKE
	1655 EZEKIEL HOPKINS
	1656 (?) JAMES CARKESSE
	1656 JOHN WEBB
1657 OWEN PRICE	1657 TIMOTHY PARKER
1657 TIMOTHY PARKER*	1660 SAMUEL LOWNES
1663 JAMES CARKESSE*	1662 THOMAS WALKER
1664 THOMAS SMITH	1663 THOMAS BRATTELL
1666 JAMES HARMOUR	1665 JAMES SAMBOURNE
1666 JOHN CURLE	1668 RICHARD REEVE
1670 RICHARD REEVE*	1670 SAMUEL CLERKE
1673 THOMAS COLLINS	1677 EDWARD BROADHURST
	1683 RICHARD WRIGHT
	1689 JOHN SMYTH
	1717 WILLIAM HANNES
1723 HENRY STEPHENS	1724 ISAAC GRIFFITH
	1728 HENRY SHEPPARD
	1740 RICHARDSON WOOD
1745 ROBERT CANE	1749 ROBERT BRYNE
1752 ROBERT BRYNE*	1752 THOMAS PRICE
	1764 JOHN RAWBONE
	1769 JOHN DOUGLAS
1776 THOMAS ROBINSON	1772 ANDREW PRICE
	1788 JOHN SLATTER
1795 WILLIAM RUST COBBOLD	1795 EDWARD ELLERTON
1798 EDWARD ELLERTON*	1798 JOHN ALLEN
1810 HENRY JENKINS	1801 GEORGE GRANTHAM

MASTERS	USHERS
1828 RICHARD WALKER	1840 THOMAS WILLIAM LAN-CASTER
1844 WILLIAM GEORGE HENDER-SON	1849 WILLIAM JONATHAN SAWELL
1846 JAMES ELWIN MILLARD	
1864 RICHARD HUMPHREY HILL	1861 HENRY EDWARD FOWLER GARNSEY
	1866 HARMAN CHALONER OGLE
	1867 H. E. F. GARNSEY**
1876 HARMAN CHALONER OGLE*	1876 JOHN HESLOP AUDLAND
1887 F. R. CHRISTIE	1887 OWEN SEAMAN
1888 WILLIAM EDWARD SHER-WOOD	1888 CHARLES EDWARD BROWN-RIGG
1900 CHARLES EDWARD BROWN-RIGG*	1901 PERCY DEIGHTON PULLAN
1930 RUSHWORTH KENNARD DAVIS	1935 ROBERT SPENSER STANIER
1944 ROBERT SPENSER STANIER*	1945 ROBERT CHARLES ARTHUR OATES
	1950 IAN WRIGHT THOMSON

III

PRIZE-GIVERS SINCE 1888

1888 THE BISHOP OF CHICHESTER
1889 DR R. H. HILL, *former Master*
1890 SIR JOHN STAINER, *former Organist of the College*
1891 THE BISHOP OF SOUTHWELL
1892 THE DEAN OF CHRIST CHURCH, DR LIDDELL
1893 PROFESSOR E. B. ELLIOTT, *O.W.*
1894 (*Prize-giving postponed to* 1895) THE PRESIDENT OF ST JOHN'S COLLEGE, DR BELLAMY
1895 PRESIDENT WARREN
1896 THE VICE-CHANCELLOR AND PROVOST OF QUEEN'S COLLEGE, DR MAGRATH
1897 PRESIDENT WARREN
1898 PRESIDENT WARREN
1899 THE BISHOP OF THETFORD, DR LLOYD, *O.W.*
1900 PRESIDENT WARREN
1901 SIR WILLIAM ANSON
1902 THE BISHOP OF LINCOLN, DR MERRY
1903 THE BISHOP OF STEPNEY, LATER ARCHBISHOP LANG
1904 THE LORD CHANCELLOR, LORD HALSBURY
1905 PRESIDENT WARREN
1906 THE VICE-CHANCELLOR, PRESIDENT WARREN
1907 DR WARRE, *late Headmaster of Eton*
1908 SIR JAMES MURRAY, *formerly a parent*
1909 THE VICE-CHANCELLOR, PRESIDENT WARREN
1910 THE BISHOP OF LINCOLN, DR HICKS, *O.W.*
1911 THE PRESIDENT OF ST JOHN'S COLLEGE, DR JAMES
1912 SIR FREDERICK KENYON
1913 PRESIDENT WARREN
From 1914 to 1918 *Prize-givings were held privately with no ceremony*
1919 DR A. E. COWLEY, BODLEY'S LIBRARIAN, *formerly assistant master*
1920 PRESIDENT WARREN
1921 REV. ECCLES WILLIAMS, *late Headmaster of Summerfields*
1922 GENERAL SIR H. WALKER
1923 VISCOUNT CHELMSFORD
1924 THE BISHOP OF BRADFORD, DR PEROWNE, *formerly assistant master*
1925 THE PRESIDENT OF CORPUS CHRISTI COLLEGE, DR P. S. ALLEN, *formerly assistant master*

1926 THE VICE-CHANCELLOR, DR J. WELLS
1927 PRESIDENT WARREN
1928 THE REGISTRAR OF THE UNIVERSITY, E. S. CRAIG
1929 PRESIDENT GORDON
1930 THE HEADMASTER OF CHARTERHOUSE, FRANK FLETCHER
1931 THE HEADMASTER OF SHREWSBURY, CANON SAWYER, *O.W.*
1932 THE BISHOP OF WORCESTER, DR PEROWNE, *formerly assistant master*
1933 SIR RAYMOND UNWIN, P.R.I.B.A., *O.W.*
1934 THE MASTER OF MARLBOROUGH, G. C. TURNER
1935 C. E. BROWNRIGG, *formerly Master*
1936 THE MASTER OF ST PETER'S HALL, *now* BISHOP OF ROCHESTER, DR CHAVASSE, *O.W.*
1937 THE WARDEN OF ALL SOULS, W. G. S. ADAMS
1938 THE PRINTER TO THE UNIVERSITY, DR JOHN JOHNSON, *O.W.*
1939 THE HEADMASTER OF CHELTENHAM, JOHN BELL
1940 THE HEADMASTER OF UPPINGHAM, LATER VICE-CHANCELLOR OF READING UNIVERSITY, SIR JOHN WOLFENDEN
1941 MAJOR GENERAL SIR ERNEST SWINTON
1942 CANON W. H. FERGUSON, *O.W.*
1943 PRESIDENT TIZARD
1944 SIR BASIL BLACKWELL, *O.W.*
1945 PROFESSOR GILBERT MURRAY, O.M.
1946 THE BISHOP OF READING, DR PARHAM, *O.W.*
1947 THE PRESIDENT OF MAGDALEN, T. S. R. BOASE
1948 LORD DAVID CECIL
1949 SIR ARTHUR SALTER
1950 THE PRESIDENT OF ST JOHN'S COLLEGE, A. LANE POOLE, *O.W.*
1951 FELIX AYLMER, *O.W.*
1952 SIR RICHARD WINSTEDT, *O.W.*
1953 CECIL DAY LEWIS, PROFESSOR OF POETRY
1954 R. KENNARD DAVIS, *formerly Master*
1955 THE WARDEN OF WADHAM COLLEGE, SIR MAURICE BOWRA
1956 THE BISHOP OF WINCHESTER, DR WILLIAMS, *The Visitor*
1957 SIR BASIL BLACKWELL, *O.W.*
1958 PROFESSOR D. H. HEY, F.R.S., *O.W.*

INDEX

R